D0277766

MEMOIRS

WILLIAM REES-MOGG

Memoirs

Harper
Press

Harper*Press*
An imprint of HarperCollins*Publishers*
77–85 Fulham Palace Road,
Hammersmith, London W6 8JB
www.harpercollins.co.uk

Published by Harper*Press* in 2011

2

William Rees-Mogg asserts the moral right to
be identified as the author of this work

A catalogue record for this book
is available from the British Library

ISBN 978-0-00-257183-8

Typeset in Minion by G&M Designs Limited,
Raunds, Northamptonshire
Printed and bound in Great Britain by
Clays Ltd, St Ives plc

LIST OF CONTENTS

LIST OF ILLUSTRATIONS

FOREWORD

In January 1977, my senior editorial colleagues gave a dinner at the Garrick Club to celebrate my tenth anniversary as Editor of *The Times*. It was a very pleasant evening for me, among people whom I regarded as both colleagues and friends. Charles Douglas-Home, himself due to become a distinguished Editor, had chosen a case of Château Lynch Bages as a present; I have only recently consumed the last bottle. I cannot recall the whole guest list. Louis Heren was in the chair, as Deputy Editor. Naturally we talked about *The Times*, with a good deal of confidence, despite the recurring problems with the print unions. We had no idea of the militant trade union crisis that was to come. Our proprietor, Roy Thomson, had died a couple of years before, but his son, Ken, had taken his place in an atmosphere of goodwill on both sides. Ken followed Roy's principle of avoiding interference with the editorial side of the paper.

I remember, at the end of the evening, walking down the front steps of the club; Peter Jay was next to me. When we were about halfway down the steps, a thought passed through my mind. This surely was going to be as good as it would get, at least in personal or career terms. Would it not have been a better conclusion to my editorship if I had taken my colleagues by surprise and announced my intention to resign in my brief speech of thanks at the dinner?

I put the idea out of my mind, even if it was ever wholly present. I could hardly wheel round on the steps of the club and ask everyone to go back to the table, so that I could make a little announcement. In any case, I knew Ken Thomson better than any alternative Editor; I could hardly leave the paper until he was completely settled in. The moment passed before it had even fully formed. Nevertheless, the intention had entered my mind, and if I had had time to think it through I would have seen that there were strong reasons for following the advice of my subconscious mind. The next four years, with the closure and then the sale of *The Times*, was a difficult period. A contrast to the mood of the dinner I was just leaving.

If I had resigned at that dinner I would have been spared the worst crisis that *The Times* faced in the twentieth century, the one-year stoppage, and I would have had another four years to develop the next stage of my life.

Ex-Editors do find it difficult to establish a second half to their careers. I remember my first Editor, Gordon Newton, of the *Financial Times*, saying of his own retirement, 'there is nothing so dead as a dead lion'. Some Editors have had successful careers in business. There is a phrase for the strategy of moving from a single big job with major executive responsibility, to the non-executive jobs which are more likely to be available. It is said that these personages have gone 'multiple'. At any rate I went multiple, and have had geological layers of different forms of employment in the period since I made a final retirement from editing *The Times* in 1982. The only trouble I have found is that the jobs one is offered after the age of seventy tend themselves to be time-limited.

In fact I have found plenty of interesting things to do since 1982, and am still writing columns for *The Times* and the *Mail on Sunday*. I am struck by the fact that most of the work I have done in journalism, in business, in helping charities, has been cyclical in character. World politics faced the threat of the Cold War and now faces the growth of terrorism. When I started in journalism in 1951 there was a liberal Conservative Government in power. Sixty years later there is a Liberal/Conservative coalition. I myself have enjoyed writing about the swings and circulating on the roundabout.

The [illegible]

I was born in the Pemb[illegible] [illegible]
an American mother a[illegible] [illegible]
was a hate sign and a [illegible] [illegible]
[illegible] that I [illegible] [illegible]
[illegible] the thought [illegible] [illegible]
born at about 4 a.m. on [illegible] [illegible]
[illegible] a child that [illegible] [illegible]
[illegible]
[illegible] point [illegible] [illegible]
[illegible] picture, [illegible] [illegible]
[illegible] [illegible]
[illegible] during [illegible] [illegible]
[illegible]

[illegible] child I [illegible] [illegible]
[illegible] [illegible]
[illegible] [illegible]
[illegible] from the [illegible] [illegible]
through express. I am [illegible] [illegible]
such a dream, which [illegible] [illegible]
birth is some and some[illegible] [illegible]

My [illegible] Beatrice [illegible] [illegible]
York, in 1892, was an [illegible] [illegible]

ONE

The Young Actress

I was born in the Pembroke Nursing Home, Bristol, England, of an American mother and an English father, on 14 July 1928. It was a hot night and a difficult labour. My mother had been determined that I should not be born on Friday the 13th, because she thought it would be unlucky. In consequence I was born at about 4 a.m. on Bastille Day, France's national holiday, and knew as a child that my birthday was a special day of celebration. I was a large baby, weighing some nine pounds, three ounces. At some point, during or after the delivery, my mother's heart stopped beating, and had to be restarted with a new drug which had recently been used on King George V. Whether my life was at risk during the delivery I do not know; my mother's certainly was.

As a young child I had a recurrent dream. I am travelling up a shaft, which has ribs. When I reach the top of the shaft, there is a light, and there are large people, giants. They assist me to emerge from the shaft. I awake, feeling that I have passed through a crisis. I am by no means the only person to record such a dream, which is sometimes explained as recalling the birth trauma, and sometimes as a near-death experience.

My mother, Beatrice Warren, born in Mamaroneck, New York, in 1892, was an Irish-American Roman Catholic and a successful Shakespearian actress. All four of her grandparents had emigrated to the United States from Ireland in the 1850s; both her grandfathers then fought for the North in the Civil War. They came from the Irish Catholic middle class, 'lace-curtain' rather than 'bog-trotting' Irish. They had experienced the famine but survived it. My mother was the eldest child of her family, and for seven years had been an only child.

I have a very vivid picture of her childhood. In the 1890s she had the regular morning treat of being driven to Mamaroneck station with her father, where he caught the commuter train into Grand Central Station. They were driven in the carriage by Arthur Cuffey, the black coachman and handyman. At that time they lived on Union Avenue, though her father later built Shoreacres, a beautiful early twentieth-century house which looks out over Long Island Sound. Her evening treat was to take the same drive to meet the evening train. They had a good quality carriage horse, called Miss Gedney, whom her father had bought from a man in White Plains.

My mother's father, Daniel Warren, started his working life as a clerk at Harrison Station, which, as every Westchester commuter knows, is the stop between Mamaroneck and Rye. He had been known as a bright lad. His father, old Mr Warren, had prospered as an immigrant and had risen to be a line manager of the New York, New Haven and Hartford Railroad. He got his sixteen-year-old son the job on the railroad.

One morning in 1881, Daniel was standing on the platform where the train to New York was about to arrive. A regular business commuter, Mr Eddy of Coombs, Crosby and Eddy, was standing beside him. Mr Eddy had a fainting fit, and started to totter. As he fell forward, Daniel grabbed him; the locomotive brushed Daniel's arm as it passed. Mr Eddy thanked Daniel for saving his life, gave him his card and asked him to call on him at his office in Wall Street. When he did so, Daniel was offered a job, rejected a flattering counter-offer by the railroad, and worked for Coombs, Crosby and Eddy, later merged into the American Trading Company, until he retired in the 1920s. He ended his career as the vice-president, which then meant that he was the executive running the business. The American Trading Company, with a strong Japanese connection and branches in many countries, became a powerful international trading house. J. P. Morgan, whom Daniel greatly admired, invited him to join his new club, the Metropolitan. Daniel replied: 'Mr Morgan, I am flattered by your invitation. I greatly appreciate doing business with you. But I am an Irish Catholic. I do not belong to the same society as you do.' Nevertheless, the American Trading Company was chosen to advise the Morgan Bank when, in the early 1900s, Morgans wanted to expand into Japanese finance.

In 1888, he made a trip through northern Mexico with eight large trunks of manufacturing samples. At the end of the Mexican National Railroad at Saltillo, he had to hire mules to carry these trunks over the mountains, which were overrun with bandits and outlaws. He remembered hiding behind a wall with a Mexican friend; some shooting was going on. His friend asked him what passport he carried; he replied 'American'. The Mexican advised him, 'Do not say "*Americano*", say "*Ingles*". They shoot Yankees; they do not dare shoot the "*Ingles*".' Such, in the high Victorian period, was the reputation of the British Empire, or perhaps just the Mexican dislike of Yankees. Daniel Warren, though his Irish ancestors had been nationalists, was an Anglophile.

He used to discuss the day-to-day problems of his business with my mother. She particularly remembered the panic of 1907. Wall Street was only saved by the rapid action of J. P.

Morgan and a syndicate he formed. Her father acted swiftly and managed to save the American Trading Company, but many other firms went under. The family took their usual summer holiday in the Adirondacks, in upper New York State, and Daniel walked with Beatrice, then fifteen, and talked himself through the stress of the panic.

My mother had been enormously influenced by her relationship with her father whom she very much admired and whom she very well understood; she thereby created for me another role model. Indeed, although I never met him – he died in 1931 and he did not come to England in my lifetime – in some respects I was more influenced by Daniel Warren than by my father. In particular my interest in business and politics comes from my American side.

From a very early age, Beatrice knew that she wanted to be an actress. She could remember, as a child of seven, joining the recitations, which formed part of evening entertainment in the age before radio or television existed. Her party piece was a sentimental poem which ended with the lines:

> Thanks to the sunshine, Thanks to the rain,
> Little white lily is happy again.

While she was at college, Beatrice told her father she wanted to go on the stage. A hundred years ago that was an unusual ambition for a well-brought-up American girl from a family of rising prosperity. Daniel replied that he would support her going on the stage, so long as she earned her own living for a year in some other way. She accepted that, and always regarded it as a sensible condition for him to have set. She taught elocution at Wadleigh High School for a year, commuting from Mamaroneck and getting off at the 116th Street Station. She could remember teaching girls who pronounced 'th' as 'd' – 'dis and dat and dese and dose and dem'.

In 1914, Beatrice went on the stage. She was given an introduction, by Granville Barker, to Margaret Anglin, who was casting for a season of Greek plays, translated by Gilbert Murray, in the Greek Theatre at Berkeley, California. Beatrice became a member of the chorus. Alfred Lunt was also a trainee, carrying a spear among the guards. He and his wife, Lynn Fontanne, were to become the leading couple of the American theatre before the Second World War. Beatrice remained with Miss Anglin's company for a couple of years. In 1916 she was playing the second lead in the Chicago opening of Somerset Maugham's *Caroline*, later retitled as *Home and Beauty*. The author, a friendly but rather shy figure, was sitting in the stalls at the dress rehearsal.

One member of the New York artistic set was Putzi Hanfstaengl, an ardent young German nationalist. He was a son of the family of Munich art dealers, and had been sent to New York to set up a local branch of the firm. They already had a branch in Pall Mall, in London. Putzi gave Beatrice a couple of the firm's celebrated reproductions, Dürer's rabbit and Holbein's drawing of Sir Thomas More, which is now hanging on our drawing-room wall. He argued heatedly in favour of Germany's historic role as the dominant power in Europe. This would have been in 1915. Beatrice did not like Putzi, though she found his intellectual range interesting. During the Second World War she remembered these conversations, and believed that German imperialism was deeply rooted, that there was a continuity between the imperialism of Kaiser's Germany and that of Hitler's. Beatrice's unfavourable view of Hanfstaengl's personality was shared by Adolf Hitler, who had employed him in the 1920s and early 1930s as his foreign press secretary.

Whereas Beatrice found Hanfstaengl's German imperialism particularly offensive, Hitler was offended by his greedy habit of taking food off other people's plates when eating in restaurants.

In 1916, Sarah Bernhardt, the great French actress, came for the last time to play Hamlet in New York. She had already lost a leg, and spoke Hamlet's lines seated on a couch. Beatrice had to play all the other parts in dumb show, and was Horatio, Ophelia, Gertrude, and, for all I know, the Ghost in mute dialogue. The producer had the commercial idea of selling equally mute chorus parts to society girls from New York. In addition to responding to Bernhardt, Beatrice had to ensure that those fashionable young ladies remained in line and did not fall off the stage. She obtained a free place on one night for her beautiful younger sister, Adrienne Warren.

She remembered Sarah Bernhardt's elocution and her professionalism. She also remembered her temperament. On one occasion, Bernhardt thought the curtain had been brought down too quickly, cutting short her applause. She turned on the stage manager and addressed him in the tones of a French Queen and the language of a French fishwife. The man operating the curtain understood the drift of her remarks, if not the precise words, and retorted by whisking up the curtain. With absolute fluency, the divine Sarah switched from her tirade to gracious acceptance of the applause of her audience. When the curtain came down, she resumed the tirade.

It was in Chicago that Beatrice first met the novelist Edna Ferber. Ferber introduced her to the Algonquin round table, and used her as copy. There is a great deal of Beatrice's character and experience in Kim Ravenal, the youngest of the three generations of actresses in *Showboat*. Kim even does the elocution exercises Beatrice had taught at Wadleigh.

In 1917 a strange incident had occurred. Beatrice was at a party with some other young women of the theatre; Edna Ferber was there. One of the girls produced a Ouija board; Beatrice had a healthy Catholic distrust of the occult, had never used a Ouija board before and never touched one again. For a while the board seemed to be pointing to random letters; the young women were asking it to say whom they were going to marry. Finally the board did start to spell out recognizable words. It pointed to the letters: GOG MOG MAGOG. None of the young women knew what these words might mean, except for Edna Ferber, who said that Gog and Magog were two wooden statues of giants, to be seen at the Guildhall in London. The word 'MOG' remained unexplained.

On the recommendation of English actors, Beatrice decided to broaden her experience with a Shakespearian season at the Old Vic, London. She sailed for England in April 1920. There was still a post-war shortage of shipping. She booked her passage on a German liner, the old *Imperator*, which had been confiscated by the Allies at the end of the war. The ship had not been perfectly converted from wartime use as a troopship, and there were still German notices forbidding Other Ranks to enter the Officers' quarters. Beatrice had to share a cabin with a young French woman who had been establishing some New York contacts for her dressmaking business. They found each other agreeable company for the voyage, and the dressmaker gave Beatrice a silk slip, which I remember seeing as a child in the 1930s. The young dressmaker was Miss Chanel.

Beatrice landed in England and went to stay with an old friend, Rosamund, who was living at Parkstone, near Bournemouth. Rosamund said she was giving a small dinner party, which would include Fletcher Rees-Mogg. She told Beatrice that Fletcher was an excellent golfer – he had a handicap of two at the Parkstone Golf Club – and a stickler for punctuality.

I have some fifty volumes of my English grandmother's diary. It records the progress of my parents' courtship:

> 10 MAY: E. F. [Edmund Fletcher Rees-Mogg] and Ed and Rosamund and Miss Warren dance. [This was either their first or second meeting.]
>
> 11 MAY: Rosamund and Miss W. (charming American) dine here. F. to works 9 to 10.30 – she and I chat, pianola.
>
> 15 MAY: F. takes Rosamund and Miss W. and me to Stonehenge. Much wind! Tea under stones!
>
> 19 MAY: v. lovely. Rosamund and B. Warren dine.
>
> 20 MAY: F. takes B. Warren to town lunch Lyndhurst, tea Sonning
>
> 26 MAY: Bea Warren comes
>
> 29 MAY: Sat 1 p.m. Fletcher and Beatrice announce their engagement.

'Sonning' is almost certainly a euphemism for 'Maidenhead'. My father gave Beatrice Warren dinner on 20 May at Skindles roadhouse on the Thames, where he proposed. Beatrice always thought that it was slightly embarrassing to have become engaged in Maidenhead. They might well have thought that Sonning, a few miles away on the Thames, would sound less embarrassing to my grandmother's Victorian ears. At all events, the time from their first meeting to the engagement was about a fortnight. She was twenty-eight; he was thirty.

They were to be happily married for forty-two years, and to have three children, two girls and a boy. They had, so far as I know, no fundamental disagreements. In their early letters they express surprise that such a gift of love and mutual understanding should have come to them.

They were married on 11 November 1920, by the Catholic priest, in the drawing room at Shoreacres, the Warrens' home in Mamaroneck. They returned to England after an American honeymoon. Beatrice was not to see the United States again until after the Second World War.

TWO

The Young Officer

My father was one of the young officers who survived the First World War. In the spring of 1914, he had caught pneumonia while working as a schoolmaster at a school in Lancashire, where he taught Latin, Greek and French. He was left with a strained heart. When, that August, he volunteered for the army, the doctors listened to his heart and rejected him as unfit. This, in all probability, saved his life.

Instead he went out to France by volunteering to drive the Charterhouse ambulance, which had been subscribed for by boys and parents at his old school. He was already a first-class amateur engineer and mechanic. He spent some months working at a French hospital at Arc-en-Barrois, but was subsequently commissioned in the Royal Army Service Corps, where he ran a mobile transport unit.

This was neither safe nor non-combatant. A fellow officer wrote that he woke every morning uncertain whether he would be called by his batman or St Peter. However, it was obviously less inevitably lethal than service in the infantry. It was also surprisingly modern. Apart from ambulance work, Fletcher's unit was the first to take mobile X-rays into the front line. His experience of X-rays proved valuable when I was X-rayed *in utero* at the Clifton Nursing Home. The matron scrutinized the

X-ray and told my parents that I had two heads. My father had seen many more X-rays than she had, and commented briskly: 'Nonsense, woman, you don't know how to read it.'

His unit was also attached to the earliest tanks, which, on average, broke down every 60 yards or so. Their job was to mend the tanks while under fire. My father considered that he had had an easy war. He shared the infantry's resentment of the inadequacy of the staff officers who did not visit the front line.

Like many young officers from the landowning class – one finds the same attitudes in Anthony Eden's memoirs – his war experience left him with a strong feeling that he ought to try to repay the privileges he had enjoyed. Some of his friends after the war were men who had been wounded, or suffered from shell shock, or had taken to drink as a result of their war experiences. For them he felt great compassion. His first cousin, Colonel Robert Rees-Mogg, a good professional soldier, had been an aide-de-camp to Field Marshal Allenby and ridden into Jerusalem in his entourage in 1917. Robert was torpedoed on his way back from Palestine, suffered from shell shock and amnesia, and never recovered. I can remember him visiting us at Cholwell, our home in Somerset, in the middle 1930s, a friendly, tall man who had lost the thread of life. Two other cousins were killed, out of a group of five, one at Gallipoli, the other in the last German advance in 1918.

I now think that I underrated the whole question of what my father had been through in the First World War. He felt, as many of those who survived did, a considerable guilt for being a survivor. The war made him feel that he should not compete in the world against people who needed the jobs. He felt that, as he had a reasonable sized estate and a reasonable income, he was in a position to lead the life of a quiet country gentleman without seeking employment and that is what he did. It was a life in which there was a lot of voluntary work and he made jobs for himself in farming which gave him an instinctive pleasure: he liked growing things; he liked having pigs; he liked having hens and he liked growing daffodils. It just about paid the wages of people who might not otherwise have had jobs during the slump.

My father inherited the long, solid, Somerset tradition of the Moggs, who had been local businessmen and landowners since at least the thirteenth century. They earned their livings as merchants, lawyers, estate agents, coal owners, bankers, clergymen, doctors, or whatever came to hand. They were involved in local government, but seem to have had little ambition to enter national politics, nor the connections to be able to do so.

In his early twenties my father inherited the family estate in Somerset, which then consisted of roughly 1200 acres and perhaps a dozen cottages, which still rented for about five shillings a week each in the 1930s and 1940s. The estate was encumbered with the death duties on his father and grandfather, and with substantial incomes payable to his sister, aunts and uncles. In capital terms he was a wealthy man, but the income that he was free to spend was not proportionate to his capital. This was the normal situation of landowners at that time, and still is today. Before the war, my father had worked briefly as a schoolmaster after spending four years at Charterhouse, four at University College, Oxford, and a further year at the Sorbonne.

By the age of twelve he had introduced me to classical Latin and Greek and even Old French. I had also been introduced to the comparative study of language. I had learned how words changed their form, so that 'W' in English would be the equivalent of 'Gu' in French, with 'William' matching 'Guillaume'. I was taught the distinction between the English words which came from Germanic roots, from Norman French, from Latin and from Greek. I have never lost this interest in words. One of our own children, when little, observed that we ought to set a place for the *Oxford English Dictionary* at the dining table, since one or other volume was so often brought out at family lunch to look up the meaning and derivation of a particular word.

When he returned from the Sorbonne, Fletcher had had difficulty in choosing a career. His father, by then suffering from depression, had gloomy visions of Fletcher going to the bad. There had been scapegraces in the family: my great-great uncle, John Rees-Mogg, in one generation and the much-loved Charles in the next. My father was never remotely likely to become a third. Nevertheless, my grandfather, William Wooldridge Rees-Mogg, would not allow my father to become a solicitor, on the grounds that half the solicitors with whom he had trained had ended in jail for dipping into their clients' funds. That was a pity, as my father would have made a first-class solicitor, highly intelligent, punctilious in detail, practical and exceptionally honest.

A friend of Wooldridge suggested that Fletcher might join the Chinese Consular Service, an absurd suggestion. Fletcher refused. Father and son negotiated at arm's length, Wooldridge in the library at Cholwell, Fletcher in the morning room, passing notes to each other. One must have some sympathy with Wooldridge, who was depressed, going blind and proved to be dying. To my great benefit, Fletcher gave me the time and love which Wooldridge had not been able to give him.

Difficult father–son relationships had been common in the Mogg family, going back to the seventeenth century: they made nasty remarks about each other in their wills. My father was absolutely determined not to repeat in his relationship with me the relationship he had had with his father. And he was completely successful. On both sides our relationship was a very affectionate one of comfort and respect.

After my father was demobilized in 1919 he went to live in Parkstone, near Bournemouth. In the last months of the war he had been serving with another young officer who was in the motor business, and was a member of the Vandeleur family. Vandeleur had decided to produce a sports car for the British market. My father set up a manufacturing business to make the chassis; the engines were substantial lorry engines from the United States. Like several other ventures by young officers selling luxury cars, this looked promising for a time, but the post-war recession knocked out the market. However, my father designed the chassis and about twenty cars were constructed. In 1921, my mother's sisters crossed the Atlantic to spend an English holiday with her. There is a picture of my American aunts and my English grandmother sitting in a Vandy, as the cars were called. It is a splendid looking car, but it does not look very economic.

In 1925 my father had the opportunity to return to Cholwell and manage his estate. He liked to grow things himself, though the farms continued to be tenanted. He kept pigs and hens and grew a large quantity of wild blackberries.

THREE

A House Built on a Hill

I am standing at the top of a little hill overlooking the back of Cholwell House. No one is there except me. It is my third birthday, and is therefore 14 July 1931. I am conscious that my birthday makes me a special person in the family for that day. Much more than that, I feel that I am very much myself, am William Rees-Mogg, and that this is a good thing to be. On a good day, after a glass of champagne, I can still feel the echo of this childish triumphalism. I am certain that the William Rees-Mogg of 1931 is the same consciousness as the William Rees-Mogg I now am.

As a boy I was much surrounded by women, in a family of two elder sisters, a mother, a maiden aunt in England, two aunts in America, an American and an English grandmother, and two maiden great-aunts who lived in St James's Square in Bath. There were also the maids and the cook, Mabel Sage. My father, myself and very distantly my clergyman great-uncle Henry Rees-Mogg were the only representatives of the male sex. I was the sole male Rees-Mogg of my generation. I did not, at the age of three or four, ask what the universe was for, what my role might be in it, or 'what is man with regard to this infinity about him'. I knew, with the certainty of infancy, which is even more implacable than the certainty of childhood, that I was myself, that I was in my proper station. I enjoyed being me.

Many children start to ask metaphysical questions at an early age. My eldest daughter, Emma, entertained the Platonic idea of the pre-existence of souls at the age of four. The early Christian father, Origen, also held that theory, as did the English poet William Wordsworth. Emma and I were walking on the lawn at Ston Easton, when she said to me, 'I understand what happens when we die but I don't understand where we are before we're born.' Her daughter, Maud, was equally interested in questions that had interested the ancient Greek philosophers when she was four. She followed the theory, which I think was first framed by Empedocles, and since popularized by Stephen Hawking, of the plurality of worlds. 'I know,' she said, 'that worlds disappear and new worlds start, but do all the other worlds have Father Christmas?'

The Elizabethan philosopher Lord Herbert of Cherbury gives a similar account of his own early development: 'It was so long before I began to speak, that many thought I should be for ever dumb; when I came to talk, one of the furthest enquiries I made was how I came into this world? I told my nurse, keeper, and others, I found myself here indeed, but from what cause or beginning, or by what means I could not imagine, but for this I was laughed at by nurse.'*

I do not remember these metaphysical problems being important to me at that age, but they have fascinated me in subsequent years. If I came into the world 'trailing clouds of glory', I cannot remember them.

William is a strong name; I never liked being called Bill. The association of the name with William the Conqueror helped as soon as I was reading history. I found myself a natural supporter

---

* *The Life of Edward Lord Herbert of Cherbury, written by himself* (Strawberry Hill, 1764).

of the Normans. I was also impressed by stories of my great-grandfather William Rees-Mogg. He was a good man of business, a local solicitor, specializing in the development of the coal industry. He built the family fortune and died a wealthy man. He had built Cholwell, where we lived. He was the dominant Victorian father figure in my family and Cholwell was his monument. The original house had been bought by the Moggs in the 1720s. It then consisted of a small Elizabethan manor house and a home farm of about a hundred acres. In 1850, William Rees-Mogg demolished the old house, which the family has subsequently regretted, and built a large Victorian country house on the hillside opposite, with a walled garden, glass houses, a conservatory and a Top and Bottom Lodge. In 1925, when my father and mother moved into Cholwell, they put in electricity and central heating. The new house was built in the Jacobean style, designed by a Bath architect who had also been responsible for the much larger Victorian pile at Westonbirt in Gloucestershire.

* * *

My first strongly political or social memory can be dated to three months after my third birthday; it relates to the General Election of 1931. The Conservative candidate is Lord Weymouth, the heir to the Marquis of Bath, supporting the National Government of Ramsay MacDonald. I am told that Lord Weymouth will be spending the day canvassing in the villages of Temple Cloud and Clutton, and that he will be bringing his daughter with him who will be left to play with me in the nursery at Cholwell.

At the age of three, I believed that all peers wore a uniform which I envisaged as being a blue velvet suit with gilt buttons. I am waiting at the front door and am disappointed when

Lord Weymouth appears wearing an elegantly cut grey lounge suit with rather flared trousers, what were then called 'Oxford bags'. He has, however, brought his daughter with him. She is of much the same age as I am. We enjoy our afternoon together, and I vaguely hope that I shall see her again. It is the first time that I am conscious of feeling the attraction of the opposite sex.

The next time I meet her it is the early 1970s and she is Lady Caroline Somerset, and we are having dinner with Arnold and Netta Weinstock in Wiltshire. At another later meeting James Lees-Milne, who thinks I am rather a prig, notes in his diary how exceptionally at ease we are together. The last time I see her she has become the Duchess of Beaufort. Like me, she has memories of having tea at Fortt's in Bath; that is where she told her younger brother, now himself Lord Bath, that fairies do not really exist. He claims that this moment of disillusionment ruined his life.

My next political memory came in July 1934. Mabel Sage, our much-loved cook, is giving me breakfast in the dining room at Cholwell, which looks out across the terrace towards Mendip. I have eaten my boiled egg with soldiers of toast. The BBC is broadcasting a news bulletin. Hitler has just carried out his Night of the Long Knives, in which Ernst Röhm and many others are murdered. I take in this information and comment to Mabel, 'Does this mean there will be another war?' She replies: 'Oh no, Hitler's not a wicked man like the Kaiser.'

I remember the German reoccupation of the Rhineland in 1936, but only as a headline in the *Daily Mail*. Our family view was that it was unavoidable, that Germany was only taking back what was German territory. We did not see it as a cause for war. The Italian invasion of Abyssinia and the Spanish Civil War had more personal impact.

I do remember the shock of Mussolini's invasion, and our sympathy with the Abyssinians. After the defeat, the Emperor of Abyssinia, Haile Selassie, went into exile in Bath, bringing members of his family with him. I was being taught to swim at the old Royal Baths in Bath by Captain Olsen, who also instructed us in climbing horizontal bars and other aspects of Swedish Drill, as physical training was then called. As I splashed around in my inflated water wings, with two princesses, Haile Selassie's granddaughters, in the water beside me, the small but benign figure of the Lion of Judah would look down on us from the edge of the pool. He is now regarded as God by the Rastafarians. There have been many worse gods.

Spain was a matter of more passionate debate, though not inside our family. As Roman Catholics, we regarded the communists, and therefore the Spanish Republican Government, as hostile to religion; they murdered priests and raped nuns. As democrats, we disliked the Fascist Franco, but also distrusted Stalinist influence on the Republicans. We did not support either side, though I think my parents may have felt that Franco would prove to be the lesser of the two evils. From the British point of view that turned out to be correct. Franco kept Spain out of the Second World War, which a communist government might not have been able to do.

However, the young men who came to our tennis parties at Cholwell saw things differently. They correctly expected the war in Spain to be merely a prelude to the war that was coming against Hitler. I heard their arguments from afar, as an eight- or nine-year-old child listening to twenty-year-old men. I do not remember if any of our friends actually fought in Spain; some of them may have felt guilty for failing to volunteer.

In the summer of 1937, our eyes were opened to what the enemy would be like. My elder sister, Elizabeth, has a gift for languages, which she may have inherited from my father, or indeed from his mother who for some of her early years kept her diary in German, and as a young woman taught in Paris. As Elizabeth was studying German, it was proposed that she make an exchange with a German girl whose aunt had made an exchange with one of our neighbours in 1900. Jutta Lorey was to come to us; the following year, in May 1938, Elizabeth was to go to the Loreys.

We did not foresee that this would be a political question. We did not realize that the political attitudes of the Lorey family were somewhat complicated. Frau Lorey was married to a Nazi judge, who disappeared at the end of the war, thought to have been killed by the Russians. Frau Lorey's sister Hildegarde, who, a generation earlier, had been the girl of the original exchange, was an anti-Nazi, but Frau Lorey herself kept quiet. Jutta was a member of the *Bund Deutschen Madel*, a fanatical sixteen-year-old Nazi child, for which she can hardly be blamed. When she made the return visit, Elizabeth spent most of her time alone or with the family's maid, Grete. Jutta was either at college or BDM meetings, Frau Lorey was out a lot and Judge Lorey had been seconded to the east. She was aware of tensions in the family, particularly during the one weekend when the judge returned home, but these seemed more personal than political. Grete was engaged to a soldier and used to take Elizabeth to the town barracks where the soldiers were very impressed by her being English. She learned excellent German which she used later when she worked as a translator at the prisoner-of-war camp in Latimer House during the war.

Jutta's visit to Cholwell was another matter. She brought with her all her adolescent fanaticism. She showed us her BDM dagger with its flamboyant inscription of '*Blood and Iron*' and its swastika. She lay on her bed in the sewing room, listening on short-wave radio to Hitler's speeches. When the door was open, I remember standing outside for a minute or two and listening to one of them. He sounded hysterical to me, a shrieking lunatic raving in a foreign tongue, but to storms of applause. I associate the crises of the 1930s with the rooms in Cholwell in which I heard different broadcasts – the dining room with the Night of the Long Knives, the sewing room with Adolf Hitler, the nursery itself with King Edward VIII's announcement of his abdication and with Neville Chamberlain's declaration of war on Germany.

We did not treat Jutta well. We suspected her of spying, probably rightly. The Hitler Youth who visited Britain were instructed to take photographs of local landmarks; German information packs, prepared for the 1940 invasion which never happened, included some of these snapshots. Jutta was a great photographer of landmarks. We could not stop her photographing Cholwell, which is indeed a prominent landmark, but we tried to prevent her photographing the tower of Downside Abbey. Whether we succeeded or not, I do not know.

We did not like Jutta, and she did not like us. The most spiteful thing I remember doing was cheating at Monopoly to make sure that she did not win. I have heard occasional distant accounts of her since the war, that she had been widowed, that she had become a hippy, that she was living in the Mediterranean. Among the evil things the Nazis did, the perversion of her adolescent enthusiasm is only a tiny mark. We knew, through her, that the Hitler regime was hysterical, evil and dangerous. It helped prepare us for what was to happen next.

When the war came Elizabeth joined the WAAF and worked as a translator. At the end of the war she worked on the repatriation of German prisoners of war and married a young German officer, Peter Bruegger, who had been classified as 'White', because he was anti-Nazi. He farmed our home farm. Though the marriage did not last, he became a popular local figure and was much loved by our children.

* * *

Until I was nine, I was educated at home. My father taught me which didn't work terribly well when I was little because he was tall and impressive and could have a short fuse. It worked extremely well when I was a bit older. I also had lessons with Miss Farr, a young woman from Bristol, who was my sister Anne (Andy)'s excellent governess. Anne was educated at home until she was sixteen because she suffered from acute migraines. Miss Farr eventually left to marry a Mr Farr and become a Mrs Farr. If I did my lesson correctly, she would stick a coloured paper star in the exercise book; if I got five stars, she would stick in a paper duck. I was easily motivated by such rewards. Between lessons I would play with Anne in the garden. My sisters, with their long legs, climbed trees which were too difficult for me. Besides I was something of a coward and they were both bold and debonair.

In 1937, the summer of my ninth birthday, I went to board at the preparatory school of Clifton College. On the night of the Munich agreement we were supposed to be asleep in the dormitory of Matthew's House, the Junior House, just opposite Clifton Zoo. There were twenty boys in my dormitory. We were excited by the prospect of war, not because we wanted war – we were too sensible for that – but because it would be so great an event. Mr Jones, our house tutor, was listening to the news on his radio, in the room below. Infuriatingly, we could barely hear it. However, we heard enough to know that, for the present, Munich meant peace, not war. I remember my feeling of disappointment as the adrenalin rush slowed.

I remember my own eleventh birthday on 14 July 1939, as the last carefree day of that pre-war summer. A special cake was baked at Cholwell. It had a cricket field, in green icing, two sets of stumps, a bat and a ball, all edible and made from marzipan. It was the custom at Clifton Preparatory School for the boy whose birthday it was to distribute his cake, so it had to be quite a large one, enough for thirty boys. The mood was cheerful, our exams were over, and we had prospect of the long summer holidays and I also had the August cricket festival at Weston-super-Mare to look forward to.

But only a few weeks later, on my sister Elizabeth's birthday, 23 August, hope was extinguished by the announcement of the Nazi–Soviet pact. With Stalin as Hitler's ally, war had become inevitable; we all knew it, in Temple Cloud just as surely as in Westminster.

On 1 September, I went down as usual to the library in Cholwell to have my morning lesson with my father. Frank Cooper, who took orders for the local grain merchant, was discussing how many bags of mixed feed my father would need for the pigs. Fletcher interrupted him to turn on the nine o'clock news on the BBC. Germany had invaded Poland. Frank Cooper left, after a few sad words. He, too, had fought in the Great War, as it was still called. My father telephoned his next contact in the network of Air Raid Precautions. He used a First World War phrase, 'The balloon's gone up.'

Two days later, we listened on the nursery wireless to Neville Chamberlain's broadcast, as we had listened only less than three years before, to King Edward VIII's abdication broadcast. Both broadcasts spoke of failure; in both there was a displeasing note of self-pity. I did not feel hostile to Neville Chamberlain, but I did not feel sorry for him either. I thought then, as I think now, that he had tried a policy of appeasement in all good faith; it had not succeeded because Hitler had always intended war. It was an honourable failure, but Neville Chamberlain's personal disappointment was a petty thing beside the disaster which had fallen on the world. Chamberlain did not sound like a war leader.

I was still of an age when I was given supper in bed. I slept in the pink room on the south-west corner of Cholwell, with windows on one side looking down the drive and on the other looking out over Paul Wood. My supper consisted of bread and honey, a banana and a glass of milk. Later in that September, I remember listening to the evening news bulletin from my bed.

The Government was concerned that in 1914 there had been undue optimism about the length of the war, and talk of 'the boys being home for Christmas'. They were anxious that this should not happen again, and put out an official forecast that this war would last for three years. I did not doubt that Britain would eventually win it. I assumed that the pattern of the First World War would be repeated, that eventually the United States would be drawn in, and that American industrial capacity would be decisive. I was, however, very interested in the question of how long the war would last, since I would have to plan my own life in terms of that expectation.

I remember doing a simple sum. Governments, I thought, are always wrong. If the Government thinks the war will last three years, it will be longer than that. It will probably last twice as long. I should, therefore, base my own planning on the war lasting for six years. I was now eleven years old. In six years' time I should be seventeen. I should not be old enough to fight before the war was over.

This judgement proved to be correct – the war in Europe ended shortly before my seventeenth birthday and the war in Japan shortly thereafter. I had to do two years' National Service, but that was in the peacetime RAF and I never regarded it as anything other than an interruption, somewhat unwelcome, in ordinary life. I do not think this attitude was unpatriotic. I was entirely prepared to join the forces. But I did decide I should concentrate on getting ahead with my school life, without thinking that I must prepare myself to be a soldier.

In fact, for the first six months, hardly anyone was doing any fighting, apart from the German invasion of Poland and the disastrous Russian invasion of Finland. At Clifton we made model aircraft out of balsa wood; the wings usually fell off mine. I remember being cold at Clifton, so cold that I used to go to bed with a torch battery in my pyjama breast pocket. I would short-circuit the battery, so that it would spread a little warmth over the area of my heart. There was also a certain amount of bullying.

One boy, in particular, was being bullied. He was a gentle, rather plump boy who came, I think, from Wales. I rather liked him. I remember discussing this with Bishop, another friend who was later killed, perhaps while still at school, in a cycling accident. I asked Bishop whether he did not think that we ought to do something about it. He gave me a political reply, based on the then unknown theory of the pecking order.

'It would be no good,' he said. 'There are twelve boys in our dormitory. Each has a position in the order. "Y" – the boy who was being bullied – is twelfth. You and I are about eight and nine. We do not have the strength to intervene. If we do, we shall join "Y" in being bullied; it will do him no good and we shall then be bullied ourselves.' I recognized the truth in Bishop's logic and, I regret to say, accepted the realities of our political situation.

The winter passed. The spring of 1940 came and with it the German invasion of Norway, the attack on Belgium and the

Netherlands, the battle for France, the fall of the Chamberlain Government, the appointment of Winston Churchill as Prime Minister. While these great events were happening, one of the boys in our house had gone down with polio; it was a mild case and he survived with little or no disability. But we were all put in quarantine, and encouraged to stay outdoors. So I heard of most of these events, and Churchill's early speeches as Prime Minister, sitting in the bright sunshine on Clifton's Under Green, listening to a junior master's portable radio.

In the West Country, life went on surprisingly normally during what we all knew was an ultimate struggle for survival. There was a German daylight raid on the docks at Avonmouth. A detachment of the Coldstream Guards, having just been taken off the beaches of Dunkirk, spent a few weeks at Midsomer Norton. We felt the safer for their presence. We all followed the daily scores of German aircraft shot down in the Battle of Britain. We now know that they were exaggerated. The fear of German invasion gradually receded. Throughout this time my basic expectation did not change. I thought we would win the Battle of Britain, I believed in Winston Churchill, I did not expect an invasion to succeed, I looked to the United States as 'the arsenal of democracy'. I felt confident that we would win in the end, as we had in 1918 and 1815.

My American aunts sent a Western Union cable in June inviting me to go to America; it even, touchingly, promised that I would be able to continue with the classics. I was rather excited by the idea, which might well have changed my life. I would, in any case, have been at greater risk from torpedoes crossing the Atlantic, than from bombs if I stayed at home. My parents took the view that they were not entitled to send me, or my sisters, if the other people of Temple Cloud could not send their children. In any case they believed in keeping the family together. I am sure that they were right, but I have always felt grateful for the invitation.

We went back to Clifton for the autumn term of 1940. A new brick and concrete shelter had been built for us at the end of Under Green; it looked like an oversized public lavatory. Thirty boys from Poole's House slept there every night, in bunks. I did not find it disagreeable; it was certainly warmer than the dormitory.

The German night attacks on the larger cities outside London started in November. Coventry was the first to be hit. Bristol came next. We were bombed in two raids, with a week between them. On the first occasion the bombs did not come very close to our shelter, though it was a noisy night and there were large fires in the central area. My parents, in Cholwell, could see the glow of the fires, and heard the bombers passing overhead. The Heinkel bombers had a particularly penetrating, intermittent drone.

The second night was more frightening. As the sirens sounded, the matron suggested that we should all say a prayer. I suggested that we should say our normal grace, 'For what we are about to receive, may the Lord make us truly thankful'!

The Luftwaffe used at that time to drop their bombs in sticks of four or five. In the middle of the raid, we heard a stick of bombs moving towards our shelter, which would certainly not stand a direct hit. The first bomb was loud enough, the second louder, the third louder still. The fourth was loudest of all, in fact about 50 yards away, and threw stones and earth on top of the shelter. It was apparent that the stick of bombs was falling in a straight line. If there was a fifth, it would land on top of us. We waited for it. It did not come. Although I was to be bombed again later in the war, in Somerset and London, that was the nearest I came to being killed.

After the previous night of the Bristol Blitz, my parents had thought of taking me away from Clifton. There was no question about that the second time, for them or for the school. I was driven out to Cholwell by one of the housemasters, Mr Hope Simpson, on his motorbike. We passed the burnt-out churches and the broken glass. My father had driven in but missed us on the way. The school evacuated itself to Cholwell House, sleeping on mattresses. The boys ate us out of the drums of Canadian honey which my mother, ever mindful of the Irish famine, had laid up in the cellar. After a few days most of them dispersed to their homes, and remain only as names in the Cholwell visitors' book. My last two terms at Clifton Preparatory School were spent at Butcombe Court, a pleasant country house about ten miles from Cholwell, within bicycling distance on Sundays.

In late May 1941 I was in my last term at Clifton Preparatory School when the German battleship *Bismarck* sunk the *Hood* in the mid-Atlantic. Only three of the *Hood*'s crew of 1421 survived. My mother and I were taken into Temple Meads Station in Bristol by my father; we went by train to Windsor where I was about to sit the Entrance Scholarship for Eton. Most public schools were by that time sending their scholarship papers to be taken at the preparatory schools, but Eton's only concession to the problems of wartime travel was to put up the scholarship candidates in the boys' houses. My mother stayed at the White Lion in the High Street; I was sent to Lyttelton's House.

The three days of the scholarship examination were interwoven with reports of the pursuit of the *Bismarck* by the Royal Navy. On the last evening, the *Bismarck* was torpedoed from the air and sank the following day. The *Hood* had been avenged. I found the exam papers rather too difficult for me. My Latin, thanks to my father, was tolerable, though hardly up to scholarship standards; my Greek was negligible; my French was of Common Entrance standard; my mathematics was scarcely up to that. However, I enjoyed the history paper and romped away with the essay, which was set on Satan's fall from Heaven as described in Milton's *Paradise Lost*. It was just my subject:

> Him the Almighty Power
> Hurled headlong flaming from th' ethereal sky
> With hideous ruin and combustion down
> To bottomless perdition.

I did not need to be asked twice to describe the fires of Hell. Lyttelton later told my mother that my essay was the best of them all.

Before we went back he had a long conversation with her, which she recounted to me on the train. He did not know whether I would get the scholarship; no Eton scholarship had ever been given to a candidate as weak in the classics. In any case, he thought that I would find the atmosphere of College too tough. He said he would be very pleased to take me into his house, whether I got the scholarship or not.

We discussed this with my father when we got home. I was also entered for the Charterhouse scholarship. My father suggested that I should go to Eton if I got the Eton scholarship, go to Charterhouse if I got the Charterhouse scholarship, and go to Lyttelton's House if I got neither. I was happy with that proposal. The Charterhouse scholarship would pay half my school fees, and I liked the idea of being a scholar. On the other hand, I much liked the atmosphere of Eton, and had been impressed by Lyttelton himself. I had even been measured for my top hat.

A few days later we received a sympathetic letter from Lyttelton saying that I had not been awarded a scholarship. Everything therefore depended on the Charterhouse exam. Fifty years later my son, Jacob, who had himself gone to Eton, heard a somewhat different story from a visiting Eton master in Hong Kong.

By this account, the 1941 examination was the last time the Provost of Eton played a part in deciding who was to receive a scholarship. The provost was Lord Quickswood, earlier Lord Hugh Cecil, son of the Lord Salisbury who was Queen Victoria's last Prime Minister. The provost, it is said, objected on quite other grounds. He did not take his stand on the fact that I knew little Latin and less Greek, true though that was. He argued that I should not have an Eton scholarship because I was a Roman Catholic. The examiners wanted to award a scholarship; the provost prevailed; no provost was ever again invited to join in the scholarship proceedings. No Roman Catholic was ever barred again.

In the meantime, my papers were written at Butcombe Court and sent to Charterhouse. They followed the same pattern; an excellent essay, good on history, weak in Latin and French, negligible in Greek and Mathematics. Indeed, in one mathematics paper I got three marks out of a hundred. I do not know why I was so bad at elementary mathematics since in my adult life I have used them more than most people do.

Robert Birley was the Headmaster of Charterhouse. The examiners spent the Friday discussing the various papers. They found it easy to award the first scholarship, which went to Simon Raven. They awarded ten others. They came to mine, and the weight of feeling was that my classics and maths were simply not up to scholarship standard. Birley, who was himself a historian, wanted to get a potential historian into the list. On Friday evening, he was not getting his own way. If they had decided then, I would not have got the scholarship.

Robert Birley was, however, a skilled chairman of a committee. He used a device which I remember using later on a critical occasion as Chairman of the Arts Council. Because he realized that he couldn't get the decision he wanted, he postponed it. On the following day, the examiners met again. I was nodded through for the twelfth scholarship. When the telegram arrived I was delighted.

There is no doubt that Lord Quickswood's intervention and Birley's persuasiveness changed my life. I know that I would have enjoyed Eton, and would have been happy in Lyttelton's House, possibly happier than I was at Charterhouse. Indeed, I might well have been too happy, too much of an Etonian; Charterhouse presented me with greater challenges. The difference extends beyond the schools themselves, to my Oxford life, to my career. If I had gone to Eton, I doubt if I would have gone on to Balliol; I might have opted for a more sympathetic political environment at Oxford. I would probably have found my political progress easier; there were plenty of Old Etonian chairmen of safe Conservative seats in the 1950s, though few are left now.

I am grateful to Charterhouse for many things. But I felt more at home at Eton, both in 1941 and later when my son Jacob was enjoying his time there. Perhaps the real advantage of going to Charterhouse was that it did not have the same dangerous charm for someone of my interests and personality. If I had entered the world of Eton, the world of Luxmore's garden and the College Library, of the cricket fields, of Thomas Gray and Horace Walpole, I might well have found it too much of a lifelong lotus land. Cyril Connolly, with whom I was later to work on the *Sunday Times*, regarded nostalgia for Eton as one of 'The

Enemies of Promise'. It was so for him, it might well have been so for me. Jacob has become a loyal Old Etonian, and Eton suited him extremely well, but he did not become addicted to its ancient charm. For myself, I think Charterhouse was probably for the best, but there were aspects of Eton, including the personality of Lyttelton himself, a remarkable and scholarly housemaster, which I would clearly have enjoyed very greatly. In the words that Senator Bill Bradley used of basketball, Charterhouse did 'teach me to use my elbows'.

FOUR

A Peak in Darien

As soon as I knew how to read, I delighted in reading. I still have the copy of H. G. Wells' *Outline of History* which Anne bound in a canvas jacket in 1934. It is a chunky book, of some six hundred pages. I may never have finished it, but I waded through several hundred pages. My first fascination was with the dinosaurs, but I was also interested in history as such. Before reading Wells, I had read *Our Island Story*, which was very imperialist, and Dickens' *Child's History of England*, which was very Protestant. I responded to his account of the Reformation by becoming equally partisan on the Catholic side. It was the Catholic martyrs I cared about; Bloody Mary became Good Queen Mary. King Henry VIII I abominated, as I still do. For Queen Elizabeth I, I had mixed feelings.

Literature forms the architecture of the mind. Shakespeare came first, even before I could read. In the winter of 1931, my mother was reading *Macbeth* with my sisters. We were in the nursery at Cholwell, with a fire in the little Victorian stove. I was three and a half years old, and had not yet learned how to read.

To my sisters' irritation, my mother insisted that I should join in the reading. She would read a line, and I would repeat it after her. My sisters felt that this procedure caused undue delay, and that Lady Macbeth was too substantial a part to be given to a three-year-old; they would then have been nine and ten years old.

I can remember moments of the reading. Most vividly, I remember the scene in Macduff's castle, when Macbeth sends his murderers to kill Lady Macduff and their son. I was young enough to identify with the son. When the murderer calls his father a traitor, the boy has the splendid line: 'Thou ly'st, thou shag-hair'd villain'. I liked that, and I admired the courage of his last words: 'He has kill'd me, mother; run away, I pray you'.

However, most of the lines I remember from that first reading come from my own part, that is from Lady Macbeth herself. My sisters thought it comic when I repeated the lines:

> I have given suck; and know
> How tender 'tis to love the babe that milks me:
> I would, while it was smiling in my face,
> Have pluck'd my nipple from his boneless gums,
> And dash'd the brains out, had I so sworn, as you
> Have done in this.

I had to ask what the words 'I have given suck' meant, and remember my mother explaining to me about breastfeeding, a practice I had only abandoned some three years before.

In this speech, Lady Macbeth is spurring her husband on to the murder of the old King, Duncan. Macbeth interjects 'If we should fail' and receives the reply:

> We fail.
> But screw your courage to the sticking-place,
> And we'll not fail.

This led to a discussion of Lady Macbeth's response. How did she say 'We fail'? Was it scornfully, as though failure was impossible, or was it fatalistically, as a consequence to be faced? In 1915 as a young actress in Margaret Anglin's company, my mother had discussed this point with old English actors in the cast. Beatrice herself was still a junior; Margaret Anglin was playing Lady Macbeth; Tyrone Power Senior was playing Macbeth; Tyrone Power Junior was being dandled on Beatrice's knee, as his father learned his lines. Tyrone Power Senior always found it difficult to remember his lines, but, like his son, he was a fine figure of a man, in the old Irish style.

The English actors in the cast opted for the fatalistic reading 'We fail', which should be said with a falling tone in a matter-of-fact way. That, they had been told by old actors of their youth, was how Sarah Siddons had pronounced it, and she was the greatest Lady Macbeth the English stage could remember. So I played the line in the Sarah Siddons tradition. My sisters were much better than I was in the role of the witches, and danced gleefully around the nursery table.

I was particularly close to my mother because when the slump came, in 1930, my parents decided that they couldn't afford a nanny, so my mother completely took over looking after me. I was two. I spent a great deal of time with her, the two of us mostly just conversing with each other. It fell to my sisters – Elizabeth was seven years older than me and Anne six years older – to get me up and dress me which was a chore they got very bored with. I had one lovely month when my American granny, Granny Warren, came over and stayed. She was in fact dying of cancer – although she kept her illness from us all. She took over the job of dressing me in the morning and I would rush along to her bedroom and she would talk to me about her childhood in the America of the 1860s.

My mother was a hugely entertaining person to be with. She had a perfect voice, a sense of timing and a sense of occasion. She had the temperament of a star, but not of a star who made excessive claims for herself. She had wit and intelligence and energy and I remember her saying she couldn't understand people being bored because she'd never been bored in her life.

As an actress my mother had considerable dress sense and awareness. She dressed in the smart, understated American style of the 1930s which was made fashionable in Britain by Mrs Simpson. She didn't spend a great deal of money on her clothes. When she got married she'd been given an allowance for her clothes, by her father, in American Trading Company preference shares. But, about a year later, the American Trading Company – under a callow new proprietor – lost most of its money and stopped paying even preference dividends. My mother felt that she had had money to buy clothes in the past but that she didn't any more. She was well dressed but thrifty.

My mother still went out on the English countryside routine of 'making calls'. The rules still really came from the carriage days: you knew the people living in the big house of their village within a seven-mile radius and you called on them – you called on houses rather than people. Therefore you had a secondary acquaintance with people who weren't in a seven-mile radius of your house but were in a seven-mile radius of a house on which you called. The calls were made in the afternoon and occasionally I was taken as a child with my mother to call. My mother had been fascinated by and had mastered the whole etiquette of calls and how Somerset ladies spoke to each other. She observed, as an actress, how old Lady Waldegrave used to talk. If you were visiting Lady Waldegrave, she would say, as the hostess, 'How kind of you to come.' And you would reply, 'How kind of you to ask me.' Beatrice discovered that she could play the Somerset ladies role better than the Somerset ladies themselves.

We were to read Shakespeare again as a family during the war. I remember that we read the English history plays, which seemed to have most to say about the dire circumstances of 1940 and 1941. Shakespeare always teaches the Churchillian doctrine: 'In victory magnanimity, in defeat, defiance'. We read *Richard II*, which contains the great patriotic speech 'This Sceptered Isle' of old John of Gaunt, 'time honoured Lancaster'. We also read *King John*, a much underrated play. I read the part of the Bastard, which also has a great patriotic speech, well suited to the worst days of the Second World War:

> This England never did, nor never shall
> Lie at the proud foot of a conqueror,
> But when it first did help to wound itself.
> Now these her princes are come home again,
> Come the three corners of the world in arms,
> And we shall shock them: Nought shall make us rue,
> If England to itself do rest but true.

In 1943 and 1944, my mother took me to see John Gielgud, first in *Macbeth* and then in *Hamlet*. London was covered by the blackout, and the plays started early, so that the audiences could get home in safety. Gielgud was not, by his own high standards, a particularly memorable Macbeth; he lacked the physical characteristics for the part.

Gielgud's Hamlet was another matter. No single actor can capture all the aspects of Hamlet's personality. No doubt Gielgud overemphasized the intellectual and sensitive Hamlet, at the expense of the active young Prince, but his was the most moving Hamlet I have seen.

It was Shakespeare who framed my mind, in terms of my vision of the world, before my experience of adult life had set in. He gave me a sense of the drama of life, and its poetry; he gave me a sense of the variety of personality and of the range from good to evil. I was fond of the wise old men, of Cardinal Wolsey, of Polonius. Indeed, my critics might think that I have made a living out of playing Polonius on the public stage; I am particularly aware of his inability to see what a comic character he was making of himself.

I did not see Hamlet as a role model, or Julius Caesar, or any of the English kings. I knew already that I was not destined to play Romeo. It was, rather, the great speeches which gave me my picture of the world. The ancient Greeks were brought up in the same way on Homer. I do not suppose many of them thought they would grow up to be a second Achilles; it was the total effect of the poetry that gave them access to a Homeric consciousness.

In wartime, one needs to turn to great literature. Shakespeare gave that, and he also gave expression to a patriotism which makes other patriotic verse sound like a penny whistle. In peacetime, one needs to understand the world as Shakespeare sees it with affection but without illusion, with caution but without timidity, with realism as well as idealism, with humility as well as ambition, with a certain melancholy. I certainly took my politics from Shakespeare. I have never doubted that he was the leading genius of the English nation. He taught me to think, to feel, to understand and to place myself as appropriately as I might in the drama of life. Like him my politics have been rooted in the human need for order and harmony. Like him I hope for the best but fear the worst. Like him I have a Catholic nostalgia for a lost past: 'Bare ruin'd choirs where once the sweet birds sang'.

It was in the first winter of the war, in January 1939, that I came across the next book which changed my life. I had caught a bad dose of influenza. The local doctor prescribed the new sulfa drug, M & B 693, which was later to be replaced by penicillin. I had to stay in my bedroom for two or three weeks. We still had a young housemaid, though she soon vanished, and I remember her coming in early in the morning to lay and light the bedroom fire, a luxury which lasted in English country houses down to – but seldom beyond – the outbreak of the Second World War.

As I was recovering, I wanted to find a book to read, so I went down to the Cholwell library. There I found a set of James Boswell's *Life of Johnson*, which had been published by the Oxford University Press in the 1820s. I could only find the first three out of the four volumes.

I lay in bed for the next ten days, entranced and delighted by Boswell. Here the romantic lines of Keats really come close to it; Boswell's *Life of Johnson* had on me the effect that Chapman's *Homer* had on him:

> Then felt I like some watcher of the skies
> When a new planet swims into his ken;
> Or like stout Cortez when with eagle eyes
> He star'd at the Pacific – and all his men
> Look'd at each other with a wild surmise –
> Silent, upon a peak in Darien.

There were many things I found attractive about Boswell's *Life*. I immediately came to share his hero-worship of Samuel Johnson:

> To write the life of him who excelled all mankind in writing the lives of others, and who, whether we consider his extraordinary endorsements, or his various works, has been equalled by few in any age, is an arduous, and may be reckoned in me a presumptuous task.

I slipped easily into the notion that I was reading the life of a congenial, great man.

Johnson is also a moralist; which is a dangerous thing to be, because it is hard to make moral judgements without becoming something of a prig and a hypocrite. To Boswell, himself constantly in a state of moral torment and doubt, it was the confidence of Johnson's morality which was most attractive. I do not think that was so in my case; no doubt I have myself been too self-confident in making moral judgements. I felt that Johnson was right to consider moral issues as essential to life. At ten I wanted to learn how to make sound moral judgements, and I wanted to know how to write good English prose. I thought Johnson could help me to learn both those things.

I respected but did not really share Johnson's Toryism. Decades later, as I was told, Michael Hartwell, then the proprietor of the *Daily Telegraph*, was discussing with Bill Deedes his possible successor as Editor. I had recently given up the editorship of *The Times*, and my name was mentioned. 'He's not our kind of Tory,' said Michael, and that closed the issue. I never have been a *Daily Telegraph* Tory, and I did not find myself a Samuel Johnson Tory either. He was a near Jacobite, King and Country, traditional Tory, although he was liberal in his views of the great social issues of race and poverty, and not an imperialist. I have always been a John Locke, Declaration of Independence, Peelite, even Pittite, type of Tory, and Johnson would have sniffed me out as a closet Whig.

It was not only Johnson's mind and personality which attracted me, but the book itself, and above all the eighteenth century. I do not believe in reincarnation, but that is the best way to describe the impact that Boswell's *Life of Johnson* had on me. I felt that I was re-entering a world to which I belonged, a world which was more real to me, and certainly more attractive, than the mid twentieth century. I felt that what had happened since Johnson's death in 1784 was a prolonged decline of civilization, the industrial revolution, ugly architecture, the slums, the heavy Victorian age, the great European wars of Napoleon, the Kaiser and Hitler. I yearned for the age of harmony before the fall. It took me half a lifetime to get used to the modern age, and I have never become particularly fond of it.

In reading Boswell, I was able to slip into the garden of the eighteenth century and regain a lost paradise. I enjoyed everything about that century, the houses, the furniture, the landscape, the paintings, the music, the literature, the letters, the politics, the people. Although this perception of the eighteenth century as a golden age has gradually eroded, it still remains quite vivid. In the years when our own family was growing up, Gillian and I lived in two fine eighteenth-century houses, Ston Easton Park in Somerset – a beautiful extravagance – and Smith Square in London. Now we live in an early twentieth-century flat in London and a late fifteenth-century house in Somerset. I delight in both of them; the eighteenth-century nostalgia has eased. But it is still the period from 1714, the death of Queen Anne, to 1789, the year of the French Revolution, which is my true homeland in history and literature.

I never suffered from Johnson's extreme fear of death, but I did feel sympathetic to his congenital melancholy. I also admired the energy he put into friendship. The passage I best remember from my first reading of Boswell's *Life* is the one in which he helped a nearly destitute Oliver Goldsmith; this account is in Johnson's own words:

> I received one morning a message from poor Goldsmith, that he was in great distress, and as it was not in his power to come to me, begging that I would come to him as soon as possible. I sent him a guinea, and promised to come to him directly. I accordingly went as soon as I was dressed, and found that his landlady had arrested him for his rent, at which he was in a violent passion. I perceived that he had already changed my guinea, and had got a bottle of Madeira and a glass before him. I put the cork into the bottle, desired he would be calm, and began to talk to him of the means by which he might be extricated. He then told me that he had a novel ready for the press, which he produced to me. I looked into it, and saw its merit, told the landlady I should soon return, and having gone to a bookseller, sold it for sixty pounds. I brought Goldsmith the money, and he discharged his rent, not without rating his landlady in a high tone for having used him so ill.

The novel was *The Vicar of Wakefield*; £60 would probably have had the purchasing power of £5000 in modern money.

That summer I was in the senior form of the junior section of the Clifton Preparatory School, a form taught by Captain Read. With war imminent, it was a time of heightened emotional tension, a time when everyone's imagination was stretched. Read was a quiet man, a good schoolmaster, who was a veteran of the First World War. I now suspect that he may have been one of those good officers who never wholly recovered from their war experience; he did not speak of it to us.

Captain Read set us an essay on 'a building we had visited during the holidays'. I wrote about the little Catholic church at East Harptree, and described, in rather sentimental terms, how it had been built by poor Irish labourers in the nineteenth century. Captain Read recognized that this was an unusual piece of writing for a ten-year-old boy, gave it a top mark, perhaps even ten out of ten, and praised it to the class as exceptionally well written.

This encouragement was very important to me. Before that I had no idea I had any special talent for writing. I knew that I was reasonably bright by the standard of the school; I usually came third in class placings, behind my contemporaries Pym and Foster, who contended for the top position. Captain Read told me I had a special talent for writing essays, and I believed him. I have been writing them ever since.

It was through my fascination with Johnson that I came to read the poets of the seventeenth and eighteenth centuries. My favourite book, one of the favourite books of my lifetime, became Johnson's *Lives of the Poets*. My mother bought for me a calf-bound set of the 1779 first edition of Johnson's *Poets*, with the works of the poets from Cowley to Lyttleton in fifty-six volumes, two volumes of index, and twelve volumes of the *Lives*. This was a fourteenth-birthday present, bought from George's of Bristol; it still has their price marked in it, of £6 15s. The first owner had been an eighteenth-century clergyman, Francis Mills, who was born in 1759. He may have bought the first volumes when he was twenty, and lived through to die in 1851 in his ninety-second year. I hope these little books gave him the lifetime's happiness they have given me.

Johnson's *Poets* covers the period from the 1620s to the 1760s. The minor poets of this period include Rochester, the libidinous Earl; Addison, one of the most delightful of English essayists; Gay, who wrote *The Beggar's Opera*; the saintly Isaac Watts, one of the best English hymn writers, and Gray, who wrote the *Elegy Written in a Country Churchyard*. When I suffered from adolescent depression at Charterhouse, I found Gray's *Elegy*, the mirror of my mood, a great comfort.

> The curfew tolls the knell of parting day,
> The lowing herd winds slowly o'er the lea,
> The Ploughman homeward plods his weary way,
> And leaves the world to darkness and to me.

In Johnson's collection, there are four major literary voices, those of Milton, Dryden, Swift and Pope; of those Swift is a great satirist rather than a great poet. Dryden is indeed a great poet, free-flowing with fire and energy, but I never found him a particularly interesting writer despite the intellectual quality of his criticism. The two great poets whom I have come back to again and again, who, after Shakespeare, have done most to shape my mind, are Milton and Pope. Milton came rather the earlier of the two; I can remember first hearing *Lycidas* read in a form room at Clifton.

Lycidas was written in memory of Edward King, a young Cambridge poet who shared Milton's idealism and died in 1637. One can imagine a young Cambridge poet of the 1930s writing such an elegy about one of his contemporaries, who might have died fighting Franco. It is a poem of the left, which foreshadows a dark future; I was reading it in just such an historic context:

> The hungry sheep look up, and are not fed,
> But swoln with wind, and the rank mist they draw,
> Rot inwardly, and foul contagion spread;
> Besides what the grim wolf with privy paw
> Daily devours apace and nothing said;
> But that two-handed engine at the door
> Stands ready to smite once, and smite no more.

These lines from *Lycidas* gave me the true thrill of great poetry then, and they still do now. When written, they were indeed prophetic of the civil war that was about to break upon England. The executions they prefigure, which may already have been foreshadowed in Milton's mind, were those of the men, such as Laud and Strafford, whom he regarded as having failed to feed 'the hungry sheep'; the young poets in the 1930s regarded Neville Chamberlain and the appeasers in much the same way. King Charles I himself, on 30 January 1649, was executed by the axe, that 'two-handed engine at the door'.

I enjoyed the poetry of public affairs; I was already storing up phrases and the rhythm of sentences which I felt I could use. If I sought to learn the use of irony and antithesis from Johnson, a line like 'Daily devours apace and nothing said', with its dying fall, became part of the inner rhythm of my early attempts at English prose.

No doubt John Milton is a greater poet than Alexander Pope; he is indeed second only to Shakespeare in the canon of English poets. But in learning how to read, which I was doing with the definite intention of learning how to write, 'elective affinities', to use Goethe's congenial phrase, go for as much as poetic merit. I learned most from the poets whose personalities I liked best. I admire Milton; I love Pope.

Although our ability to classify poets by political temperament has often been denied, it seems to me that it is sometimes quite obvious. Alexander Pope loved Horace, a natural conservative among Roman poets. Pope took the view 'whate'er is best administered is best' – not a radical view of politics, he admired the Augustan ideal and detested what he saw as the contagious vulgarity of Grub Street. Milton was a man of the left, a radical progressive, a supporter of Cromwell, a hardline servant of the revolutionary government. Had he been a young Frenchman in the early 1790s, he would have been a Jacobin; if a young Russian in 1917, he would have been a Bolshevik.

I knew perfectly well at the age of ten that my own political temperament belonged to the conservative type, that I had no political sympathy at all with Milton's radical progressive point of view. I had read about Cromwell in my early history books and saw him as an enemy. The poet who was to have the strongest influence on me was bound to be one who shared the temperament of rational conservatism. I found such a poet in Alexander Pope. He has been the friendly guide to my literary life.

His critics have said that Pope is not a poet at all, but, in effect, a brilliant prose writer, using verse as his medium for expressing what they would regard as merely prosaic thoughts. He is indeed an unusual poet; he was a cripple, marked by the effects of a tubercular disease of the spine in childhood. He was some inches short of five foot in height. Such an experience has its impact on the development of personality. As with blindness, certain aspects of life are cut off, but other aspects are intensified. Language, and the control of language, became his resource, into which he focused an astonishing energy.

In no poet does one feel to the same degree that each line has been packed with an intensity of meaning, so that phrase after phrase comes to the reader primed to explode, not as a sparkler or grenade, but with a nuclear energy. I do not know if I appreciated this when I first read Pope; Shakespeare and Blake are great poets who are highly accessible to children; Pope is a poet of argument, and the arguments are often mature in character. Later I was to realize that Pope's arguments compress whole books into a couplet or two. Take these opening lines in the second book of *The Essay on Man*:

Know then thyself, presume not God to scan;
The proper study of mankind is Man.
Plac'd on this isthmus of a middle state,
A being darkly wise, and rudely great:
With too much knowledge for the Sceptic side,
With too much weakness for the Stoic's pride,
He hangs between; in doubt to act, or rest;
In doubt to deem himself a God, or Beast.

Each couplet is a tablet of stone. Although both are great poems, the preference between *Lycidas* and *The Essay on Man* is inevitably a temperamental one; it is the choice between the radical's sense of destiny and a conservatism tempered with scepticism. I was already seeing the world through Pope's eyes rather than Milton's. For me Milton might be the greater poet, but Pope was far more sympathetic.

The virtues of the best prose include clarity, energy, rhythm, strength and concentration of meaning. No word should be wasted; words should have colour as well as logical coherence. These are the lessons of Pope; everyone who aspires to write good English prose, and particularly journalists, who have to write too much of it, too fast, should read Pope, not occasionally but regularly. In any case such a habit is a great, and reliable, pleasure. If one has the right temperament for it.

FIVE

But we'll do more, Sempronius

In September 1941, my father drove me for my first term at Charterhouse in his green 1932 open Lagonda, using some saved petrol coupons; I remember our happy feeling of companionship. The setting of the school is beautiful, and even then I appreciated it; the old school buildings, the best Gothic of 1870, look out over the green, where later I was to watch Peter May as a thirteen-year-old batsman; he became one of the finest English batsmen there ever was. The green itself is at the summit of the steep hill which runs up from Godalming; the view stretches out to Haslemere. Around the school there were walks in its extensive grounds, and beyond that the Surrey countryside, though Surrey seemed brown and scrawny compared to the green meadows of Somerset.

In summer the setting was delightful, but in autumn, winter and spring, it was cold, almost as bone-chillingly cold as the Charles River in mid-winter, if one walks back across the bridge from Harvard to Boston. My father had been cold at Charterhouse; I was cold. Nevertheless, I was quite happy in my first year. I was a fag in Verites, which was my house; 'fag' was then an innocent word, which meant that I had to perform minor domestic tasks and run errands for the monitors. My own house monitor soon discovered that he would do better to polish his own shoes than have me polish them.

I was in the scholars' form, and found myself sitting next to Simon Raven, on the alphabetical principle. He was as good a classical scholar as I was a bad one, and was soon moved up a year into the fifth form. The quiet and elderly form master of the Remove, Mr Lake, had taught my father when he was a young man, and shared my enthusiasm for the novels of Anthony Trollope.

My great-grandfather had been to Charterhouse, in the time of Thackeray; my grandfather had been to Charterhouse, less than ten years before the school moved out of London and down to Godalming in Surrey; my father had been to Charterhouse in the years before the First World War. None of them had been happy; all had received a sound classical education and retained a loyalty to their old school. For much of the time I was not happy, or in good physical health, but I too retain an affectionate loyalty for Charterhouse.

Institutions are like people; one has a temperamental affinity with them, or a temperamental unease. I doubt if I have an '*anima naturaliter Catholica*', a naturally Catholic soul. Left to its own devices, my soul is rather inclined to Protestant liberalism. I do, however, have a naturally Catholic temperament; I enjoy the personality of the Church of Rome, as well as being thankful for its graces. I love the ancient institutions of Somerset. I love the institutions of the United States. In another life I would have liked to have been born in Boston, preferably in the 1860s, studied at Harvard and – if my career flourished – become a Senator for Massachusetts during the Presidency of Theodore Roosevelt. I related reasonably well to Clifton College, saw the appeal of an Eton I did not go to, am loyal to Charterhouse, rather disliked Balliol – which returned the compliment – but enjoyed Oxford, and particularly the Oxford Union, had a liberal education at the *Financial Times*, worked well with the *Sunday Times*, have had by far my greatest professional loyalty to *The Times*, seriously disliked the institutional BBC, was happy and useful at the Arts Council and enjoy a peaceful old age in the House of Lords. Balliol and the BBC, out of all those institutions, I did not take to. They were not my cup of tea, and most decidedly I was never theirs.

One story illustrates how Charterhouse sees the world. My daughter Charlotte, who was a sweet rebel as a teenager, had left Cheltenham Ladies College in disfavour; it was, in my view, the College's fault rather than hers. I remember writing to the Chairman of the Board of Governors a letter which contained the sentence: 'You make the girls unhappy and then punish them for being so'. We decided that Charlotte should, if possible, take her A levels at Charterhouse. They received a letter from Cheltenham, which, apparently, warned them against Charlotte in strident terms. Their reaction was to decide at once that they ought to take her. I was an Old Carthusian, which constituted a bond; Charlotte's education was in difficulty; they obviously ought to help. That is how sympathetic grown-ups think. It is not how all schools would have reacted. So Charlotte became the fifth generation of Rees-Moggs to go to the school of Addison, Steele, Blackstone, Wesley, Thackeray, Max Beerbohm and Robert Graves.

At the start of the autumn term of 1941, the war was shuddering towards its tipping point. Germany had invaded Russia, and at first had been having every success. The Russian winter was holding the German army before Moscow. Towards the end of my first term at Charterhouse, the Japanese bombed Pearl Harbor, and the United States entered the war. After that, there was never any doubt who was going to win. Of course, Pearl Harbor came as a great relief to the British; the Japanese had given us an invincible ally. Despite the loss of Malaya and then of Singapore, the turn happened in the last months of 1941, and every schoolboy knew it.

At Christmas the scholars were promoted to the Special Remove, which was then taught by a charismatic man, Bob Arrowsmith. He would have regarded the word 'charismatic' as new-fangled, possibly blasphemous and certainly vulgar. He had three great enthusiasms: Charterhouse, cricket and eighteenth-century literature. He found that I shared all three; having discovered in the nets that I was a hopeless duffer at cricket, he particularly encouraged my interest in the eighteenth century. He received antiquarian booksellers' catalogues, and left them for me on his desk; he got me to read Gibbon's *Decline and Fall*; he let me explore the minor eighteenth-century poets, such as William Shenstone; he introduced me to the great classical scholar Richard Bentley, and to the eighteenth-century letter writers. In those days, when his arthritis only showed in a slight limp, he was a great walker and we went on country walks together and discussed what Gray had written to Mason, or John Wilkes's reply to Lord Sandwich. 'You will either die of the pox or by hanging.' 'That depends, my Lord, on whether I embrace your Lordship's mistress or your principles.'

For some boys, probably the majority, Bob Arrowsmith was a great teacher. We used to imitate his drawling vowel sounds. 'My dear Sir', he would say, and it was easy to imitate that. With those he did not like, he could be more alarming. Max Hastings, who has edited both the *Daily Telegraph* and the *Evening Standard*, was later to have him as a housemaster. I believe that Bob tried to be kind to him at an unhappy period of his life, but I do not think Max has ever forgiven him for his inability to reach a common ground of sympathy.

In February 1942, I asked Bob whether, in addition to my ordinary school work, in which I was rather idle, I could write a weekly essay for him. It never occurred to me, nor, I think, to him, that I was putting him to any trouble. For the next couple of terms, I wrote these essays. I remember one of his comments. I had been reading Bacon's *Essays* and was writing in similarly short, staccato sentences. Bob said that my essays reminded him of the Book of Proverbs. None of those essays survives, and I imagine they expressed antiquated prejudices in antiquated language; indeed, Bob would have liked that. But those weekly essays, with their echoes of Bacon, or Addison – I was reading Addison's *Spectator* – Johnson or Gibbon, helped to teach me how to write. I tried to imitate Addison's conversational style, but could not resist a rhetorical antithesis. One should get a big style as a teenager, so that one can tone it down later on.

My first year at Charterhouse was a good one, particularly the summer, when I spent my spare time divided between the cricket field, at least as a keen scorer, and the excellent school library, with its huge patent Victorian stove in the middle.

It was after I had returned to Somerset for my first summer holiday that I fell ill, and for the next couple of years that illness changed my school life, even leading to a suggestion by J. C. Holmes, my housemaster, that I should go on indefinite leave to try to recover my health. I remember the first illness being diagnosed by Dr Brew, the jovial and very old-fashioned Somerset doctor from Chew Magna. He was a farmers' doctor, and was full of farming stories, such as that of the old farmer who had not been to the end of the garden for six weeks, and commented, 'you'd better send a ferret up'n'. He listened to my symptoms, felt the area of my liver, and diagnosed the infectious jaundice which had become epidemic in the unsanitary mass feeding of wartime. It would now be diagnosed as Hepatitis A.

I have never felt so horrible; I had less than no energy; my urine was the colour of mahogany; I was struck by the depression which is a symptom of the disease. The illness and convalescence lasted from late July into October, when I did manage to go back to Charterhouse, but I do not think my energy or my spirits fully recovered so long as I was still at school.

I do remember one happy moment when I was at home, but had started to recover from the acute stage. My mother wanted to cheer me up. I had set my heart on a set of the Pickering 'wreath' edition of Christopher Marlowe, which I had seen earlier in the summer in George's Bookshop, at the top of Park Street in Bristol. It was priced at £2 5s. That would now be the equivalent of about £75; if I saw the same set in a bookseller's catalogue, I would now expect it to be priced at about £350.

I have the books in front of me as I write. They are bound in a Victorian half-green morocco, an excellent, clean copy. I put a regrettable rubber stamp of 'W. R-M.' in the end fly leaves, and stuck my great-grandfather's armorial book plate, which is far more appropriate, in each volume. I also put a red ribbon as a book mark to each volume; two of the three still survive. The title pages read: '*The Works of Christopher Marlowe. Volume the First (Second, Third)* [wreath ornament] '*Marlowe renown'd for his rare art and wit Could ne'er attain beyond the name of Kit.' London: William Pickering, Chancery Lane; Talboys and Wheeler, Oxford; J. Combe and Son, Leicester. MDCCCXXVI.*'

This birthday present introduced me to Christopher Marlowe, and for a year or more I was drunk on his plays. I read the plays in quite a careful way. In Act II, Scene II, of *Tamburlaine the Great*, there is a line which Pickering's edition reads as 'His arms and fingers long, and snowy-white'. My pencil note, slipped in, reads: 'Sinewy is now the generally accepted emendation to snowy-white'. It would indeed be surprising if Marlowe had praised Tamburlaine for his lady-like hands.

I found my imagination stirred by all of Marlowe's plays. I delighted in the bravura poetry of *Tamburlaine the Great.* I wrote to John Gielgud, asking him to put on a performance of *The Jew of Malta*, not realizing how anti-Semitic it was, but taken with the beauty of the verse.

I realized, of course, that *The Tragical History of the Life and Death of Dr Faustus* was Marlowe's masterpiece. The closing scene, in which Faustus faces his death and damnation, is of Shakespearian quality.

> O lente, lente currite noctis equi!*
> The stars move still, time runs, the clock will strike,
> The devil will come, and Faustus must be damn'd.
> Oh I'll leap up to heav'n! – who pulls me down?
> See where Christ's blood streams in the firmament:
> One drop of blood will save me; oh, my Christ!

My imagination was so gorged with Marlowe that, when I went back to Charterhouse, I wrote two full-length tragedies in my version of Elizabethan blank verse. The plots were full of murders, and were placed in sixteenth-century Italy, about which I knew next to nothing. I remember that one of the more sinister characters was called Bagnio. These plays are lost, which I cannot regret.

Unfortunately, jaundice is a disease which produces clinical depression, and I suffered for the next two years from an adolescent depression which, though intermittent, was at times acute. I remember a degree of exhaustion which made it hard to rise from a chair, even when I was sitting in a draught. In such a depression, as many will know only too well, all pleasure,

---

* Horses of the night run slowly, slowly.

interest and zest disappear from life. At the time I had never seen television, but the effect of depression is to grey the world, as though one was turning the colour control from vivid to black and white.

The school authorities were naturally disturbed, but fortunately they were flexible. I sometimes went to class, and sometimes not. I often stayed in bed until lunchtime, and occasionally did not get up at all. Admittedly I read a lot in bed, so the time was not wholly wasted. Somehow I stumbled through School Certificate with respectable but not scholarly marks. The two matrons at Verites, Mrs Lewis and Mrs Peel-Yates, fluctuated between wondering whether I was malingering or was so seriously ill that they should no longer take responsibility for me. They were, however, very kind.

The school doctor, a healthy-minded man, was convinced that I was a malingerer who ought to be restored to ordinary school discipline. My physical symptoms, which were not extreme, centred on my sinuses. He sent me to a Harley Street ear, nose and throat specialist, Mr Gill Carey, who had the background of an international rugby player, from New Zealand, or perhaps from Australia. He was, in my life, the good physician who may have saved my sanity. He examined the X-rays and shone a torch into the back of my mouth. He saw that my sinuses were in no great disorder. I left the room; he then told my mother that I was reasonably healthy in my sinuses but tired and run down; that I was not a malingerer, but should not have any pressure put on me; that I should be permanently excused from games and the Officers' Training Corps, but might, if I wished, play an occasional game of cricket in the summer, as I seemed to enjoy that. He wrote a letter to the school doctor to that effect.

That solved the school and the games problem, and thereafter the depression gradually abated, though it was only at Oxford, six or seven years later, that I had the last attack of it which I can remember. During the more acute phase of the depression I had suicidal ideas. I talked about suicide to my friends, including Gerald Priestland, who later became the much-admired religious correspondent of the BBC. Suicide ends the career of Somerset Lloyd Jones in Simon Raven's *Arms for Oblivion* novels, a character which is loosely based on the less agreeable aspects of my schoolboy personality.

I argued with Bob Arrowsmith that both Socrates and Jesus Christ had committed suicide, because they could both have avoided their deaths; it was not his sort of argument, and it embarrassed him, though he tried to frame a reply. I never actually made any attempt at suicide, but I can remember looking at my father's wartime pistol, and wondering how it worked. I can also remember a moment in Charterhouse chapel when I simply wished that I could be removed from an earth which I found so pointless and returned to what seemed to me a lost state of happiness. I could not understand what I was doing in this strange and ugly century, when the eighteenth century had been so much better.

Literature continued to be a great consolation. I read Edgar Allan Poe, a sinister though romantic author I cannot now stand. I also read Shakespeare, and when, in 1943, I saw Gielgud's *Hamlet*, the Shakespearian melancholy – 'Oh that this too solid flesh would melt' – summed up my mood precisely. So did Gray's *Elegy*, which I read in a state of acute depression. Gray's elegiac depression offers a benign and calming alternative; one is still depressed, but in a nostalgic style.

Undoubtedly depression affected, and even dominated, my period at school. Nowadays it would probably have been diagnosed and I would have been put on some mood-altering pill, which might or might not have improved it. I am, however, glad to have experienced it, and even gladder that it has not so far recurred, as I rather expected it to, in later life. It gave me an understanding of the shadowy side of my own nature, and a better sympathy with the tragic condition of human life. I think it gave me somewhat more insight than I might have had into the gusty emotional weather of adolescence in others. Depression – if it is survived – is an exploration as well as a disaster.

In my worst year, from the autumn of 1942 to the summer of 1943, I was taught by a most sympathetic master, V. S. H. Russell, nicknamed 'Sniffy'. He was not a very good teacher in his class, but he was a brilliant teacher outside the classroom. He was a man of wide learning, and sympathetic to anyone who was going through a bad time. He was the housemaster of Hodgsonites, and I used to drop round to his house after school to talk over school gossip, in which he delighted, and about literature and the progress of the war, where, of course, many of his recent pupils were fighting.

Arrowsmith and Russell were both classicists. They believed that the study of the languages of Latin and Greek provided the only sound basis of education; this belief had dominated public school and grammar school education in England since the time of Erasmus and Linacre. Up to my fifteenth birthday, I received, without the floggings which used to accompany it, the same classical education as John Locke would have had at Westminster under the great Busby, Horace Walpole would have had at Eton, or as my father had under Thomas Ethelbert Page at Charterhouse. It was more limited in scope than modern systems of education, more vigorous in its mental discipline and more intense. I am glad that I belonged to the last generation educated in the culture of ancient Greece and Rome.

The grammar and public school classical teaching retained its imperial purpose when I was at school. Clifton and Charterhouse were a practical training for, among other things, governing nations and fighting wars. This faded away within a few years of the independence of India, which brought the British Empire to an end. Britain no longer needed to train boys to become colonial officials; deference to authority slipped away from the national culture and education.

By the end of my second term in the Classical Under Sixth it became clear to me that I was never going to make a classical scholar, even of the humblest kind. Nevertheless, there had to be a battle if I was to change my specialization. The classical side of Brooke Hall, which is the masters' common room at Charterhouse, would not easily give up. Arrowsmith advised strongly against a change; Russell, as was his nature, was less dogmatic; Irvine opposed it though with decreasing confidence. My housemaster, Jasper Holmes, was a scientist, but was well aware of the strength of the classical side in Brooke Hall, from which he had sometimes suffered his own reverses in Charterhouse politics.

I wanted to switch to the History Under Sixth, which would lead naturally to Robert Birley's History Sixth. That in its turn would lead to reading history at Oxford. I was increasingly strongly convinced that that was what I ought to do. However bad I was at the classics, I was good at writing essays, and had always read history.

During the period of this minor, but, to me, crucial, struggle, an incident occurred which nearly led to my changing my house as well as my form. There was a Jewish boy in Verites whose family background was unhappy, and whose conduct was erratic. He was so unhappy that at one time he tried to set fire to the school pillar box. He was nonetheless intelligent, and he was a friend of mine. I remember once going to a meal with his mother. Perhaps she had pressed him to bring a friend home. I knew therefore that his home was not happy, and that he resented about equally the authority of Charterhouse and that of his non-Jewish stepfather who, even to me, lacked charm.

In Verites he was unpopular. No doubt there was anti-Semitism in it. He was accused of being dirty, of not having taken a bath for a long time. This was not all that unusual; hot water was rationed and we only got one bath a week, so we must all have been pretty grubby. A group of sixteen-year-olds dragged him to the bathroom, stripped him and put him in the bath.

I was present, protesting and horrified at what was happening. I was not able to prevent it, though my protests may have helped to shorten the ordeal. I went to Holmes, as the housemaster, who took less action against the bullies than I thought appropriate. I wrote to my mother, saying that I could not tolerate staying in a house where this sort of thing could happen. In this there was no doubt some desire to take advantage of the situation for my own ends, as well as a genuine horror and shock at the Jewish boy's humiliation. I suggested that I should be transferred to Birley's house, Saunderites.

Strangely, it did not occur to any of us that there was a parallel between the ritual humiliation of my friend, who had come to hate Charterhouse, and Nazi anti-Semitism. The event happened, after all, in 1943. I did raise the issue of bullying and the issue of anti-Semitism. I did not myself raise the parallel of Nazi anti-Semitism. Neither Holmes, Birley, nor, indeed, the bullies saw it in that way. The bullies themselves were not particularly thuggish boys, as I remember. They seemed to be acting out some very primitive role, like chimpanzees setting on a weakened companion in the rainforest.

I am not sure how closely my bid to move house, which failed, and my bid to move from Classics to History, which succeeded, were linked. I do not regret having stayed in Verites; it was not my spiritual home, and Holmes was not a particularly sympathetic housemaster, but we had a mutual respect, and I was certainly more trouble to him than he was to me. Later, when Birley made me Head of the School, Holmes refused to make me Head of Verites, a disjunction of office which had last happened when William Beveridge, later the author of the Beveridge Report, was Head of the School. That, too, suited me perfectly well. I liked the prestige of being Head of the School, but was happy to forgo the chore of running Verites.

The move to studying history was a joy and a turning point, one of the crucial decisions of my life, all the better for having been achieved after a struggle. Robert Birley, later to become the head of education in the British Zone of Germany and Headmaster of Eton, was an inspired teacher of history for a sixth-form student. Even then, I took a Tory view of the world, more so than I do now, and was always willing to argue the Tory case. Disraeli was right; Gladstone was wrong, even about Ireland. Birley found that amusing; he was himself a man of liberal views, later to distinguish himself in the struggle against apartheid in South African education. Some of his liberalism was bound to rub off on me, as it did on James Prior, who was in the same History Sixth, and as it had on Edward Boyle, an earlier Eton pupil of Birley's, who, as a rising Conservative Minister, resigned over Suez.

The summer of 1944, when I had my sixteenth birthday, was a happier one. The depression was still lurking, but was seldom too unpleasant when the sun was shining and there was good cricket to be watched on the Green. My closest friend at Charterhouse, one of the closest friends I have ever had, was Clive Wigram. Clive was the son of a distinguished Jewish doctor, who had cared for Asquith in his last illness. Because he was Jewish, Clive had been sent to the United States early in the war, but his father fell ill and he came back in 1942, earlier than most of the refugee children. He was more mature than the rest of us, and was a year older than I was; he found it difficult to take schoolboy life seriously, and even Robert Birley misread his character as a result. Birley mistook Clive's maturity for cynicism.

Clive and I would go for gentle walks in the Charterhouse grounds. On one such walk we were discussing the fact that we had not been invited to join the Literary and Political Society, an ancient Charterhouse society. The reason for our exclusion was that the Lit and Pol was run by Harry Iredale, a senior French master with snowy white hair, who disliked us; he had never been made a housemaster because of his progressive views, which were largely derived from George Bernard Shaw. He saw Clive and myself as sinister and reactionary; we saw him as pretentious and superficial. The poor man had suffered a tragedy, some time in the later 1920s, when he had taken a boy out punting on the River Way. The boy had fallen overboard and been drowned.

As we walked beside Under Green, the idea came to us of setting up our own literary society. I am not sure who had the idea first; it came into our heads together. We thought it should cover much the same subjects as the Lit and Pol, but from a more conservative point of view. We decided that it should be set up so as to capture the high ground of Carthusian prestige. We would match Iredale by two patrons from Brooke Hall; one was to be Russell, always a willing co-conspirator in school politics, the other Mr Thomson, the senior science master. He introduced me to Sung Dynasty Chinese pottery, of which he had a fine collection.

Clive and I discussed an appropriate name, and decided to call it the Thackeray Society. William Makepeace Thackeray, the

Victorian novelist, was one of the most eminent of the Carthusian authors; there is a long-standing Thackeray Prize for an English essay, which I was later to win, narrowly beating Simon Raven into second place. We thought that the school would soon accept the Thackeray Society as an established institution.

I remember some of the early meetings the society had, usually in Russell's drawing room at Hodgsonites. Clive and I had selected the best of the next year's group of boys, most of them scholars. One of them was Dick Taverne, the brightest of the scholars of the year below mine. We took entrants a year younger than the Lit and Pol, during their summer in the fifth form, so that we could catch the best candidates before the Lit and Pol could get hold of them.

My own contributions were marked by my interest in a classical and even stoical human culture. I persuaded the society to have a play-reading session in which we read Addison's *Cato*, on the grounds that Addison had been an Old Carthusian. *Cato* is a play which justifies suicide in a noble cause, and that may have influenced my choice; I think it was more the stoicism which attracted me.

> 'Tis not in mortals to command success,
> But we'll do more, Sempronius; we'll deserve it.

I still feel an attachment to the play, which has many connections for me. It is a link to the Thackeray Society, to Russell and Clive Wigram. It is a link to my youth, and what it was like to be sixteen. It is a link to George Berkeley, my favourite Christian philosopher, and to Alexander Pope. Both Berkeley and Pope were present on the first night the play was performed in April 1713.

On that first night, the part of Marcia, Cato's daughter, was played by Anne Oldfield, the leading actress of the period from 1710 to 1730. I think Pope fell in love with her and was rebuffed, since he attacked her more than once in barbed verse. She had an illegitimate son, Charles Churchill, who married Maria Walpole, Robert Walpole's daughter by Mary Skerritt, also born out of wedlock. My son-in-law, David Craigie, is a descendant of that romantic match between an illegitimate Churchill and an illegitimate Walpole. For me, Addison's *Cato* is ringed about with the happy coincidences of life. Four of our grandchildren are descendants of Anne Oldfield.

In the early autumn of 1944, I discussed with Robert Birley the prospect of going to university. I knew that I wanted to go to Oxford. I was drawn by its romantic and political character and slightly repelled by the intellectual puritanism of Cambridge. I had no strong family connection with any particular Oxford college; my father had gone to University College, but his uncles had gone to various other colleges, and my ancestor John Rees had gone to Jesus. Birley recommended that I should try for a scholarship at Balliol, his own old college; he had himself won the Brackenbury Scholarship, which had been held by various other well-known figures, such as Cyril Connolly and Hilaire Belloc. In terms of prestige, the Brackenbury was then the best known history scholarship at Oxford.

I was only just over sixteen and had been a history specialist for no more than a term and a half. Birley warned me that I was too young and did not really know enough history to get a scholarship, but suggested I should enter for Balliol, to see what the examination was like. I was delighted with the challenge.

The examination was taken over a couple of days, and the candidates stayed in college. I remember how cold it was, with an early December snow covering the paving stones outside the

Sheldonian. I took with me a copy of Richard Hooker's *Ecclesiastical Politie*, a first edition which I had bought from George McLeish of Little Russell Street. I imagine that I found an opportunity to work in some quotation from Hooker, intended to show the breadth of my reading. The set essay was a quotation from Shakespeare's *King Henry VIII*, in which Cardinal Wolsey says to Cromwell: 'Fling away ambition, by that sin fell the angels'. At the age of sixteen, I was not at all willing to fling away ambition, which was my ruling passion at the time. I wrote an essay defending ambition; how I got over the problem of the fall of Lucifer I do not now remember.

There was an oral interview, in which my confident assertions were gently probed. Two young Balliol dons, still serving in the army, took part in it: Richard Southern, a serious-minded medieval historian, who later became the President of St John's, and Christopher Hill, the Marxist historian of the seventeenth century, who later became Master of Balliol. Southern was too ascetic, too serious, too medieval for me, and I was too frivolous, too partisan, too eighteenth-century for him. I was never to find it easy to learn from him, which was my fault; he never found much pleasure in trying to teach me, which was also my fault, since he was both a good historian and a good man.

Christopher Hill was much more my type of historian. As a good Marxist he looked for broad explanations of historic events. He saw, and taught, history as a series of challenges and responses, which could be explained by identifying underlying social and economic forces. He had an ebullient Celtic temperament. Although we were on different sides of the ideological fence, and disapproved of each other quite strongly, we were also quite fond of each other in an adversarial way. I have always been grateful for his Marxist teaching; Marxism is only one of the ways of looking at history, and is only partly true, but it is a form of analysis all historians need to have experienced at some point.

The history dons sat round the fire in the Dean's room, and made me feel welcome; I knew I had done quite well. I was back in Somerset on my Christmas holiday with my parents when the telegram arrived, telling me that I had won the Brackenbury. I had won it, as I now think, because I had the basic qualities not of a good historian, but of a good journalist. I had trenchant opinions; I wrote with vigour at short notice on any subject; I was manifestly clever, without being particularly consistent, accurate or profound. I showed promise. Indeed, my whole educational career was based on showing promise.

When I received the telegram I was filled with delight; I felt like Marlowe's Tamburlaine. 'Is it not passing brave to be a King, And ride in triumph through Persepolis?' Was it not passing brave to have won the Brackenbury Scholarship at the age of sixteen? I have never felt such an uprush of pleasure at any subsequent success, at becoming President of the Oxford Union or Editor of *The Times*, agreeable though success always is. It is the moment of success which gives the greatest satisfaction; the life of a Prime Minister must be anxious and exhausting, but the hour of appointment, or of winning a General Election, must feel very good. The hour I got that telegram from Balliol was good in that way. Of course, if one is going to have a success, sixteen is an enjoyable time to have it.

I paid for it, in a way I have not had to pay for any subsequent success. I went back to Charterhouse in the January, having achieved a Balliol scholarship and having at least a couple of terms of relaxation ahead of me. The old depression came back, more severely than it was ever to come again. I sat in my study at Verites, unable to concentrate, unable to take pleasure in anything, wholly lacking in energy, let alone zest. I had not expected to react so badly to something which had given me so much delight. The black mood passed as spring came, but for a couple of months I felt lower than I had felt high on receiving the telegram.

That year I edited *The Carthusian*, which was a senior position in the school. I spent a good deal of my leisure time with Clive Wigram, on whose judgement I greatly relied. I remember a walk with him when we discussed the relative evils of the Hitler and Stalin regimes. I said that Stalin's was the more totalitarian of the two, and that a private individual had a better chance of preserving some normality in Germany rather than Russia. Clive agreed, but pointed out that such an option would not be open to him, because he was a Jew, and Hitler would kill him. At that time, early in 1945, we still had no real knowledge of the Holocaust, but Jews knew that Hitler was a Jew killer. It was only when British troops liberated Belsen in May of 1945, and the first photographs of the starving or the dead appeared, that we began in Britain to realize that the evil that had happened was even worse than the war itself.

In the summer, the war in Europe came to an end. Rather to my surprise, Birley asked me to stay on for an extra term and be Head of School. I had not been considered a likely candidate for the job, and, in any case, everyone assumed I was leaving. I was conspicuously unathletic. I was a thorn in the side of my housemaster, who was opposed to the whole idea. I was seen in the school as a weedy intellectual, and there were doubts as to whether I could maintain discipline. Few headmasters other than Birley would have considered it. I think that part of his motivation was the desire to show that an intellectual could be Head of School.

I do not think that I made a particularly good one. I compensated for my apparent lack of authority by being too decisive in some cases. The benefit of my being Head of School was not to Charterhouse but to me. I would previously have thought of myself as the sort of person who edits the school magazine but does not become the Head of School. My self-image came to include the idea of exercising authority. I have never subsequently found it worrying to handle the political relationships in such positions of authority as I have held. As Editor of *The Times* or as Chairman of the Arts Council, I have found the simple leadership skills which I first learned at Charterhouse were useful, and if I made some of the mistakes of the learning process while I was still at school, that is as it should be.

SIX

Everyone Wants to Be Attorney General

I went up to Balliol in January 1946, just after the war. Balliol, a left-wing college, was then full of Labour triumphalism, following the General Election in the summer of 1945. The mood lasted about a year to the summer of 1946. It was quite unlike the political mood at any other time in my life. The Labour majority was a large one, people believed that this was a revolutionary event; they believed that the old ways of doing things had been thrown out. It was widely felt that the conservatism of the pre-war era had been not only morally repugnant, but also intellectually contemptible; it was a more complete ideological rejection than that of 1997. It was further held that figures like William Beveridge and J. Maynard Keynes had shown how it was possible to run society in a much more scientific and effective way. Conservatism was dead, and disreputable; the future lay with Attlee socialism, Keynesianism and the Beveridge Report. I did not agree.

Ideologically I was swimming against the tide in post-war Balliol. I took the view, best set out in Hayek's book *The Road to Serfdom*, that universal state controls, including substantial state ownership and very high taxation, involved a serious loss of liberty. I held the connected belief that liberty was the key to economic and social development and that, by restricting liberty, Britain was putting shackles on its future performance. Margaret Thatcher, an Oxford contemporary and acquaintance, was taking the same view at the same time and in the same environment, but in 1946 we were a small minority, either among students or in Britain as a whole.

Balliol itself possessed a set of values which was distinct from the other Oxford colleges. It was a strange mixture. There is an extremely attractive feeling that Balliol is a special place, that there is a friendship throughout Balliol which crosses the boundaries of opinion. On the other hand, there was a self-congratulatory side to some Balliol men, which must have seemed rather ridiculous to the outside world. Balliol was, indeed, attracting and producing the best undergraduates. It was regarded as *the* academic college and merited this reputation. The Norrington Table had not yet been brought into existence, but Balliol was getting, fairly effortlessly, a high quota of Firsts. The many brilliant undergraduates included George Steiner, the literary critic, Bernard Williams, the philosopher and future Provost of King's, and, among distinguished lawyers, George Carman, Lord Hutton and Lord Mayhew.

Among my first actions after I arrived at Oxford was to join the Oxford Union and the Oxford University Conservative Association (OUCA). The Union was the key institution in my life at Oxford. When I arrived it was dominated by people who had come back from the war. Being only seventeen, I was a schoolboy among people who were ex-officers and had been in battle. It was quite difficult to get myself into, and succeed, in a society which was dominated by people with much greater experience. I countered this by being very active indeed, not only managing to get myself elected, after only my first term, to the Committee of the Conservative Association, but also, at the end of my second term, to the Library Committee at the Union. I was an eager beaver, running round, working on university politics and getting to know people.

Ever since I had been at Charterhouse, where I founded a Conservative Society, I had sought out senior politicians as part of a learning process; they were almost a continuation of my school teachers, and were often generous with their time. I wrote to Leslie Hore-Belisha after the Conservative defeat in 1945, when he had lost his seat. Before the war, he had been, briefly, the great modernizer of British politics. In the National Governments of the later 1930s he modernized the transport system, introducing driving tests, the Highway Code and pedestrian crossings, marked by lights which were known for many years as Belisha beacons. Next, he was appointed to, and modernized, the War Office. He retired some twenty of the senior officers of the army, appointed Lord Gort as a new broom, and prepared the British Army for war in 1939. Without Belisha's reforms the army could scarcely have formed the British Expeditionary Force in 1939, or, indeed, had the resilience to escape from Dunkirk.

These reforms were a material achievement, for which he was not much thanked. The old guard almost always wins in the end. Anti-Jewish prejudice was used to destroy Hore-Belisha. Early in 1940, he went as Minister for War to review the defences in France. He observed, and reported to the Cabinet, that there was a gap at the end of the Maginot Line. The French complained. Neville Chamberlain, with relief, took the opportunity to dismiss Belisha. Those who called him 'Horeb-Elisha' and 'the Jew Boy' had won.

I think Leslie Hore-Belisha saw himself as a second Disraeli. He was a brilliant speaker, a very modern publicist and a Minister capable of radical reorganization of his department. I cannot remember just how I first met him, but when I was at Oxford I attached myself with enthusiasm to his unfortunately waning star. I canvassed for him in Coventry South, a seat he failed to win back for the Conservatives in 1950. I exchanged lunches with him, going to his Lutyens house behind Buckingham Palace; we corresponded when I was in the RAF. He, too, had been President of the Oxford Union when he was at Oxford. By the 1950s he had very few disciples, and I think he was pleased to have a supporter. I learned a good deal from him.

I must have started the correspondence about the same time as I won the Brackenbury Scholarship, and presumably made some expression of my own political ambitions. At any rate, I remember one striking sentence in his reply which reflected both his own adolescent ambitions and what he saw as mine. 'At the age of sixteen,' he wrote, 'everyone wants to be Attorney General.' I remember a few other of his remarks. He told me that the perfect length for a speech in the House of Commons was no more than eight minutes; after that one would lose the attention of the House. His old seat had been Devonport, which in 1945 was won by Labour. He decided to move to the marginal seat of Coventry South, and commented of Devonport, 'if they don't want me, they shan't have me'.

My political ambitions were already well formed. I believed I would become a political lawyer. I planned to read for the bar (I actually joined Gray's Inn in 1948 or 1949), and to stand for Parliament. My imagination was fixed on a career as a Member of Parliament. I have always enjoyed politics, political company, debate, argument, even committee meetings. To me it is a stimulating and natural environment.

Shirley Williams once described me, in a flattering phrase, as 'a young sage' at Oxford, someone whom people would seek out for advice on matters relating to their own careers. Robin Day was the guru of younger Oxford politicians, advising them when to stand and for what office, but I studied the game of Oxford careerism with almost as much fascination as he did. I used to lunch with Robin Day at the Committee table in the Oxford Union. Later in life we lunched together at the Garrick Club. When Robin died I made a calculation that I had lunched with him more often than with anyone else outside my family. We always talked politics.

I got off to an early start in seeking political office at Oxford, as did our son Jacob in the late 1980s. He became President of OUCA and Librarian, though not President, at the Oxford Union. At the end of my first term I was elected to the Committee of OUCA. One of the senior members of the Committee was Margaret Thatcher and in the summer term she stood for the office of President. There were eleven members of the Committee with the right to elect the President. I voted for Margaret Roberts, as she then was, and she was elected by – as I remember it – seven votes to four.

She invited me to be the Meetings Secretary for the following term and I accepted with some glee. It would have meant greeting the outside speakers, who ranged between retired Cabinet Ministers and the rising young stars of the party, such as Reggie Maudling. I also looked forward to working for Margaret, who seemed in the immediate future to be the leading figure in Oxford Conservative politics and whom I liked.

This agreeable prospect was taken away from me when Sandy Lindsay, the Master of Balliol, who was made a Labour peer in 1947, decided to give my place in the college to a demobilized ex-serviceman. This meant that I only had two terms at Balliol in 1946, and I had to do my own National Service in the middle of my time at Oxford, which I resented. It was indeed contrary to the commitment the college had made when I came up. I was not able to take up my post as Meetings Secretary and had to go round to Somerville College to apologize to Margaret for my inability to accept her offer. In retrospect, I naturally regret not having worked more closely with her. When I returned to Oxford, two years later, she was in the hierarchy of ex-Presidents. By the time I became President of OUCA myself she had gone down from the university. Nevertheless, we retained a friendly acquaintance, which always gave me access after she became Leader of the Opposition and Prime Minister. I was not a member of the inner team of friends and advisers, but I think I was regarded, if rather remotely, as 'one of us'. We never imagined at that time that Margaret was to become the first woman Prime Minister, though we knew how disciplined she was and how determined to achieve her objectives.

In 1946–8, I served two years in the RAF. The first winter was that of the 1947 fuel crisis. For most of those who lived through it, 1947 was one of the most unpleasant years of their lives. It started with an exceptionally cold winter in which supplies of coal ran out. These were fuelless days, electric fires burned only a dull red, and crowds suddenly discovered the fascination of tropical plants at Kew Gardens and tropical birds at various zoos around the country.

The fuel crisis broke the reputation of the Attlee Government for administrative competence. For years afterwards the Conservative Party speaker's handbook carried a much-loved quotation from Emmanuel Shinwell: 'There will be no fuel crisis, I am the Minister for Fuel and Power and I ought to know.'

I spent that winter as a National Service clerk in a Nissen hut at Flying Training Command Headquarters in Reading,

Berkshire. We burned anything we could lay our hands on, except the snooker table, in an effort to keep the hut warm; we failed.

In the spring of 1948, I was sent on a course to Wellesbourne Mountford in Warwickshire to be turned into an acting sergeant in the RAF Education Corps. That I enjoyed.

Wellesbourne Mountford is situated close to Stratford-upon-Avon where I went to the Shakespeare Memorial Theatre; and I managed to stay with my cousins who then lived in the beautiful village of Clifford Chambers. Their house was said to have a rather sad association with Shakespeare. In 1616 he went there for a drinking party, returned home flushed with mulled wine, caught a chill which turned to pneumonia, and died. I do not know whether the story is true.

We had a splendidly crazy wing commander who was in charge of the course. He was concerned that we should have brightly polished boots, something I was still no good at. He told us a long and rambling story about a Canadian Mountie who was sent into the wilderness to capture an outlaw. It took him three years to find his man and three years to bring him back. Nevertheless, when he returned with his prisoner, he walked into his station with his Mountie uniform impeccably pressed and his boots shining like the sun.

As the education sergeant when I returned to the Reading headquarters I was not exactly fully employed. Consequently, I arranged to have tutorials on seventeenth-century history at Reading University, for which my tutor was paid three guineas a time.

I tried, and failed, to teach an illiterate WAAF recruit to read. I taught young officers general knowledge for their officer's promotion exam. I remember telling them, with all the authority of a nineteen-year-old, that they would acquire an excellent grasp of current affairs if they read *The Times* every morning over breakfast.

I drafted a general knowledge quiz to find out what, if anything, they did know. That project had to be dropped when I put the quiz in front of my education officer, who was a squadron leader. One of my multiple-part questions required the candidate to sort biblical characters into the Old and New Testaments. Unfortunately, the squadron leader had not read his Bible. He thought Moses was a figure in the New Testament, and scolded me for setting a quiz which he regarded as unreasonably difficult.

In the sergeants' mess we drank our beer and the occasional whisky and soda. I was the only teenager in a group of middle-aged men. They saw my life as quite divorced from their concerns, but we wished each other well.

The following year, I left the RAF and returned to Oxford University. As a sergeant I fear that I had failed to impress my Commanding Officer. He wrote a reference in my leaving book: 'Sergeant Rees-Mogg is capable of performing routine tasks under close supervision.' I only wish that were true.

It was the autumn of 1948 when I returned to Oxford. I was now twenty. I had had the advantage of two years in the RAF, which had transformed me from a callow recruit to a sergeant in Education. I had kept in touch with Oxford life through my friendship with Clive Wigram, who was himself elected as President of the Union. In the spring of 1948, I came up to Oxford for the last time wearing my RAF uniform with its largely unpolished boots. Clive and I went to watch some college races on the river. We met two delightful girls, both of whom were acquaintances of Clive. The dark-haired one was Val Mitchison, daughter of Naomi Mitchison, the novelist, later to become Val Arnold-Foster; the blonde was Shirley Williams, the daughter of another novelist, Vera Brittain. I remember thinking what a delightful place Oxford was, if one could stroll the towpath and meet such delightful young women. I did not realize that Val and Shirley had already become stars of Oxford society.

It was Shirley who chose public life. Even in those days people discussed the question of whether Shirley would become Prime Minister. If anyone had made a book on it, she would have been the favourite and Margaret would have been the longer odds.

My relations with Margaret and Shirley have pursued tranquil paths from that day to this. All three of us have ended up in the House of Lords, that bourne from which no traveller returns. I have never had a cross word in either my relationship with Shirley or Margaret, or for that matter with Val; all of these young women I first met at Oxford came to my eightieth birthday party at St John's Smith Square. Friendships which last for sixty years must be regarded as a rare blessing.

Returning to Balliol in 1948 was strange. Both Balliol and I had changed. In 1946 I would have been seen as very young, very political, probably not very likeable, still immature and very much making my way in the world that I had chosen. A Conservative zealot, perhaps. I returned from the RAF more or less as a grown-up. By then, I was a contemporary of some of the younger dons and I was relaxed and more self-confident about my position. My contemporaries from 1946 were now at the head of affairs at the Union, and I was able to rejoin them in relatively senior positions in Oxford's political world. I had to restart my political career, but I did not have any particular difficulty in doing that. I was able to restart nearer to the top of Oxford politics than when I had gone down.

Among my tutors, after 1948, the strongest influence was Marcus Dick, a philosopher rather than an historian. It was he who first introduced me to my beloved Somerset philosopher,

John Locke. I doubt if Marcus thought that seventeenth-century political thought, with its variations on the doctrine of the social contract, was a particularly important branch of philosophy, but it has moulded my thought.

As an undergraduate in the late 1940s, I developed four heroes, Locke for liberty, Walpole for administration, Keynes for economics and Churchill for national defence. I believed in Locke's principle of religious tolerance, and had found repugnant the orthodox Catholic idea that there was 'no salvation outside the Church'. I believed, in Thomas Jefferson's phrase, in the right 'to life, liberty and the pursuit of happiness' and in Locke's formulation of 'life, liberty and estate'. I believed that liberty included the right to own property. I believed in equality before the law and equality at the polling booth, but I did not believe in equality in the socialist sense of an equal distribution of income or capital. My mother had brought me up to have the horror of slavery which all good Yankees share. I was shocked by segregation and apartheid.

As an historian, I came to see the way in which strong pragmatic Prime Ministers had provided a stability for the State, which had allowed people to develop their own interests and careers. I became a professed admirer of the great pragmatists: Cardinal Wolsey, Robert Walpole, and in a different way, Pitt the Younger and Lord Salisbury. I warmed to the idea that administrative stability, even bought at a relatively high price, was the essential foundation of good government.

As someone interested in economics, though never a properly trained economist, I fell under the spell of Maynard Keynes. I never met the great man, though I came close to doing so. I had met his brother, Geoffrey, through book collecting. Geoffrey visited us in Somerset to encourage me as a young collector. He also invited me to tea in Hampstead in 1946, and said his brother would be coming. Unfortunately Maynard was detained by the debate on the American loan in the House of Lords; a fortnight later he was dead.

I then entirely accepted the basic Keynesian orthodoxy. I thought that his *General Theory*, published in 1935, had given the answer to the problem of economic cycles – that you can simply add to public expenditure to ease a downturn in the economy. I thought that modern economic theory meant that really damaging economic conditions, like those of the 1930s, would never happen again. It was not until the 1970s that I realized, as the world was forced to, that Keynes had not found a general theory, but a theory for the particular circumstances of the 1930s. Nevertheless, Keynes' theory helped to give the world economic stability for twenty-five years: a very long time for any economic theory to work.

Winston Churchill's 1946 Fulton Speech, when he first talked of 'the iron curtain', and called for resistance to Soviet expansionism, also had a great impact on me. I read the article in *Foreign Affairs* which first analysed Stalin's objectives and called for a policy of containment. When Douglas Wilson and Tony Berry, the youngest son of Lord Kemsley, who owned the *Sunday Times*, produced *Conservative Oxford*, I wrote about the issue of world communism; Margaret Thatcher wrote about her father's great interest, the reform of local government. I had no idea she would become one of the major external influences in destroying the Stalinist system.

During my time at Oxford I discussed these ideological problems of Conservatism with two of my closest friends, Clive Wigram and Sir Edward Boyle. Clive was now reading law at Oriel; Edward Boyle had come to Christ Church via a wartime period at the Bletchley decoding centre. Just as I owe a great deal to Marcus Dick, I owe a great deal to Clive and Edward. Clive later married Pamela Maxwell Fyfe, the daughter of David Maxwell Fyfe, who was then the Conservative Home Secretary and later Lord Chancellor. Maxwell Fyfe was nothing like the right-wing figure that is now portrayed, but a man of moderate views and friendly temperament. Pamela was the perfect wife for Clive, and their marriage was one of the happiest I have ever seen.

How can one describe Clive? How does one describe people of outstanding ability who die young? He died in 1956, in his thirtieth year, from Hodgkin's disease. His last three or four years were spent under sentence of death. If he had lived to a normal lifespan, he would inevitably have risen to a leading position in the law, and perhaps in politics, though he was beginning to put the bar ahead of his political interests. At Oxford he became President of the Union in a period of extremely strong competition; he might have become Master of the Rolls, Lord Chief Justice, a Lord of Appeal, Lord Chancellor, one of those high legal offices; who can tell? He would have been a better Lord Chancellor than most I have known.

Our approach to politics was as different as our psychology; it was no accident that he became a lawyer and I a journalist. He once summed up the difference by saying that I was drawn to classical rules of order, because my temperament was naturally romantic, and that he was drawn to romanticism because his temperament was naturally more lawyerly – I forget what precise word he used. He had, indeed, the strongest natural judgement I have ever known; one could come to him with any issue, political, professional or personal, and he would provide a perfectly balanced judgement that was decisive and full of insight. I am sure that many of the mistakes of my life happened because I lost the benefit of that sure advice when I was only twenty-eight.

Clive was not an observant Jew, and had a sceptical view of all religion, though he was buried with Orthodox Jewish rites. His strength of mind, his realism, his respect for law, all seem to me to have been developed by the Jewish culture in which he lived. He was sensible about money, but did not exaggerate its importance. His Wigram cousins were successful property developers in Cardiff and London; at one point he was invited to join the firm, which would have given him the chance to make millions in the post-war property boom. He declined the offer because he thought the law was more important and worthwhile.

I suppose that the main influence that Clive had on my own intellectual development was his combination of judgement, pragmatism and a sense of long-term realities. I do not possess those qualities in the way that he did, but at least I recognize their value. He had a penetrating habit of hitting on vital questions. Once, shortly after I had joined the *Financial Times*, we were walking near his flat, on the south side of Regent's Park. He asked me what my ambitions were; did they really lie in journalism or politics? Did I want to become Prime Minister? I thought that was beyond me. Would I feel that I had succeeded in life if I became a Cabinet Minister? I said that I would. Would I feel I had fulfilled my ambition if I became Editor of *The Times*? I had literally never thought of it, and replied to the effect that of course it would fulfil my ambitions completely, but that it was a job which nobody could get except by unusually good luck. I did, however, agree that I would rather be Editor of *The Times* than a Cabinet Minister.

My other great friend of that period, Edward Boyle, was a little older than Clive and myself. At Eton he had been tutored by Robert Birley, which was something of a link between us. He had in childhood inherited a baronetcy, a country house in Sussex, run by his mother, and a substantial family fortune. His culture was that of the old intellectual families; he would have been at home in the period of Arthur Balfour. In fact, he made no bones about his family's comparatively recent success in Victorian business. I remember canvassing for him at a by-election at Perry Bar, in Birmingham; we were staying in a vast and gloomy Victorian railway hotel. Some family problem came up at dinner. 'It was not for this,' he said, 'that grandpapa boiled soap.'

My political ideas and Clive's remained in a more or less stable relationship to each other in the years of our friendship. Edward Boyle's moved in an opposite trajectory to mine. He started from a position which, if not to the right of mine, certainly put greater emphasis on traditional English values. He believed in the structure of the traditional English society, including the Church of England. Perhaps one would then have compared his views to those of Lord Halifax, Chamberlain's Foreign Secretary. He was, however, reading Karl Popper's *The Open Society and Its Enemies*, so there must have been elements of Austrian liberalism in his thinking.

By the end of his political career, when he decided in the late 1960s to leave politics, Edward had moved to the left, and no longer felt comfortable with the Conservative Party. Ted Heath urged him to stay in the Shadow Cabinet and greatly regretted his loss. I had moved in the opposite direction. In particular I disagreed with his support for the replacement of grammar schools by the comprehensive system. Edward defined the difference in our politics: 'I am a moderate, but I am not an extreme moderate like William.'

Again, it was the impact of his temperament which counted for more than his particular views. When, in the early years of our marriage, Gillian and I stayed with Edward in Sussex, he was amused that I took Laurence Sterne's *Tristram Shandy* upstairs to read in bed. Later, he sold the house, and sent me a parcel with the set of Sterne's works inside. He inscribed it '*To William, my best friend during twenty years of politics. Edward Boyle 3.8.70.*' I would like to think that was true, and am still touched by it. Eleven years later, at the age of fifty-seven, he, too, died a premature death from cancer. Both men were a loss to English political life in my generation.

My biggest difficulty in 1948 was the return to academic work. When I went up straight from school, with the impetus of Birley, I was a good historian from an examination point of view, and my results in the term when I went down into the RAF could have been converted into a wartime First. When I returned I had lost the desire to do that kind of study and was not even writing very good essays. I dawdled.

I was elected President of the Union for the summer of 1951. This was undoubtedly important in my life. It confirmed my self-image. I had taken time to learn to speak. I had been defeated for every major office in the Union; defeated for Secretary, defeated for Treasurer, defeated for Librarian, though I had later become Librarian, and defeated a couple of times for the Presidency. I was what one might call an old lag at the Union. I was, by the time of my third campaign for the Presidency, inevitably a very familiar Union figure; I had been around, on and off, for five years and I had the broad goodwill of the Union debaters.

I had initially decided not to stand for the Presidency in my last term because I thought that I ought to devote my energy to getting a good degree. Specifically, I had promised the college that I would earnestly give time to studying history, which would not have been compatible with the Presidency.

It was Dick Taverne who changed my mind. It was another of those odd coincidences which can be so important in one's life.

I was walking through the front quad in Balliol and ran into Dick, a contemporary at Charterhouse, Balliol and nowadays the House of Lords. Dick, like myself, had already held the office of Librarian of the Union, which ranks immediately below the Presidency; he could well have wanted to run for President in what was going to be the last term for both of us.

Dick asked me why I would not run for the Presidency for my last term. I replied that I had told the college I would not. He said that he had definitely decided that he was not going to do so because he thought that he could get a First if he concentrated on work between that time and the exam. He did indeed get his First. Dick put to me the direct question: 'Would you rather have a First, supposing that that was the issue, than be President of the Union?'

That persuaded me. I went off to my history tutor, who was a very likeable Australian called Hugh Stretton, and explained my problem. His reply was that the college would not mind; the college would like me to be President of the Union and would like me to get a First; but was perfectly happy to leave the choice to me. He went on to say that his personal view was that whether I got a First or not would depend on whether the examiners liked my style. They might give me a First because what I wrote was interesting, and they well might not, but he did not think that the work I would do between now and then would make the difference. He advised that, as far as he was concerned, I might just as well go for the Presidency if I thought that I could get it. And I did. The members of the Union had got so used to me being around by then that they thought it was about time. I got a respectable Second.

In October 1951, I went with Dick Taverne on a debating tour of the United States. The Union, having received an invitation from the English Speaking Union, which organized the tour, set up a committee to make the choice. The three main candidates were Dick Taverne, Jeremy Thorpe and myself. The unanimous view of the selection committee was that Jeremy Thorpe was unquestionably the best speaker of the three of us. He was, however, regarded as a difficult man. The committee thought that as a team Dick Taverne and I would work better together. They chose us.

My first visit to the United States took me to fifty or more colleges in New England, the Midwest and the South. Dick and I only lost one debate, which was in a prison. I got to know my American cousins and stayed with my aunt, Adrienne Kelly, and her husband, Austin. They were most generous. I loved America and for the following fifty years made regular visits. Culturally I feel half-American, all the more so because I later discovered that on my father's side I was descended from John Winthrop, the father of New England.

Just before we left for America I was having tea in a shop off Carfax in Oxford with Robin Day. We saw two beautiful girls at another table. Robin went across and introduced us, a thing I should not have had the confidence to do, but I was glad he did. I became a lifelong friend of Diane McTurk, who is now known as the 'otter lady' of Guyana. She has been responsible for the conservation work of the Rupununi Trust.

SEVEN

'A University Extension Course'

When, in my last term at Balliol, I became President of the Oxford Union, *Isis*, which was the undergraduate magazine, published the customary profile of me as incoming President. It was largely written by my friend Shirley Williams, and included the correct statement that I read the *Financial Times* over breakfast.

The *Isis* profile was cut and sent to the *Financial Times* by their press cuttings agency. It landed on the desk of Garrett Moore, later Lord Drogheda, the *Financial Times*' Managing Director. He sent it downstairs to Gordon Newton, the Editor, with a note saying, 'We are recruiting undergraduates from Oxford. Might it not be a good idea to have a look at one who actually reads our newspaper?'

Gordon Newton then contacted Roy Harrod, Keynes' biographer, who was an economics don at Christ Church and a *Financial Times* contributor, to ask if he knew me. By a further piece of good fortune, Roy had addressed a study group on Keynesian economics which I had organized in the previous year for the University Conservative Association. He gave a favourable reference to the *Financial Times*.

Three days before I started my final exams I got a note from Roy Harrod asking me whether I would like to go and see

Gordon Newton, with the implied possibility that I might be offered a job. Until then, it had not entered my head that I might become a journalist. My intention was to read for the bar, and I had already started eating dinners, which was the necessary initiation to the education of barristers. Indeed, I am now one of the oldest perpetual students at Gray's Inn, since I later paid fifteen guineas to be allowed to remain a member of Gray's Inn, as a student, for the rest of my life.

Once I began to think about the *Financial Times*' offer, it seemed an ideal place to start work. I was interested in the development of economics and finance; I was interested in the City; I was interested in how investment worked and I thought that the issues of public affairs and Government were largely economic issues. In any case, I had taken only too many exams and did not relish the bar exams.

The *Financial Times* then had a rather strange method of training young journalists. It set us, right from the start, to write centre-page features. I doubt if the features we wrote were very good, but the method seemed to work reasonably well; feature writing of that kind followed on easily enough from writing essays at university level. The paper did not assume much prior knowledge of finance or economics. I learned most of the economic theory I possess at the *Financial Times*.

Previously, I had already learned a little about finance, but not much more; I had dabbled in stocks and shares. My father had been very interested in investment for much of his life. I had read *The Economist*, the *Financial Times* itself and the *Investors' Chronicle*. Consequently, I had a little knowledge; I had even been invited to join a firm of Bristol stockbrokers. Inadequate as it was, my early interest in investment proved quite an advantage. Most graduate trainees lacked even this basic introduction.

The *Financial Times* in the 1950s was, to borrow Dr Johnson's phrase about Pembroke College in his time, 'a nest of singing birds'. A lot of bright graduates had joined the paper because it would get them into journalism. My contemporaries included Shirley Williams herself, who had already done a brief spell on the *Daily Mirror*, Samuel Brittan and Nigel Lawson. The atmosphere was that of a senior common room of young dons. We ate our meals together; we stayed for drinks after work, and there was a running debate about the issues which the paper was itself discussing. It was no surprise that I found the atmosphere educative and stimulating. I learned more in my early years on the *Financial Times* than I had in my later years at Balliol. I found the practicality of the *Financial Times* attractive, just as I had found the socialist assumptions at Balliol unsympathetic.

I regard the *Financial Times* as my post-graduate education. The three best periods of my educational life, when I learned a lot and rather fast, were my years being taught the classics by my father, my two years in the History Sixth form at Charterhouse under Robert Birley and my first three or four years at the *Financial Times*, under Gordon Newton. I strongly agree with David Kynaston's remark in his excellent *The Financial Times: A Centenary History* that, for graduate trainees, the *Financial Times* 'was rather like a university extension course in which the trainees learnt far more than they had done at university'.

One of the first projects I proposed to Gordon Newton was that I would like to write about the finances of Fleet Street. I thought that Fleet Street ought to be regarded as a business like any other business, that it had its own problems and that it would be interesting to our readers to discuss them. At this time, in the early 1950s, there was hardly any newspaper reporting of press affairs. Gordon Newton readily saw the point; and he saw that I would benefit from visiting the Fleet Street bosses and asking them about the state of their businesses. Gordon recognized that I would learn a lot, but he was characteristically nervous that it might not come out too well, that my proposed piece might cause offence, or that I might make the *Financial Times* look ridiculous if I got things wrong. He said that I might by all means write this feature, but I must not expect him to publish it. So, I went round and saw people like Cecil King, who was then running the Daily Mirror Group, and the Managing Director of the Mail Group. I learned a great deal about Fleet Street. The piece was never published.

The *Financial Times* was a very small newspaper in those days, with a staff of about sixty, working out of a Victorian house in Coleman Street, in the City. There was only a small group of us who were the bright young graduate trainees; most of the staff were non-graduates, some of whom found us irritating. Ours was undoubtedly a very privileged position which would not normally arise or would be difficult to recreate in modern conditions.

Partly because of the size of the staff, I had a close relationship with Gordon Newton from early on. It was a tough relationship; he was a demanding taskmaster, particularly in one's first years. He was also a great Editor. The first leading article I wrote was the obituary leader on Sir Stafford Cripps, whom I had admired. Gordon felt that Cripps had stood for left-wing socialist policies of which the *Financial Times* had thoroughly disapproved. He therefore thought that my first draft was too enthusiastic. I had to rewrite that leader three times before it went into the paper. It was a good discipline.

I was surprised to learn, years later, that Gordon Newton had told a colleague of mine that whenever he decided that he wanted me to rewrite a leading article he used to go downstairs to the canteen and have a glass of brandy before summoning me to his room to order the rewrite. I was quite in awe of him, and had no idea that I inspired any counter-awe. I liked his directness; I found him a sympathetic character, with his sense of detail and his sharp practicality.

Surprisingly, for an editor, he suffered from malapropisms and strange pronunciations. He had no idea of the pronunciation of foreign languages. He pronounced the world guillotine as 'gully-ot-ine' and remarked that the opera critic was going to review the new Wagner production of 'The Wallcure'. Gordon also mixed up his phrases. All of his young men had their own favourites. For its surrealist flavour, mine was 'that man is grinding his own horse'. He was also cautious. The Foreign Editor, Andrew Shonfield, once wrote a somewhat controversial leader. Gordon paused on reading it, tapped his teeth with his pen, and then added the words 'or maybe not'. When I became an editor, I often felt tempted to follow his example.

I was lucky to start my career as a journalist under his guidance. By his sympathetic selection of recruits, his meticulous care for editorial detail and his gradualist approach to the development of the paper, Gordon made the *Financial Times* the outstanding newspaper success of the 1950s. It was a time when interest in economic, financial and industrial affairs was growing, years which saw the rise of Siegmund Warburg and the new merchant banking.

The fact that Gordon Newton was a non-writing editor was an advantage from the point of view of his staff. It focused the whole of his attention on what they were doing. This may have been a shortcoming of mine when I became an editor. I was always a writing editor. Of course, writing editors inevitably concentrate on their own copy. On the other hand, they can use their own writing to establish the tone of the paper on major issues.

In addition to Newton himself, I saw a certain amount of Garrett Drogheda. I think I was the only recruit to come, by an accidental circumstance, through the Managing Director's office. I was hugely flattered when, after I resigned from the *Financial Times*, Garrett rushed out and bought me a gold Omega watch at Asprey as a farewell present. One does not normally expect to get a gold watch after one's first eight years in journalism. This was a typical Drogheda gesture; he was as enthusiastic as Gordon about the development of the paper through the development of talent.

I also fostered a valuable relationship with Brendan Bracken, who was the Chairman and had the role of proprietor. I had first met him at the Oxford Union. I admired him because of his wartime work for Churchill and his having been the most loyal of Churchill's supporters before the war. He, too, believed in encouraging youth, and he also believed in journalists. He said once in a Chairman's speech to an Annual General Meeting of the *Financial Times* that 'the capital of this company is the brains of its journalists'.

The key focuses of the *Financial Times* in the 1950s were, as set out under the title on the front page of the paper, 'Industry, Commerce and Public Affairs'. My job was to write about public affairs; it has remained so ever since. In professional terms, I am a child of the *Financial Times*. However, throughout the 1950s I saw myself as a politician who was earning a living in journalism. In the early 1960s, and particularly after my marriage in 1962, I came to see myself as primarily a journalist and ceased to put my name in even for the safest Conservative seats.

After I had been at the *Financial Times* a couple of years, Paul Einzig, the City economist who was then the lobby correspondent, fell ill. I was still on the Features staff, and Newton asked me whether I would work in the lobby job for three or four months until Paul returned. I saw this as an ideal opportunity to broaden my political as well as my journalistic experience.

I was very fortunate, because my few months as a political correspondent coincided with the last months in which Winston Churchill was Prime Minister. I heard his last great speech to the House of Commons, in which he reviewed the threat that the hydrogen bomb posed to world peace, or, indeed, human survival.

At that stage of his career, Churchill was loved even by the great majority of his political opponents. Everyone knew that his resignation could not be long delayed. Everyone saw that he was the last great hero of Britain's period of historic dominance. Not only would we not see his like again, no subsequent generation would see any leader like him. He had a national admiration no British Prime Minister had enjoyed since the Duke of Wellington, more than a hundred years before.

All his last speeches had this quality; all personal ambition, all party political interest had been prised out of them; they were solely concerned with the welfare of his country and the dangerous future of the world. For the younger members of Parliament, or for young journalists in the Press Gallery, he gave an example of magnanimity in politics, founded on historic achievement.

The lobby itself worked in a way which would now seem old fashioned. There were formal lobby meetings, held, I think, only once a week; they were sometimes taken by Lord Swinton who, as Secretary of State for the Commonwealth, had been given responsibility for public information. As all Government decisions were announced first in the House of Commons, these meetings provided very little new information.

There were a few leaks, as there are in every government. While I was in the lobby, I was not well enough connected to be a beneficiary of these leaks. I do not think any politician wanted to leak to the *Financial Times*; in those days we were still thought of as having a narrow City audience, though the next Prime Minister, Anthony Eden, was an avid and even hypersensitive *Financial Times* reader.

Of my contemporaries among *Financial Times* colleagues, one of the most striking was Nigel Lawson, Thatcher's second Chancellor. I was delighted when Nigel came to the paper. Not only was he highly intelligent, he was also bumptious in that he had lots of energy, and he was not afraid to show it; he knew that he was clever, which he was, and he put his energy and his cleverness both into his work for the paper and into his conversation. He believed he would go far, and so did I. I enjoyed that. If there were others on the paper who found his energy and cleverness a bit much, I was certainly never one of them.

Later on, Nigel's ability forced me to take a key decision when I was on the *Sunday Times*. I was the Political and Economic Editor of that newspaper, a double bill which reflected the fact that there were very few journalists then, far fewer than there would be now, who could handle both politics and economics. The interweaving of politics and economics gave me a professional advantage, and significant influence, on the *Sunday Times*.

Denis Hamilton, then the Editor, asked me whom I would recommend as a possible City Editor, a post I had already held. I recommended Nigel, aware that I would be breaking my own monopoly combination in economics and politics. If Nigel had accepted, I would have created my own competitor. In making this recommendation, I remember thinking that Nigel and I were either both going to be a success, or we might both fail. I thought I should put the interests of the paper as I perceived them ahead of my personal career interests. Nigel Lawson, perhaps fortunately for me, went to the *Sunday Telegraph*. Later, he took the opposite decision from mine and moved from journalism to politics.

In 1954, I persuaded Gordon Newton to introduce a Saturday column called Finance and the Family. It was then an innovation, though personal financial advice has now become a universal feature in newspapers and broadcasting. Ann Temple's Human Casebook, an 'agony aunt' column in the *Daily Mail*, gave me the idea.

We established a committee to which we appointed a solicitor and an accountant. My role was to sort the letters and send them to the appropriate specialist; the specialist would then send back a reply a couple of days later. We would print both the original readers' letters and the reply. Sometimes, we received very touching letters. I remember one from a lady in Belfast, concerning a problem about a will, which started with the striking sentence 'I am illegitimate and a spinster'. We advised her to make a will rather than risk the problem of an intestate estate.

The following year, after John Appleby's departure to the *Daily Telegraph*, I became the Chief Leader Writer, the leaders being one of the main ways in which we covered public affairs. Even then the leading articles were not particularly party political, though the paper's assumptions were more Conservative than they are today. Brendan Bracken would not have agreed to the *Financial Times* becoming a supporter of the Labour Party; he held views which would now be described as Thatcherite.

In 1956, within four years of my joining the paper, Russia invaded Hungary. Like other newspapers, we were distracted by the Suez crisis from thinking enough about Hungary. However, even if Britain, or, more importantly, had the United States felt differently, there was very little assistance we could have provided. The Soviet Union was armed with nuclear weapons and had not the least intention of leaving Hungary on a voluntary basis. We could no more have saved the Hungarians in 1956 than we could have saved the Czechs in 1968.

A year earlier I had been approached by a small publisher, Rockliff, with a proposal that I should write a life of Anthony Eden, which I agreed to do. I met the Prime Minister, and remember a pleasant conversation with him about his childhood, sitting in deckchairs in the garden of No. 10 Downing Street. That was the old house which still looked and smelled like a genuine eighteenth-century town house, where one could imagine Walpole or Pitt as likely to stroll in from the House of Commons. The refurbishments of the Macmillan era destroyed the historic illusion; the modern Downing Street is an office decorated in the style of a grand hotel, not a home with a history.

The life was written; it is not, in retrospect, a bad little book. It introduced me to Eden, an opportunity for an ambitious young politician and, indeed, for a young journalist. In 1955, I was, so far as I know, the only member of the staff of the *Financial Times*, except Paul Einzig, the political correspondent, who had access to the Prime Minister. I do not remember that Gordon Newton believed in talking to Prime Ministers. However, the Managing Director of the *Investors' Chronicle*, Bobbie Allen, was Eden's parliamentary private secretary. In the following summer, he asked me whether I would join the group of speech writers, organized by Central Office, who helped prepare the Prime Minister's speeches. I was to assist with the economic passages.

Relations between journalists and politicians have varied over time. I doubt if nowadays any member of the staff of the *Financial Times* would be allowed to do any political speech writing, certainly not the Chief Leader Writer and certainly not for a Prime Minister. However, Gordon Newton agreed to this new role when I consulted him. Eden was not an easy man for whom to write speeches. He was always extremely courteous; I never saw the least sign of his apparently hysterical temper. However, he treasured his image of moderation, and thought that any striking phrase was likely to damage rather than enhance that image. Whenever we wrote a good line for him he would strike it out.

I had tried my hand at a small number of speeches, and got perhaps a paragraph into one or another, when, in July 1956, Gamal Abdel Nasser, the President of Egypt, announced the nationalization of the Suez Canal. This was a huge strategic challenge to Britain. In economic terms, Suez was the route by which the Western world, including Britain, got oil from the Persian Gulf. In political terms, the nationalization was a challenge to Britain's control of the oil countries of the Middle East, to British influence on Iraq, Saudi Arabia, Kuwait and the other Gulf States. Eden correctly saw that Nasser, as a successful Arab nationalist, would become immensely powerful in the Middle East if he managed to keep the Suez Canal, which he had seized. British influence in the Middle East would be destroyed; we would cease to be a world power. He failed to see that British influence depended on American support. It was, of course, against the interest of the United States to undermine Britain, since Britain protected the West's access to oil. Nevertheless, that is exactly the course President Eisenhower followed.

This was an extremely important news story for the *Financial Times*; it was also an opportunity in terms of my political career. In the summer, the British Government went through a process of negotiation, including the creation of a collective body called the 'Suez Canal Users' Association'. John Foster Dulles, the US Secretary of State, was particularly unwilling to help Britain, though prepared to offer sufficient support to string Eden along.

At first the Labour Party, then led by the undoubtedly patriotic Hugh Gaitskell, supported Eden's determination to resist Nasser. By the end of July 1956, that phase had already passed. The Labour Party increasingly came to argue that everything should be referred to the United Nations, although it was obvious that the UN would do nothing to recover the canal for Britain. Labour policy was theoretically idealist, but practically impotent. Eden also had critics inside the Conservative Party, who had been opposed to the withdrawal from the Suez Canal bases in 1954. These included Julian Amory, Harold Macmillan's son-in-law, and Angus Maude, father to Francis Maude, who was to become the critic of successive Conservative leaders forty and more years later.

In the meantime, a by-election was called for early September 1956 in the safe Labour constituency of Chester-le-Street, a mining seat in County Durham. I had agreed with Gordon Newton that I would not look for a seat until I had been at the *Financial Times* for at least three years. That ruled out the 1955 election, but left subsequent elections open, with the paper's approval. In July 1956, I put in for the Conservative candidature of Chester-le-Street, and won it, against the formidable competition of my friend Peter Tapsell, who later sat in Parliament for most of the next half-century. I wanted to fight a by-election with a view to taking a Conservative-held seat at the following General Election, which actually came in 1959.

I fought Chester-le-Street on the theme of standing up to Nasser. I remember going round the streets of the town with a loudhailer telling the Durham miners not to appease Colonel Nasser. In terms of public opinion, Eden's policy had their sympathy, but trade union loyalty meant that the Labour candidate had their votes. There was a 3 per cent swing to Labour, despite all my efforts, which I robustly described as a 'sign of support for the Government in these difficult times'. I greatly enjoyed the campaign. In those days, Durham Tories still wore red rosettes because they had been the colours of King Charles I in the battles of the civil war. I handed out balloons with 'Vote for Rees-Mogg' on them.

When I got back to the *Financial Times*, it was becoming increasingly clear that Eden would have to go to war with Egypt or face defeat. I was not in any way privy to his plans, but I was still on the speech-writing team. In late September, I was asked to write a complete speech with which he could open the Motor Show. He was going to France, and would have to be handed it at the airport on his return. I used the help of my colleagues at the *Financial Times*, including the motoring correspondent. The speech was a rhapsodic celebration of the spread of the automobile – 'a car in every garage'. Its enthusiasm was quite un-Eden-like. He read it out at Olympia without any variation; next day we solemnly reported the *Financial Times*' view of the future of the motor car as delivered by the Prime Minister. Even nowadays journalists sometimes get uncomfortably close to politicians. Unfortunately, Mr Eden had not been in France to experience for himself the joys of touring by motor car but, rather, had been plotting with France and Israel to invade Egypt. It turned out to be not a good plot.

The next task was to prepare for the Conservative Party conference. Like the conference of 1963 or 1989, this was to be the final conference of a Conservative leader. Like them, it was to leave its own scars.

The conference was at Llandudno in North Wales, on the pier. The speech writers went up to Llandudno on the train. This was the first conference at which I can remember security guards being needed; by now, the unavoidable security precautions have destroyed the free exchange of political conversations which made the old conferences of all parties so enjoyable. The terrorists in 1956 were not Egyptian, or a threat to the Prime Minister, but Greek Cypriots from EOKA, and it was the Colonial Secretary, Alan Lennox-Boyd, who was their theoretical target. He had armed officers outside his door, but no EOKA terrorists appeared.

I think we wrote rather a good speech for Llandudno. Lord Salisbury had written an even better one for himself. That was read out by Anthony Nutting, as though it had been his own, despite the fact that Nutting was an Arabist, and was to resign over Suez. He got a standing ovation. Eden had a standing ovation as well, for his argument that Nasser had his hands on our windpipe, or at least on our oil pipe. My contribution was this line: 'Mr Gaitskell has said that "socialism is about equality", but I say to you, "Conservatism is about opportunity".' That also got applause. I was always at ease with Eden's belief in 'property-owning democracy', a phrase which he introduced to British political debate.

Late in October, Bobbie Allen asked me to call round to see him in his small office on the right of the front door in Downing Street. When I arrived he sat me down and swore me to secrecy. Israel had moved forward into Egyptian territory. The French and British governments had sent an ultimatum calling on the Egyptians to withdraw, on pain of a Franco-British attack. His understanding was that a naval force would be setting out from Malta that evening, and that the paratroopers would be landing in the Suez Canal zone the following morning. Would I come in at 8.30 the next day to help write any speeches the Prime Minister might have to deliver? I said that I would.

I went back to the office and wrote the first of the *Financial Times*' leaders on the Suez campaign. Like many other people, we supported the campaign at the beginning, but became steadily more cautious as it seemed likely that it would fail. This pragmatic view was held widely among the general public. This is the pattern of human nature in risky enterprises, well demonstrated in subsequent events such as the increasing unpopularity of the Iraq War. If events recover, governments may regain their original support, if not, not. One passage from a *Financial Times* leader, which I must have written, and Gordon Newton must have approved, stated, 'The Government has taken on a grave responsibility. It was right to do so.' That represented the *Financial Times*' line before we had any knowledge that there had been a conspiracy with France and Israel.

Both Anthony Eden's Suez and Tony Blair's Iraq War started with genuine concern for Britain's national interest, which included access to oil as well as influence in the Middle East. Eden genuinely believed that Nasser was a threat to peace, just as Blair genuinely believed that Saddam Hussein was a threat. In both cases there was a public reaction when it became apparent that the action was not based on reliable information – in the Suez case there was a deliberate conspiracy, in the Iraq case there was the 'dodgy dossier'. Suez proved that Britain could not dominate the Middle Eastern balance of power without American support. Iraq proved that the United States could not dominate the balance of power in the Middle East, even with British support. In both cases legitimate initial intentions were not enough.

The following morning I turned up at Downing Street a few minutes early. On time, I was shown, with a couple of other speech writers, into Eden's bedroom in the upstairs flat. He was sitting up in bed, wearing blue pyjamas, looking in all other respects like a young First World War subaltern ready to go over the top. He greeted us with friendly courtesy, thanking us for coming at an inconvenient hour. Like Tony Blair, he always had excellent manners.

The same pattern was followed for three or four mornings. The navy and the paratroopers took far longer to arrive than had been expected. It was said that the navy took longer to get from Malta to Egypt in 1956 than Nelson took in 1797 at the Battle of the Nile. The Prime Minister would take confidential telephone calls in front of us – he trusted his speech writers, though he no longer trusted one of his press officers, whom he believed to be briefing against him to certain parts of the left-wing press. This press officer was forbidden access to the private office downstairs. The Foreign Office adviser in the private office was Philip de Zulueta, who later became a close friend and godfather to our son Thomas.

Eden's telephone calls did not sound very encouraging. There was a suggestion that the Foreign Secretary, Selwyn Lloyd, should go to New York to address the United Nations. I think Selwyn favoured it, but Eden decided that his inner team should stick together in London. There was at least one conversation with Guy Mollet, the French Prime Minister. '*Ah, mon cher ami*', Eden began. It was increasingly apparent that the Eisenhower administration would be as obstructive as possible. Dulles was anti-British; Eisenhower had never liked Eden; the presidential election was an added embarrassment. Today, we can reasonably look back and reflect that Eisenhower's Suez policy led to George W. Bush's decision to invade Iraq forty-five years later. Eisenhower himself came to think that he should have backed Britain against Nasser; in that case the Anglo-French conspiracy might never have arisen and America might have assumed the British role as the main external influence in the Middle East. The pro-Western Iraqi government of Nuri el-Said might have maintained power. By invading Iraq, President Bush was, in effect, trying to reverse the outcome of American policy in 1956.

In early November, Gordon Newton must have had a discussion with Brendan Bracken, who spoke to Eden. My double role was becoming difficult. The *Financial Times* had to be free to distance itself from Eden's Suez policy, and I had to write the leaders which took the more distant line.

Brendan Bracken extricated me from my role as speech writer. On the last morning, Eden could not have been more charming. He said that he understood that difficulties had arisen, and thanked me for my help. I was both relieved and disappointed. It simplified my work at the *Financial Times*, but it had been fascinating to be on the bridge, in however junior a capacity, in an historic crisis of such proportions.

Harold Macmillan, who succeeded Eden as Prime Minister in January 1957, had been the leading hawk at the beginning and became the leading dove at the end. Rab Butler, with whom I continued to be in contact, was doubtful throughout, but worked to help prevent Iain Macleod from resigning. He thought that it was his duty to minimize the damage to the Conservative Party. My closest political friend, Edward Boyle, did resign, a decision which shaped the future of his political career. The Suez crisis demonstrated the limitations of British power and was a great political storm from July 1956 to January 1957. However, in retrospect, it changed less in British politics than might have been expected. When Eden resigned as Prime Minister, Macmillan beat Butler on what was then a Cabinet vote. He returned to the domestic issues which made his Government popular. When he said 'We never had it so good' he may have sounded complacent, but it was the simple truth. The next General Election in 1959, in which I stood for the second time in Chester-le-Street, was held in a prosperous period and won with an increased majority.

The weekend before Eden resigned, I was staying with Rab Butler in Essex. He knew that Eden's prime ministership was doomed, and he hoped to succeed him as Prime Minister. Macmillan persuaded the Conservative Party that it was Rab's opposition that had prevented Eden carrying the Suez campaign to success. In fact, Macmillan became leader by blaming Rab for his own switch of policy. Suez was a useful lesson in the shifting positions of politicians in a crisis.

In 1957 the *Financial Times* changed hands, from the Crosthwaite-Eyre family to the Pearson Group. This move, instigated by Brendan Bracken, was a mistake, at least in terms of price. Bracken was by then certainly ill; he died a year or so later. He did not then trust Oliver Crosthwaite-Eyre to carry on his tradition. Crosthwaite-Eyre, whom I met when I was in the lobby, was a Conservative Member of Parliament, a difficult man to deal with, and Bracken had never had much respect for him. Bracken, the leading trustee of the Crosthwaite-Eyre trust, sold the *Financial Times* for, as I recall it, £650,000 to the Pearson Group. He thought the Pearson Group was large and stable and could be relied upon to keep the *Financial Times* as an English institution far into the future. I differed with his view on this, but was far too junior for my opinion to count. I thought that the price was absurdly low, that the Pearson Group would be relatively dull as an owner, perhaps too large in scale and most likely too risk-averse.

The British Aluminium takeover battle of 1959 was a moment of modernization for the City and for the *Financial Times*. This deal was influential not so much for its size but because it represented the new City against the old. Acting for British Aluminium was Siegmund Warburg, the newest and most entrepreneurial of all the merchant bankers. The arena for the battle for control of British Aluminium was the press, particularly the *Financial Times*' influential Lex Column, of which the junior partner was then Arthur Winspear. Arthur rapidly became convinced that Warburg were right. By the standards of the time, it was daring for the *Financial Times* to back Warburg, the new City, against Lazard, the old. This choice had most important consequences. It helped Warburg to win the British Aluminium battle, it cemented their reputation and it developed the idea of the *Financial Times* being on the side of the more dynamic, the more active, firms. It gave encouragement to the idea of the contested takeover as the way of changing British industry. It marked the death of gentlemanly capitalism and started a whole series of movements which ended up eventually with Big Bang and the domination of American firms like Goldman Sachs. Siegmund Warburg, whom I later came to know quite well, was a central figure in the new London banking. Another friend I made at Warburg is Sir Ronald Grierson, who also worked on the bid for British Aluminium. We subsequently worked together at GEC and when he was Chairman of the South Bank.

EIGHT

Thank you very much for … *the* Sunday Times

After I returned from fighting the 1959 General Election in Chester-le-Street, where the result was another Labour majority in excess of 20,000, I had a discussion with Gordon Newton about the possible development of the *Financial Times*. I proposed that we should have a daily column, to report on the personalities and events of business and the City. I had been the Chief Leader Writer since 1955, and I offered to take six months away from leader writing to start the column. I advertised in *The Times* for a junior and received about ninety replies, including one from Gillian Morris, who was working in the press department at Conservative Central Office. Her application was backed up by a very strong recommendation from her boss, the Conservative press officer. She was interviewed for the job, but it went to someone else, although I liked her the best. Another of the defeated candidates was Jilly Cooper.

Before the column, which we called Men and Matters, had even begun, I had the offer of another job. I was having lunch with William Clarke, a very distinguished City Editor at *The Times*. He told me that he had been offered the position of City Editor of the *Sunday Times*. I urged him to take it on the grounds that he would be given a byline on the *Sunday Times* and would become a known figure; *The Times* did not have bylines until

1967, when I introduced them, to the regret of some old *Times* hands. William told me that he had decided to turn down the *Sunday Times* offer because he valued his *Times* position more highly. About a week later, I received a letter from Harry Hodson, then the Editor of the *Sunday Times*, asking me whether I would be interested in the City editorship. I had already argued the case for William Clarke to accept the job, and I had been convinced by my own arguments. I had an interview with Denis Hamilton, the Editorial Director of *The Times*. Apart from my desire to have a public platform, I thought that Roy Thomson would be the newspaper proprietor of that time.

When I told Gordon Newton, he expressed appropriate regret, which, indeed, we both felt. I admired him as an editor, liked him as a man and felt a debt of gratitude for the opportunities he had given me. He made only one stipulation, that I should get the new column started. I delayed joining the *Sunday Times* until June 1960. As City Editor, I had my own column, and I had to edit the City page which had an excellent economic column written by George Schwartz, a first-class monetarist economist and a delightful colleague. Fifteen years later he would have been a fashionable economic commentator; in 1960 he was regarded as out of date though a good writer. The tide which was to inspire Thatcherism had not yet turned.

When I knew that I was moving to the *Sunday Times*, I had to find someone who could organize the City office. I immediately thought of Gillian. I wrote a letter to her, offering her the job, and I invited her to join me for tea at the Ritz, where I outlined the work to her, and she accepted.

In fact I had seen Gillian before these job interviews. The first time was at a Conservative press briefing. I was struck by her because she reminded me of my mother. She happened to have her hair parted in the middle, in a style similar to my mother's hairstyle in a photograph taken in about 1913. The first time we were introduced was at a meeting of Harold Macmillan's at the Alexandra Palace. We were introduced by Susan Chataway, as she then was, who was working with Gillian, handing out copies of Harold Macmillan's speeches. On that occasion, a member of the League of Empire Loyalists, dressed up as an old lady in a wheelchair, got to the front of the audience; he whipped out a megaphone and started to heckle the Prime Minister before being removed by stewards.

Gillian and I worked together in the City office, which was in the Gray's Inn Road, from June 1960 to October 1961. It was a very happy period. Gillian was – as she always has been – very good at her job, was very popular with the *Sunday Times* staff, and made life enjoyable for all of us. My own work was going well. I was pretty inexperienced to be a City Editor, so I wrote a light and readable column. In fact, the financial advice I gave, which included recommending GEC shares from the first weeks of Arnold Weinstock's management, made money for our readers. I was forming a good relationship with Roy Thomson. I liked him very much. I could hardly not like a benefactor who gave me a job, gave me promotions, and subsequently bought *The Times* and made me Editor.

In October 1961 Gillian and I went out together socially for the first time. I arranged to take her out to dinner. My sister Anne was down in Somerset recuperating from an acute attack of pancreatitis, so after dinner we went back to 8 Westmoreland Terrace, the Pimlico house I was sharing with Anne. I proposed and was accepted. We still have the elegant Swedish sofa on which I proposed. I remember buying it in Heals in the early 1950s, when I regarded it as the height of Scandinavian chic.

We were married by Father Alfonso de Zulueta in the Church of the Holy Redeemer, Chelsea. Lord Kilmuir made a little speech at the reception which was held in St Pancras Town Hall, where Tom Morris, Gillian's father, was that year's mayor. My marriage has been extraordinarily happy. Gillian is much more practical than I am, and we have been able to share and absorb the inevitable crises of life.

Our first child, Emma, was born on 17 December 1962. My father had died on the 12th, and I was in Somerset for his funeral, which was due to be held on the afternoon of the 17th. When I heard that Gillian was in labour I travelled back to London by train and spent the night in Queen Charlotte's Hospital. Emma was born early in the morning and I then returned to Somerset with my father-in-law, Tom Morris, in time for my father's funeral at Cameley church.

Shortly before the birth, I had said to Gillian that I thought we might as well stay on in Westmoreland Terrace for a few more months. That December the snow came early in London. We had recently been outbid for a house in Lord North Street, behind Westminster Abbey. It was later the house in which Harold Wilson lived in the early 1970s. No. 13 Cowley Street – which is an adjoining street – then came up. I visited Gillian and Emma in hospital, and we bought it, on a twenty-seven-year lease from the Church of England. The site had originally formed part of the outer garden of Westminster Abbey. The street had been developed, as a speculation, by Barton Booth, the early eighteenth-century actor, who had been the first to play the hero's role in Joseph Addison's *Cato*.

Cowley Street is a delightful row of Georgian houses, built in about 1720, in London brick. Number 13, whether because the house next door was bombed, or because it was built in a marsh, had floors with quite a steep slope. From the attic one can see the towers of Westminster Abbey, and the Victoria Tower, and at night one can hear the striking of Big Ben. It was for us a wonderfully happy house. We brought home to it a further three children, all born in Queen Charlotte's – Charlotte in 1964, Thomas in 1966 and Jacob in 1969. Veronica Crook, from Wrington in Somerset – a descendant of the Wrington rector who baptized John Locke – joined us as our nanny in 1965 and has been with us ever since, filling several roles, including canvassing for Jacob, for which he has been teased in the gossip columns.

The weekend after Gillian and I became engaged I had been invited down to Essex to stay with Rab Butler and his wife, Molly. I rang up to say that I had just become engaged and would hardly leave Gillian on our first weekend as an engaged couple. Molly immediately invited us both down, the first of a number of weekends we were to spend with the Butlers, either in Essex or Trinity College, Cambridge. In the 1970s they were also our guests in Ston Easton. Either then, or shortly afterwards, Molly told Gillian that they were expecting in due course to leave Smith Square, and take a flat for their retirement. When they did, she suggested that we might like to move to their house, No. 3 Smith Square, as we would need a larger house for a growing family. In the event, they decided to move in 1970. We then bought the house from them, on a valuation of their Essex land agent, which proved to be very fair.

Smith Square is only a short distance from Cowley Street and forms part of the same village of early eighteenth-century houses. Number 3 is a large house; it was extended by the width of an extra room at the back and at that time had a surprisingly large garden, running down the length of the cottages in Gayfere Street, with a large and beautiful London plane tree in the middle. The house faces across the square to St John's Church, a magnificent early Georgian building which had been converted to a concert hall after it, too, was bombed in the war. Number 3 had also been severely bombed, and Rab Butler had been forced to leave it and seek shelter with Paul Channon's father, Chips Channon, in Belgrave Square. After the war, Rab and his first wife, Sidney, had moved back into Smith Square, which was later redecorated by Molly after her marriage to Rab.

We lived in Smith Square for twenty-six years. For the first eight we were living in Smith Square at one end, and Ston Easton Park in Somerset at the other end, of our weekly lives. Gillian ran two large houses with calm efficiency. We entertained in both, giving dinner parties in London in the dining room which Sidney Butler had installed when Francis Bacon was her interior decorator. It had a curved roof and was rather long, like an underground carriage as it might have been designed by Sir John Soane. I loved the idea of living in two such fine homes, the finest Palladian house in north Somerset and one of the best Georgian houses in London. They provided an improving, if somewhat theatrical, setting for an Editor of *The Times*. They were perfect family homes, and Gillian made the best of them. They cost an increasing amount to run, in the inflation of the 1970s. They provided the glory years I was lucky to have. In 1979, after we had sold Ston Easton, Annunziata was born, in a Bath hospital, and Smith Square was her childhood home, all the more so as she went to London day schools.

Shortly after moving into Cowley Street I graduated from the purely financial role of City Editor of the *Sunday Times*, to Political and Economic Editor. I could fairly be described as a young progressive Conservative, with friends in the One Nation group. My closest political friends, including Rab Butler and Edward Boyle, were both on the left of the party. I did a good deal of political speaking, often to young Conservatives.

I gave up my own political ambitions in 1963. I felt strongly that Alec Douglas-Home was not the right man to become the Leader of the Conservative Party in succession to Harold

Macmillan. I believed this partly because of my loyalty to Rab Butler, and partly because Alec Douglas-Home, though very knowledgeable about foreign affairs, had no contribution to make in home affairs. With Alec as Leader, the Conservative Party could not even attempt the job of modernization which then seemed to be the central problem for the Government. Britain in the early 1960s had failed to grasp the post-war opportunities which had been exploited by the United States, Germany and Japan. We were becoming an overmanned post-industrial power.

When Alec became Leader, Iain Macleod and Enoch Powell decided to resign from the Cabinet. I resigned from my Conservative committees, the Policy Committee and the Conservative Political Centre. My reasons were similar to those of Macleod and Powell. Additionally, I was coming to think that I would have a more interesting career in journalism than I was likely to have in politics, and would perhaps enjoy influence over a longer period.

I had initially aimed to enter Parliament in 1959, and had spent the summer of that year failing to be nominated for safe Conservative seats such as Chichester, St Albans and the Isle of Wight. It was after I missed the Hallam Division of Sheffield by a single vote on the executive that I decided to fight Chester-le-Street again in the 1959 General Election. The Conservatives were, to my mind, likely to go out of office in 1964. The 1959 intake of new members would always, therefore, have a crucial advantage as against the 1964 intake. Put simply, the best of the 1959 intake would have at least some contact with the Government; some of them did indeed become Ministers. There would then be, I supposed, at least a full Parliament before the Conservatives got back in and before the 1964 intake would have their chance to get into Government in any form.

After 1959 I had served on the Central Policy Committee of the Conservative Party, a confidential committee mandated to prepare Conservative policies for the next General Election. Iain Macleod was in the Chair and Harold Macmillan attended at least one of our meetings. It became apparent that Macmillan had won the 1959 election without having a clear idea of the policies he would pursue after that. He was also put under great pressure by the charismatic example of President Kennedy in the United States. In 1959 the idea of having a relatively elderly Prime Minister was perfectly acceptable to the public. However, Kennedy brought in the cult of youth. All over the world, heads of government were expected to belong to the new generation; Harold Macmillan had chosen his image as 'the wise old man'. Now all politicians were expected to possess high levels of energy and spirit, to look and behave like young men rather than paternal figures. Wise old men were out. A similar transformation occurred when Tony Blair entered government. William Hague was chosen as a young man to lead the Conservatives in the hope that he would make his party seem young. In fact he seemed a young fogey.

The issue of age became particularly embarrassing when Harold Macmillan ran into the Profumo crisis in 1962. John Profumo, a likeable but run-of-the-mill Minister, had an affair with Christine Keeler, who was also having an affair with a Russian diplomat. Profumo denied the affair to the House of Commons but, when it emerged that he had lied, he had to resign. This escalated into a summer storm of public scandal, with a serious effect in discrediting the Government. I visited Harold Macmillan the night before he replied to the Commons debate on the subject, and gave him bad advice. He explained to me that he was not much in the company of the young and had no idea that this affair was going on. This seemed to me to be a truthful and legitimate defence of his position. One would not have expected Harold Macmillan to be going out to nightclubs, nor to be living with the fast set of the early 1960s. However, when Macmillan repeated this defence the following day in the House of Commons, it was ridiculed and used against him. He was portrayed as an old fuddy-duddy, totally out of touch with anybody under fifty.

The *Sunday Times* covered the Profumo affair in great detail and very successfully. We had young reporters nipping in and out of the office to see the various witnesses. In June 1963, all the gossip was about whether the Prime Minister himself would survive. I went round half the members of the Conservative Cabinet asking them who they thought ought to become the next Prime Minister. The other half honourably refused to talk to me. The two main candidates were Rab Butler and Quintin Hailsham, although both men faced vigorous opposition from some colleagues. No one mentioned Alec Douglas-Home, the then Foreign Secretary in the House of Lords, as somebody they regarded as a potential leader.

My canvass of the Cabinet, though interesting, did not provide much insight into what was to happen next. In the early autumn, the Conservative Party went up to Blackpool for the party conference. On the first day a message came from Harold Macmillan saying that he was in hospital and that he would not be able to continue as Prime Minister. The message was, I seem to recall, delivered by Alec Douglas-Home to the conference. It was Alec who had actually got the decision out of the old man. He himself left the impression that he was not a candidate, but would help to oversee the process of choosing a successor.

The announcement came as a complete surprise. We were having a public meeting of the Conservative Political Centre; because I was the deputy chairman of the CPC committee, I was sitting on the platform. The meeting was to be addressed by Lord Hailsham. Lord Hailsham provided a climax to his speech by announcing that he was going to throw his hat in the ring. He hoped, he went on, that he would receive enough support to become the next Leader of the Conservative Party and therefore the next Prime Minister.

I was not quite sure what to do. I supported Butler not Hailsham. As a journalist I was reluctant in any case to get too involved in the new Hailsham campaign. As a figure on the platform I did not know whether to join in the standing ovation or to sit glumly while everybody else stood up. I looked round and saw that Martin Redmayne, the Chief Whip, had decided to stand up, though I knew that in fact he was not the least in favour of Quintin becoming Leader of the party. I concluded that if the Chief Whip could stand up, I could appropriately stand up, too. So I stood up. In any case, I was very fond of Quintin who was a great man, though not necessarily a particularly wise one. The whole conference was a period of surprises. It was all very exciting.

My time at the conference was much more enjoyable because this was the first party conference after my marriage. Gillian was with me and we were having a thoroughly enjoyable social life. There were buckets full of champagne to keep people happy while they debated who their next Leader should be. Randolph Churchill, who always added to the excitement of any occasion, was there, campaigning for Quintin.

Throughout that party conference week I was able to talk in his room at the Imperial Hotel to Rab Butler. Rab in my view possessed the best understanding of the changes the party needed to make. He had the handicap of being the front runner, and Quintin the challenger. The possibility existed that the party might turn to one of the younger men, either Reggie

Maudling or Iain Macleod. On the closing day, Rab addressed the conference. It was not a bad speech – Rab was far too professional for it to be that – but it was not the exciting rallying call which might have seen him home.

I did not know all the intrigues that were going on, but I certainly had the sense that Alec Douglas-Home could not be ruled out as a possible candidate. I wrote a piece that week, for the *Sunday Times*, recommending Rab Butler: he was best able to take the party on to the next stage; he had a very good grasp of the possible reforms in the domestic area, particularly social reform. Indeed, in his work on education, Rab had been one of the architects of the original welfare state.

His challenger, Hailsham, nonetheless, was a delightful man, an intellectual man, a hilarious man, a man capable of brilliant oratory, of exciting an audience, a man of colourful views. What disturbed the Conservative Party was the idea that they might be putting themselves into the hands of a leader whom they thought had unpredictable judgement. Quintin was over the top. Rab, by contrast, was a safe pair of hands. He had been a front-bench figure for thirty years. His humour was more subtle. Hailsham was too manic and Rab was too calm.

I became actively involved in Butler's campaign, both urging him to press ahead and urging other people to support him. Many of my friends, including Denis Walters and Ian Gilmour, were supporting Hailsham.

This sort of link between journalism and politics may then have been commoner, and perhaps more accepted. On the left, for instance, there were journalistic politicians, like Michael Foot, Tom Driberg, Dick Crossman. Nowadays, it is not all that different; many journalists have close and partisan relations with politics, as, for instance, Michael Gove on the Conservative side, or Alastair Campbell, who was a political correspondent for the *Daily Mirror* before becoming the press spokesman for Tony Blair. Historically, some politicians have always tried to influence public opinion through their own journalism. Among Conservative leaders Bolingbroke, in the early eighteenth century, and Salisbury and Disraeli in the nineteenth, were highly effective in their journalism, as was Winston Churchill in the twentieth. Politics and journalism cannot really be separated because politicians are dependent on public opinion. Julius Caesar wrote eulogies on himself and Walsingham employed Christopher Marlowe as a spy.

The week after we all got back from Blackpool was very intense. Early on in that week I was told by a *Sunday Times* colleague – I did not ask and still do not know his source – that the new Leader was going to be Alec Douglas-Home, that it had all been fixed. I rang Iain Macleod, then the Party Chairman, who was having lunch with Reggie Maudling, the Chancellor. I told them that the *Sunday Times* had the information that it was going to be Alec Douglas-Home. It came as a complete surprise to both of them. Later, after Alec Douglas-Home had become Prime Minister and was forming, or had formed, his Cabinet, I wrote in support of the position of those, pre-eminently Powell and Macleod, who had refused to serve under him. I took the view that it had all been a stitch-up, which it had been; moreover, that it was fixed that the whips had consulted Members of Parliament in a way which was in fact neither open nor fair. I described the episode as one which demonstrated that the Conservative Party, if it ever had been, had ceased to be run by gentlemen. I doubt if politics ever was a gentlemanly sport.

Macmillan himself had sewed up the succession with the aid of an inner circle. Having decided that he did not want Rab Butler to succeed him, due to an ancient distrust between them, he had been in favour of Hailsham, but switched his support to

Douglas-Home. Macmillan genuinely thought that Rab would not make a good Prime Minister. This is a legitimate judgement for an outgoing Prime Minister to make of one of his colleagues, if that is what he thinks. However, Macmillan had not approved of Hailsham coming out into the open too early, nor in such an excited manner. So, he dropped the idea of Hailsham and took up the idea of Alec Douglas-Home.

There had been a meeting on the Scottish island of Islay between the Chairman of the 1922 Committee, Lord Margadale, and Ted Heath, an ex-Chief Whip. The combination of the Chairman of the 1922 Committee and a powerful, if retired, Chief Whip is extremely powerful. This pair had decided, in the course of the late summer of 1963, that they would back Alec Douglas-Home, and at this meeting they started that ball rolling.

Ted's personal interest in supporting Alec may have been that he knew he could not himself get the leadership of the Conservative Party at that time. He may have believed that, if Alec Douglas-Home got the job, he would appoint Ted Foreign Secretary. As Foreign Secretary, Ted would have expected to succeed Alec. If that was Ted's plan it did not entirely work, because, to Ted's intense indignation, Rab Butler agreed to serve under Alec, on the condition that he became Foreign Secretary. It was a post he had always coveted, having been the Under Secretary of State for Foreign Affairs in the 1930s when Lord Halifax, in the House of Lords, was the Foreign Secretary. Rab, therefore, had a feeling that he was going back to his old home at the Foreign Office, a place central to his political interests.

Later, when I came to know him, I liked Alec very much as a man. Everybody who dealt with him did. He readily forgave me for my criticisms of him, though, to her credit, his wife never did. For all his skill in foreign affairs, his ignorance of domestic politics was considerable. He had first to fight the Perth by-election to re-enter the House of Commons, and to confirm his prime ministership. He was asked about comprehensive schools. At the time there were pilot schemes of comprehensive schools in a few local authorities, but Labour Party policy was to roll them out across the country, which they were indeed to do two years later. Alec replied: 'You tell me what a comprehensive school is and I'll tell you what I think about it.' Nor was economics his strong suit. He made the foolish remark that, when matters of the economy were being discussed, he had to get out his matchbox to be able to count, an ironic joke against himself but probably not far from the truth. The trouble was that he was the right man in the wrong place at the wrong time. I felt that he should have known his limitations.

Alec's leadership regrettably turned the Conservative Party away from addressing the problems which people of my age all thought ought to be addressed. His failure left Harold Wilson free to make the theme of modernization almost a monopoly of the Labour Party in the run-up to the 1964 General Election, as Tony Blair did before 1997. The Conservatives were not in a position to pretend that Alec Douglas-Home was connected, in any way, to the white heat of technology. Still, because Alec fought the 1964 General Election in his honourable and attractive way, the margin of victory for Labour was much smaller than might have been expected. Ideologically, the Conservative Party did not move too far to the right, but it failed to address the modernization. It offered no development. The country clearly recognized the failure.

In the summer of 1965, I wrote a column arguing that Alec should step down. Ted Heath had already started a movement to get him to do so. Ted by then hoped that he himself could win the leadership, which he did, beating Reggie Maudling. I supported Ted, because I thought that Reggie lacked the drive to take the Conservatives back to power.

In proposing Alec's resignation, I wrote a rather condescending piece which I now find irritating to read. I compared Alec to the amateur captain of the second eleven who comes into the first team and does rather a good job for the time being, but must not be regarded as a permanent fixture. It may be that my cricketing metaphor impressed Alec; he had himself been an excellent cricketer. Hugo Young, in his last book, *Supping with the Devils*, says that my piece represented an exercise of direct influence which no columnist would now be able to enjoy. For, after reading the article and thinking I was right, Alec went out into the rose garden and decided to resign. Few other Prime Ministers' minds work in this way. Often, they do not really care whether the people who say they should resign office are right or not. Alec did. He was, in an unusual way, a detached man, as well as a thoroughly honourable one.

This kind of influence for a journalist is no longer possible as there are simply too many columnists. I was then in a very favourable position. I was the only political columnist with a column every week to write for the *Sunday Times*, then, as now, the most influential of the Sunday broadsheets. I enjoyed making strong judgements, and was encouraged to do so. I rarely enjoyed giving a simple descriptive review of the current political situation. I aimed to be more analytical, more forensic, less sketchlike. I wanted to get people to believe what I believed.

International affairs became very tense during the period I was at the *Sunday Times*. I was very close to Henry Brandon, the long-standing and well-connected Washington correspondent. I was not expected to write a weekly piece about foreign affairs, but, if I happened to be abroad, or had recently been abroad, I had the latitude to write about that as well. American politics were then extremely interesting. John F. Kennedy was elected President of the United States a few months after I joined the *Sunday Times*. Whatever else might be said about him, he was, from a journalist's point of view, the most stimulating, most interesting President of the modern age. I never met him. Still, in 1963, I did go to JFK's last press conference, with Henry Brandon. I remember Kennedy's impact. He was discussing Laos, part of the Vietnam issue. The press conference, I felt, was designed to support a decision to make a greater commitment to Vietnam. He was not preparing the minds of the correspondents for partial or complete American withdrawal. My impression could be put in the sentence 'The boy stood on the burning deck'. Here was a young figure facing the issues of the survival of the human race, certainly the survival of liberty against communism. Kennedy appeared gladly to assume the burden upon his shoulders and to respond with courage and determination. I felt sympathy for him.

Despite public opinion which compared the two men unfavourably, Kennedy had a good relationship with Harold Macmillan, based on their shared sense of irony, along with a family connection. Macmillan had married the daughter of one Duke of Devonshire and Kennedy's sister had been married to an heir to the dukedom. Kennedy possessed the feeling of wit, not that he was always making witty remarks, but there was a slight edge to the way he replied to journalists' questions. Additionally, he possessed, and was surrounded by, a group of very admiring friends in Washington, who were themselves very gifted people. Henry Brandon would have dinner parties when Gillian and I visited, and we would meet some of the best and the brightest from the Kennedy entourage. I remember a meeting with McGeorge Bundy, who was then a young White House figure, the Special Assistant for National Security Affairs. At the dinner were several other members of Kennedy's circle. They were extremely highly educated, mostly Ivy League, Harvard, Yale, Princeton, figures with detailed academic knowledge of their subjects rather than the more superficial knowledge which political administrators tend to have.

Washington was full of able people who happened to have found an outlet for their abilities in government, and it was extremely enjoyable. It was natural to sympathize with Kennedy and admire him. Subsequently, this rather rosy picture of Kennedy has undoubtedly been tarnished by what we have come to know about the Kennedy family, about his personal conduct and about his sex life. I did not meet Jackie Kennedy until after his death. I did not warm towards her. She had this strange, very artificial-sounding voice, a sort of funny soft, little girl's voice. I thought she was in some sense phoney.

Of course, as everybody who was alive then does, I recall exactly where I was when the news of the assassination of Kennedy came through. I was standing in the *Sunday Times* building in Gray's Inn Road, by the lift on the editorial floor, waiting to go home. It must have been 6.30, or thereabouts, in the evening. It was a Friday night. I pressed the lift button, the lift was coming. Someone told us the news. We then threw ourselves into recreating the paper that we had originally prepared. All of us who took part in producing the paper thought that it was the best *Sunday Times* we had produced. I remember how proud we felt of it. The remaking of the paper was led by Pat Murphy, one of the great Fleet Street professionals, but we relied heavily for our coverage on Henry Brandon who had been in Dallas at the time of the assassination.

Following the assassination, the light went out of the Democratic Party. Only with the nomination of Barack Obama did it again become a party favourable to ideas and ideals, which it was when Kennedy was alive. Even if one thinks that Kennedy's message was partly bogus, the impact on the Democrats, and the impact, through the Democrats, on American public life, was very real. The impact on the British electorate was that we wanted a Kennedy of our own. Harold Wilson, no Kennedy, heaven knows, had to pretend that the Labour Party was the Democrats and that he was Kennedy, and that he would be able to give us an extra dimension in politics. Perhaps the real tragedy of Wilson was that he lowered the expectations of politics.

There were high hopes when Wilson was elected Prime Minister in 1964. I came fairly quickly to doubt his commitment to modernization. I questioned several of his key Cabinet appointments. For instance, Jim Callaghan was not the right person to appoint as Chancellor of the Exchequer. He was not a modernizer, and was reluctant to face major changes, as, for instance, devaluation or trade union law. Still, one should never underrate Jim Callaghan. He was a robust personality and a canny, good politician. He turned out to be a better Prime Minister than he was a departmental Minister.

When Labour came to power in 1964 devaluation of the pound had become inevitable. The pound had ceased to be competitive in trade terms, particularly against European manufacturers. Callaghan resisted devaluation for too long. His handling of the issue was naïve. Devaluation to Callaghan was a matter of national honour. Consequently, he was deeply upset when he had to devalue and he insisted on soon leaving the Treasury. He did not see devaluation as something which might become necessary to correct an imbalance, and therefore something to be approached in a dispassionate spirit. He was particularly unsuited to being Chancellor, being at once too emotional and too simplistic.

The pre-eminent achievements of the early Wilson administration were probably the social policy reforms undertaken by Roy Jenkins in his justly well-regarded period as Home Secretary. I was opposed to the abortion law. I thought that it would inevitably lead to abortion on demand; it grossly undervalued the life of the potential child. Moreover, I thought the Abortion Act would encourage people to treat abortion as a matter of social convenience. My point of view on abortion is a straight Catholic view, I have no doubts about it. However, I felt that as a newspaper we had to understand and make judgements in terms of the broader public opinion of a non-Catholic, and increasingly non-Christian, society. In those terms as well, the abortion law was far too lax. So there I had no political sympathy with Roy Jenkins.

As a Catholic I also questioned the aims of his reforms of the divorce law. Admittedly, we had an unsatisfactory divorce law. Simplification was necessary, but 'no fault' divorce was intended to make divorce easier, and that, in my view, undermined marriage.

I was, however, in favour of Roy's abolition of the death penalty. There had been various cases, even in my time, in which the guilt of the person executed was either not demonstrated or at best doubtful.

I was also in favour of reforming the laws on homosexuality. Prior to the reforms people were blackmailed and jailed for conduct between consenting adults. That, obviously, did a great deal of harm, causing suffering. It was a blackmailer's charter.

The combined effect of the Jenkins reforms took liberalism to the point of libertarianism. It tended to weaken the moral order of society and to encourage promiscuity rather than stability. The promiscuity which one sees in the early years of the twenty-first century does huge harm; huge harm to the institution of marriage; huge harm to people's lives. However, I think Jenkins' reforms were inevitable and, with the exception of the abortion reforms, justifiable. He had the *Zeitgeist* with him. Taken in the round, Roy's reforms were a very important achievement. In proposing, piloting and implementing these reforms, Roy Jenkins was a man of his time; he had the broad moral attitudes of European society. Similar reforms were passed at more or less the same time, even in very Catholic countries, like Italy (though not in Ireland or Poland), and also in most of the states of the United States, although the abortion law in the United States was changed by the Supreme Court, not by legislature.

The *Zeitgeist* to which Jenkins was responding was a post-war wave of relaxation of previous customs. A similar relaxation had occurred in the 1920s, also a decade of post-war liberalism. In the 1920s, however, this was confined to a rather small group of the upper-class young. The bright young things of the twenties were often the children of relatively wealthy parents. In the 1960s, instead of it just being the 'top' 5 per cent who were affected, the changes extended to the whole of the middle class.

The *Sunday Times* was very close to the *Zeitgeist* with its colour supplements and Snowdon pictures. In 1967 there was a pop song by the Scaffold which had the line 'Thank you very much for ... the *Sunday Times*'. Admittedly the song's next words gave thanks for the 'napalm bomb' but we felt that the song reflected the *Sunday Times*' iconic status. The *Sunday Times* was the paper which was closest to the movement of culture. It was where the action was.

The *Sunday Times* employed people who were influential in this cultural movement. Mark Boxer, the first editor of the Colour Magazine, certainly was; Lord Snowdon also. Snowdon had additional prestige with his connection to the Royal Family.

That aside, he was a brilliant young photographer, an aesthete and connected by blood to the aesthetic movements of the 1920s. His mother came from a famous artistic family and Cecil Beaton was some sort of a cousin. At any rate, Snowdon was a leader of this so-called movement. The *Sunday Times* also had people, notably Brian Glanville, who understood the new fashionable culture of football. We certainly had journalists who moved in the circles of the fashionable London set, the Carnaby Street set, the photographers, the hairdressers, indeed. It was not a world that I felt I had too much to contribute to and yet, at the same time, I felt that it was right that the paper should be interested in the changes that were taking place. Newspapers do not generate these societal changes, but certainly a newspaper which articulates them attracts interest and possesses value.

Partly because of the Colour Magazine, the *Sunday Times* became very interested in issues of layout. We had the benefit of Robert Harling, a brilliant layout adviser, who contributed to the visual quality of the paper. Harry Evans was another central figure. His forte was combining a strong story with a strong display. Harry was a journalist who certainly had a better understanding than I did of the new world that was emerging, this world which was a mixture of new politics, new fashion and new age. When I first met him, he was closer to his Manchester Welsh origins with a strong loyalty to what he regarded as his working-class roots and still married to his first wife, Edna, whom we much liked. He later married Tina Brown, herself a brilliant journalist, who was very loyal to him in the great *Times* stoppage of the late 1970s.

Harry was a colleague whom I much admired. He was to become a very gifted Editor of the *Sunday Times*.

I did not feel particularly close to the culture of the sixties. During my time on the *Sunday Times* I was ambivalent towards it. I saw its importance in newspaper terms but I knew I was much better at understanding the political, governmental and business worlds, which were still in the hands of people whose value systems were more old-fashioned. Nevertheless, I was excited by being connected to a new powerhouse of energy, despite never being, or thinking of myself as, 'one of us'.

This urban, recently working-class, aesthetic outlook frightened the Conservative Party. They did not know how to handle it. Maybe Iain Macleod understood it pretty well. He was not representative, though. The Conservative Party was still very much in the hands of an older social order, as the choice of Alec Douglas-Home demonstrated.

The 'generation gap' was truly a 1960s development. It represented something real. Prior to the 1960s, there existed a remarkable homogeneity of outlook between parents and children. The concept of a culture, distinct to young people and created by young people, was unknown. Gillian and I were fortunate in that our children were not teenagers at the height of the sixties. These two divergent cultures were most dangerous when parents were completely in a 1950s or pre-1950s set of attitudes and children were swept up by 1960s attitudes.

Representative of this clash of cultures was the 1960 *Lady Chatterley* trial. It was an absurd trial. I could not get worked up about it. Having some law, which limited, as it were, the flow of pornography into the community, was not in itself wrong. However, that particular judgement, which tried to exclude *Lady Chatterley's Lover*, was mistaken. D. H. Lawrence is a serious literary figure and his book was not pornography. I was not, however, one of those who thought no censorship of any kind should exist. Without censorship, or without effective censorship as you now find with the internet, the most terrible pornography, including child pornography, may become freely available. This is bad for society and dangerous to its victims.

In 1965 I joined the Garrick Club, on the suggestion of Denis Hamilton. It has changed its character a good deal since those days. We were then a club for actors, publishers, journalists and lawyers, convenient for the Law Courts and not too inconvenient for the Gray's Inn Road, where I was then working. We had a notable history, full of rows between eminent literary figures, and a wonderful collection of theatrical paintings. We were not perceived as a particularly fashionable club, like White's and Brooks's, nor was the club particularly rich. There was a waiting list, but it was quite short.

Now the club is much wealthier, thanks to our share in the literary estate of A. A. Milne, the popularity of Winnie the Pooh and the multi-million deal with the Disney Corporation. We are also a highly fashionable club with the longest waiting list in London. But the members are drawn from the same professions. The difference is attributable to the change in the status of the media professions, from their comparatively humble ranking in the 1960s to their present degree of celebrity. The Garrick even has a list of celebrities, such as Jeremy Paxman, whom it has blackballed – a decision which was rightly revoked.

The great virtue of the Garrick is that it is a conversational club, unlike those clubs at which members will bring a book or a newspaper to accompany a frugal and solitary lunch. From the start, I was invited to sit at what was then regarded as the *Times* table, the far corner table on the left as one entered the coffee room. *The Times* never had anything like a monopoly of the table, but it had come to be associated with leading *Times* figures over the years. Indeed, there was a myth, rather like the myth that the papacy alternates between thin popes and fat popes, that the editorship of *The Times* alternated between Garrick editors and editors who belonged to the Athenaeum, where there was less gossip, and, it was said, a more meagre cuisine.

I have enjoyed the conversation at the Garrick, and particularly at that table, for nearly forty years. Certainly the Garrick is a place for those who are obsessed by the news of the day. There is always a choice of Garrick views, improved in quality by the information of the journalists and the legal experience of the judges.

It was at this table that I lunched frequently with Robin Day. Robin had a genius for conversation. He was serious about conversation, in the way that Samuel Johnson was serious. He believed it should involve argument and the clash of views and, in such debates, like Samuel Johnson, he wanted to win. He was at his best in argument with those who enjoyed the same cut and thrust, like the outrageous old Mr Justice Melford Stevenson. But he was also very good at drawing out the shyer or younger members. He was a sensitive person and alert to the sensitivities of others.

For better or worse, Robin created modern television journalism in Britain. He had trained as a lawyer and practised briefly and impecuniously at the bar. His sole forensic triumph, by his account, was a case of alleged indecent exposure, in which he secured an acquittal by convincing a perhaps elderly jury that his client, far from wishing to expose himself, had a problem with his prostate. How Robin failed at the bar is beyond belief; he had all the gifts, had already been a renowned President of the Oxford Union, but in those days he could not survive on two-guinea briefs and only a thin supply of them.

When he joined the original ITN team of newscasters, he saw the opportunity to use the techniques of cross examination to get the truth out of politicians. In those days, both sides behaved better. Interviewers, even if pressing, were polite and politicians had not yet discovered that it is quite unnecessary to answer questions – it is always possible to answer a quite different question which has not been asked. Robin pinned down the issues on television, as he did in the Garrick Club.

Years later, when, in 1986, I retired as the Vice-Chairman of the BBC, Robin's career with the BBC was almost over. He had been replaced by younger and less talented men. It was then the custom for the BBC to give a farewell dinner for the retired Governors. I invited my family, and I invited Robin. By that time the senior management of the BBC, who had a high opinion of their own importance, did not like me. Indeed, some of them cordially disliked me for my failed attempts to change the BBC, as I thought, for the better. In those days the BBC was run by producers who had been promoted to the senior ranks of the bureaucracy.

Producers do not like presenters. Indeed, one even sympathizes with that. Producers create the programme. Much of the time, though never with Robin, presenters merely read out the words. I made the usual sort of after-dinner speech, thanking people – though I doubt if I had much thanking to do – and making polite remarks about my guests. I said that I was quite unimportant – they did not disagree – that the Governors were also unimportant – we were not what broadcasting was about. Again they agreed. I went on to say that the senior management, the Managing Director, Television, the Director General himself, were not what mattered to the public. I then pointed to Robin and said that he represented real broadcasting, the creativity of broadcasting. He was what the public cared about. That was not what they wanted to hear. But it was true. Robin's death robbed the Garrick Club of its archetype.

NINE

Sadat's Viennese Ideal

In July of 1966, when I was thirty-eight, Denis Hamilton told me I was to be appointed Editor of *The Times*. Denis was then the Editor of the *Sunday Times* and I was his Deputy Editor. Denis was on the Board of the Thomson Organization and had been negotiating on behalf of Roy Thomson to buy *The Times* from the Astor family of Hever. Lord Astor, as Major J. J. Astor, had acquired control of *The Times* after Northcliffe's death in 1922, but now the family, feeling it then neither had the answers for *The Times* nor the share capital to rebuild it, had decided that it would sell the paper to Roy Thomson.

During the negotiations for the sale, Denis called me into his office, told me that *The Times* was now likely to be bought by Thomson, and informed me that, in the event of this sale going ahead, he thought I would be the best person to be Editor. This decision was taken, without, so far as I know, any great consideration of the alternatives. There were two other members of the staff of the *Sunday Times* who might have been considered for the job: Frank Giles, the Foreign Editor, and Harry Evans, Assistant Editor on the home side. It was pretty obvious to me, and I think it was pretty obvious to Denis Hamilton also, that if the choice were between Harry Evans and myself, then Harry was a natural Editor for the *Sunday Times* and I a natural Editor of *The Times*. Frank later succeeded Harry in 1981 as Editor of the *Sunday Times*.

I think this was the right temperamental choice. Harry proved to be a brilliant Editor of the *Sunday Times*. He relished the excitement of each weekend, the campaigns, and the circulation of 1.4 million.

In prospect, I was aware of the historic legacy of preceding editors. Still, I thought *The Times* needed bringing up to date, as all newspapers do from time to time. I had considerable respect for Sir William Haley, my predecessor, but felt that his *Times* was distant from my generation. He was twenty-five to thirty years older than me. Of the other long-serving previous editors of the twentieth century, there were Geoffrey Dawson and R. M. Barrington-Ward. Dawson in fact held the post for two periods. However, his reputation was hopelessly marred by his support for appeasement and the fact that he had failed to support tough-minded coverage of the Nazi regime. Barrington-Ward had taken *The Times* to the left in his period at the end of the war and immediately after the war. One can understand why Barrington-Ward took those decisions but they did not seem to me, in the late 1960s, to have been the right decisions: they came before the Cold War and they underrated the tyranny of the Soviet Union in the same way as Dawson had underrated the tyranny of the Nazi regime. I had no desire to move back to their kind of editorship, with the appeasing of dictators. Nor did I want to be as close to Government as Dawson had been to Neville Chamberlain.

For a few months William Haley remained as a non-executive Chairman; he was not an easy man to know. I never established even a friendly formal relationship with him. He was, however, a master of a traditional kind of journalism. He had brought *The Times* up to very high standards, encouraging journalism which was responsible and accurate. But his *Times* lacked excitement; perhaps he thought excitement was rather vulgar, but he was not attracting new readers into the paper. I thought that an opening up of the paper was absolutely necessary; necessary for survival.

Part of the challenge for an incoming Editor was the organizational structure of the paper. Denis Hamilton became the Chairman and Editor-in-Chief and also had the executive responsibility for Times Newspapers. I thought his title of Editor-in-Chief inappropriate for the structure of *The Times*. *The Times* had always been a paper in which the Editor was the Editor. Editors of *The Times*, including Geoffrey Dawson, had fiercely guarded their independence from their proprietors. The Editor-in-Chief is a sort of intermediate title, suggesting that there may be somebody who is entitled to give editorial instructions to the Editor. While I was obviously grateful to Denis Hamilton – he had promoted me on the *Sunday Times*, he had chosen me as Editor of *The Times* and we got on well personally – still I was concerned to make sure that his role did not in any way reduce my independence. To set out my position, I sent Denis a memo to outline what I took to be our relationship. I used the phrase 'the Captain does not cease to be responsible for his ship even if he has a senior officer on board who is responsible for the whole fleet'. I admit that if I had been Denis Hamilton and received such a memorandum I should have been irritated by it. But Denis accepted the memorandum and our relationship worked reasonably well. I did not ask his advice (and he seldom offered it) regarding the line the paper was taking.

The only area in which I did take much advice from Denis concerned personalities: he was a very good judge of journalists and of their potential. He suggested one or two people who might be worth looking at for the early appointments. The most important of these was Michael Cudlipp. Denis had brought Michael to London from the *Manchester Guardian* to be News Editor of the *Sunday Times* when he was only twenty-four. At the start of my editorship he was appointed head of *The Times* home news gathering operation, which he reorganized. Michael later became Deputy Editor.

Iverach McDonald, whom I inherited as my Associate Editor, had been foreign correspondent before the war. He was the only man who interviewed both Hitler and Stalin. He was one of the Young Turks on *The Times* in the Dawson period and fought to get stories warning people about Nazi Germany into the paper. He was very much a Highlander, very softly spoken. He put on one side any feelings that he should have been Editor and greatly helped me to avoid mistakes when I first arrived. He steered me round the course of avoiding giving offence to the members of the staff. He even contributed a very great maturity and wisdom to my first couple of years, and I was very sorry indeed when he retired.

Another key influence was John Grant, who was defence correspondent and then became the Managing Editor of the paper. I delegated to him the administration of the paper. In the period when trade union relations were really difficult, a great responsibility fell on him. I remember John saying of one of the trade union officers that he never left John's office without leaving 'a turd in his teapot'. John also very successfully ran a good deal of the recruitment.

Roy Thomson, the proprietor, was as hands-off as Denis Hamilton. Asked once on television about the relationship between his political views and those of his editors, he replied: 'I'm a very rich man; like most very rich men I have very right-wing views. I own two hundred newspapers; it would be quite ridiculous if all of my newspapers had to have the same views as me.' Roy Thomson's attitudes to newspapers derived from his experiences in Canada where he had owned small local newspapers. There was only one rule he applied to his editors: that they should serve their communities. As a proprietor, so long as he was satisfied that one of his editors was genuinely concerned to serve that community, and not pursuing some personal end, Thomson felt he had to support the editor even when personally he would have come to a different conclusion.

I was left free, therefore, even on the most important issues. When I first took *The Times* on a strongly pro-European line – we supported the original Labour Government application to join the European Community – I realized after we had written two or three pro-European leaders that I did not know what view Roy Thomson, as a Canadian, took of Britain joining the European Community. As it turned out he shared our pro-European line, on the grounds that Europe needed a continental market like that of the United States. But I did not feel that I had to ask him. I was grateful for my independence, both to Denis Hamilton and Roy Thomson.

The urgent task for an incoming Editor was the modernization of the paper. This was recognized throughout the paper itself. Indeed, the first radical modernizing step had been taken by Haley six months earlier, in May 1966. That was the decision to put news on the front page. This was radical because *The Times* had, until then, retained a traditional eighteenth- and nineteenth-century newspaper layout with personal advertisements on the front page. This format was retained for quite so long partly because it was thought that the old front page marked *The Times* out from other newspapers. There was *The Times*, and there were other newspapers. It was also a considerable source of revenue; once news came onto the front page there was never again a personal advertisements column which had the same pulling power. However, the old front page had not given the day's news. That was tucked away in the centre.

Haley's decision shifted the whole balance of the layout of the paper, but this shift had not been fully implemented at the time of my appointment. There was still a great deal of work to be done in reorganizing the format of the paper. My aim was to make *The Times* a modern newspaper for contemporary and younger readers. I was influenced by my *Sunday Times* and *Financial Times* experience, and by the example of the two Editors who had trained me, Denis Hamilton and Sir Gordon Newton at the *Financial Times*.

My first major innovation was the introduction, in January 1967, of personal bylines. Haley had not believed that bylines were right. He thought that journalists ought to be giving impersonal news, that it was a bad idea to allow the egotism of journalists to show through, that the anonymous newspaper was therefore inevitably superior in quality to the journal in which reporters' names appeared. He admired the anonymity of *The Economist*, he had retained it in the *Times Literary Supplement* and he wanted to keep it in *The Times*. I disagreed with this, believing, then as now, that journalists do their best work if they know that they are to receive some individual credit for it. I thought that it would be extremely difficult to attract the sort of journalists whom I hoped to have writing for the paper if they were to remain anonymous, particularly at the time when every other paper in Fleet Street was giving the journalists their bylines. For a journalist, his name is his career.

Certainly, the introduction of bylines had a strong impact on *The Times*. The quality of journalism changed. The previous detached tone of the old *Times* was very attractive, but the signed journalism was more colourful and sometimes more energetic. Undoubtedly the old *Times* staff had a selfless devotion to the paper and to their craft which may have been reinforced by anonymity. I would not say that the quality of the journalism was always improved with the introduction of bylines, but it became different, and inevitably it became more personal.

A further innovation was the launch, in April 1967, of The Times Business News. The idea for this went back to my experience on the *Financial Times*. In the early 1950s we had felt on the *Financial Times* that *The Times* ought to be our great competitor. But it was not. *The Times*' City columns of the 1950s, though scholarly and serious, lacked colour.

This idea of the opportunity for a competitor to the *Financial Times* was still in my mind when I went to the *Sunday Times* as the City Editor. After a period as City Editor, I had received the rather strange byline of the Political and Economic Editor. It was then that I got Denis Hamilton's enthusiastic agreement to start the Sunday Times Business News, the first separate business section in a Sunday newspaper. On our first Sunday the section was in profit, with £60,000 of advertising. I thought that it was natural that such a separate section would also succeed in *The Times*. *The Times*' readership had always included a large number of business people, often with investments, or other financial interests. If The Times Business News was a success, we could, I believed, provide for people who did not need the full professional services of the *Financial Times*. In its initial impact, however, this new challenge did more good to the *Financial Times*, which broadened and improved its coverage, than to *The Times*.

To run The Times Business News, we brought Tony Vice, who had also been the founding Editor of the Business News at the

Sunday Times. He had proved a first-class Editor. We recruited a staff, which included some very good people, but we did it all somewhat too fast. Too many of the people we recruited, though experienced in finance, had too little experience of journalism. Consequently, we ran into two problems. First, too many mistakes were made, giving us a reputation for inaccuracy. Secondly, there was the problem that people who did not read the Business News simply discarded this section; they often discarded it in a very public way on the commuter trains into London. The littering of the trains with this section was not good for us. The advertisers came to believe that it was a throw-away section.

The star of our new recruitment to the Business News was Peter Jay, whose work was to change national economic policy. More than anyone else, he introduced monetarism to Britain. He came to *The Times* from the Treasury as Economics Editor in 1967, holding the post with distinction for a decade. In 1969, believing that the paper needed a better understanding of the US economy, I asked Peter to spend a year in Washington as economic correspondent. While there, Peter gained an understanding of the 'Chicago school' and of the work of Milton Friedman. He formed a deep familiarity with the body of modern monetarist thought in the United States. His exposure to these new theories led Peter to conclude that you could not cure inflation by direct price or wage controls. Moreover, he believed that the whole policy of price controls, to which both parties in Britain were at that point committed, distorted the economy. He agreed with the Chicago school that inflation was essentially a monetary phenomenon, one that could only be stabilized by control of the money supply rather than by direct control of prices. This is a familiar argument now. That it is so owes much to *The Times*, and much to Peter's work.

Peter soon became a friend; he was a major personal and professional asset to me as Editor. He was the son of Douglas Jay who had himself been on *The Times* as a young journalist and had then been a Labour Minister in the Attlee Government; Douglas was a member of the group around Hugh Gaitskell in the Labour Party. Peter himself had a very brilliant career at Winchester and Oxford and was widely seen as one of the brightest and best of his generation. From Christ Church, he had entered the Treasury, where he was seen as a high flyer. Peter was successfully recruited to *The Times* through Hugh Stevenson, an Oxford friend of his, who had already decided to join. Hugh later became Editor of The Times Business News.

He stayed with the paper until the late 1970s when he was appointed Ambassador to the United States. I remember Peter coming to tell me that David Owen, the Foreign Secretary, had offered him the Washington job. Both of us saw there would be charges of nepotism, because Peter was married to Jim Callaghan's daughter, Margaret, but I felt, and said: 'What a loss for the paper, but what an opportunity for you.'

Peter's conversion to monetarism and his subsequent conversion of *The Times* proved to be of political importance. We were early converts. We were able to exert influence both professionally and personally. Professionally, through pieces published in *The Times* and personally because Peter had his own direct influence with the Government. He had excellent access to Jim Callaghan, both before and after Jim became Prime Minister. He persuaded Callaghan and Denis Healey, as Chancellor, that monetarism was the most effective way of controlling inflation; that a Labour Government could not spend its way out of trouble. While Margaret Thatcher also became a monetarist, under the influence of Keith Joseph, the Callaghan Government in the mid 1970s had already made the first change of policy.

In addition to convincing Callaghan and others in opposition and government, Peter converted me from a broadly post-Keynesian view to a monetarist view of what caused inflation and how you ought to stop it. I took some time to be converted. Probably, I now think, rather too long. Nonetheless, *The Times*' position had become monetarist by 1974.

As a young editor, I was well aware of the political influence of the paper which still enjoyed a haze of its nineteenth-century power. However, the great influence of what were broadsheet newspapers lies in helping to set the agenda rather than in moving broad public opinion. It is the mass circulation tabloids which can influence elections. *The Times* exerts its influence on professional and international opinion. A quality newspaper can succeed, when it gets this right, in raising items which it thinks are very important onto the agenda of other media. It can influence the agenda of the BBC and other broadcasters, and sometimes even the agenda of the Government. Leading articles carry weight proportionate to the quality of their information and their argument. However, readers only pay attention to leading articles which are strongly projected. When we wanted a particular leader to receive attention we gave it greater length than other newspapers were then giving. We also gave more striking headlines, such as the 'Who breaks a butterfly upon a wheel?' which is still attracting attention over forty years later. I wrote some of these longer, attention-seeking leaders myself, but not all of them.

Although I wrote about one leader a week myself during my editorship, I tried to run the newspaper in a collegiate way, particularly among the leader writers. We had weekly leader writers' conferences. These would be attended by the four or five most regular leader writers with other members of the staff who would write a leader when their subject came up. We would discuss all the major issues as they arose.

I differed from some other editors before and since in that the leaders and letters were my most direct personal responsibility. Obviously news is more important – it is the central function of a newspaper – but no editor can have the same direct control of the whole news process that is still possible on the leader page. I edited directly all the leaders on their way into the paper. I would have a conversation beforehand with the leader writer about whatever the subject was, we would then agree the line and I would then, when he had written it, make any changes I felt desirable. I reinvented the long leader, which could run up to 1800 words and which took the whole of one side of the leader page. I wrote most of them myself. Sometimes, the leader would have represented my immediate reaction to events, but most of the time I was trying to develop themes which had the information of our experts behind it and represented an agreed opinion of the paper's staff. I was particularly keen to involve the younger leader writers in the discussions.

In addition to overseeing the leaders, I also oversaw the letters page with especial care. Working with Geoffrey Woolley, the Letters Editor, I chose which letters we were going to run. I regarded the readers' opinion as expressed in the letters as part of the development of the opinion of the paper, a unique contribution which *The Times* could make. Somewhere in *The Times* readership there would always be an expert on every conceivable subject; they often knew more than we did, or than the Government. I wanted to offer the readers the opportunity to be heard. The only criticisms that I had about the expanded letters page, that I can remember, were from some members of the staff who thought I too often allowed in letters criticizing them, and who were upset by it. I took the view that if members of the staff expressed a definite view with which our readers, or some of our readers, disagreed, it was a very healthy process to have a sharp debate about it. Journalists are professional critics; they should not themselves be oversensitive to criticism.

Within the context of the leaders and letters page and across the paper more generally, I aimed to set the agenda of *The Times* in the areas of politics and economics. These were, after all, the interests which had led to my appointment. Additionally, I followed broad international policy, particularly over relations with Europe, the Soviet Union, the Middle East and the United States.

Nonetheless, there were areas on which I failed to develop a clear personal view. The continuing crisis in Northern Ireland was a notable example. This I largely left to Owen Hickey, the senior leader writer, who had been on the paper well before I arrived. Owen had a home in the Republic of Ireland and he was a devout Roman Catholic, but was also a Unionist in sympathies. In personal terms, I admired Owen and he reluctantly tolerated me. I did not decide to leave Northern Ireland to Owen because I underestimated its importance. On the contrary, throughout the 1970s it was a central political issue. I simply thought Owen understood Ireland better than I did. I knew that I did not know what ought to be done about Northern Ireland. I occasionally visited Ulster only to return even more baffled than when I set out. I shared Owen's perception that the moderate Unionists in Ireland, like Brian Faulkner, Prime Minister of Northern Ireland from March 1971, were not being well treated by the Heath Government. I was suspicious of the Government decision, though it had almost unanimous backing in the House of Commons, to abolish Stormont. My experience of sitting in the Press Gallery had been that whenever the whole House agreed on anything it turned out to be wrong. I thought this about the abolition of Stormont. But I never felt wholly satisfied that the moderate Unionism of *The Times* was particularly helpful in the public debate.

My attempts to report, understand and explain public policy continued to bring me into close contact with politicians. At the time of Wilson's election victory in 1964, I was still on the *Sunday Times*. In that election, we had advised people to vote Conservative, if only because we thought most of our readers were Conservatives. Still, we thought it was time for a change, though there were Labour Party policies which we disagreed with fairly strongly. At any rate the *Sunday Times*' welcome to Harold Wilson was perfectly friendly; we had accepted his opposition propaganda about modernization. When the time came for the purchase of *The Times*, Roy Thomson, Denis Hamilton, Harry Evans and I had an embarrassing dinner with him. It was the autumn of 1966. Labour had just won a large majority at the General Election. Roy Thomson had reached his agreement to buy *The Times* from the Astors, but the deal required Government clearance. If the Government referred the deal to the Monopolies and Mergers Commission, on the grounds that Roy Thomson already had more than enough newspaper circulation, that could have blocked the deal. At that time, as we have seen, Roy Thomson owned two hundred newspapers in different parts of the world.

The argument *for* the deal was that *The Times*' financial situation was pretty bad and that the country might lose it altogether unless a strong newspaper proprietor was prepared to take it over. There was, therefore, a very reasonable argument to say that the Government ought to wave the deal through on national interest grounds. However, Harold Wilson thought that this was an opportunity to gain some political advantage. He invited Roy Thomson and his colleagues down to Chequers. I was invited as the prospective Editor of *The Times*.

At dinner, Harold Wilson raised the question of David Wood, then the political correspondent of *The Times*, an excellent journalist, very experienced and indeed very fair-minded. David had reported criticisms which were already being made of the Wilson Government. These criticisms had upset Harold Wilson; he may have suspected David of being a closet Tory. Wilson, more or less openly, proposed terms to us that he was prepared to allow the purchase of *The Times* by the *Sunday Times*, which would obviate the necessity of involving the Monopolies Commission, but in return he would expect David Wood to be fired. There was an awkward pause. Roy, Denis, Harry and I adopted exactly the same tactic: we hoped that if we gave no reply, Wilson would assume that he would get what he wanted. We hoped he would take our silence for consent. None of us, naturally, had the least intention of carrying out our side of the proposed bargain. So we sat there looking down at the fine Chequers china, and the conversation passed on to the next subject. After dinner Roy Thomson, who had instructed his driver to remain at Chequers throughout the meal, decided he would be happier in his own bed and left for home.

After Thomson left, Wilson's conduct became less dangerous, but more ridiculous. This was the time of the independence of Rhodesia and Ian Smith. There had recently been a meeting concerning Rhodesia aboard a warship called *Tiger*. As Wilson began to talk of this meeting, he called for a bottle of brandy. This was not a good move. Denis Hamilton hardly ever drank at all, I never drink brandy, Harry Evans was just about capable of consuming two small glasses of brandy in the course of an evening. The rest of the brandy bottle disappeared down Harold Wilson. There were no other guests. He kept us up until three in the morning telling us how he had outmanoeuvred the white

Right: William c. 1935.

Below: Cholwell, 1936.

Bottom: Fletcher, Beatrice, Aunty Molly, William, Elizabeth and Andy in 1936.

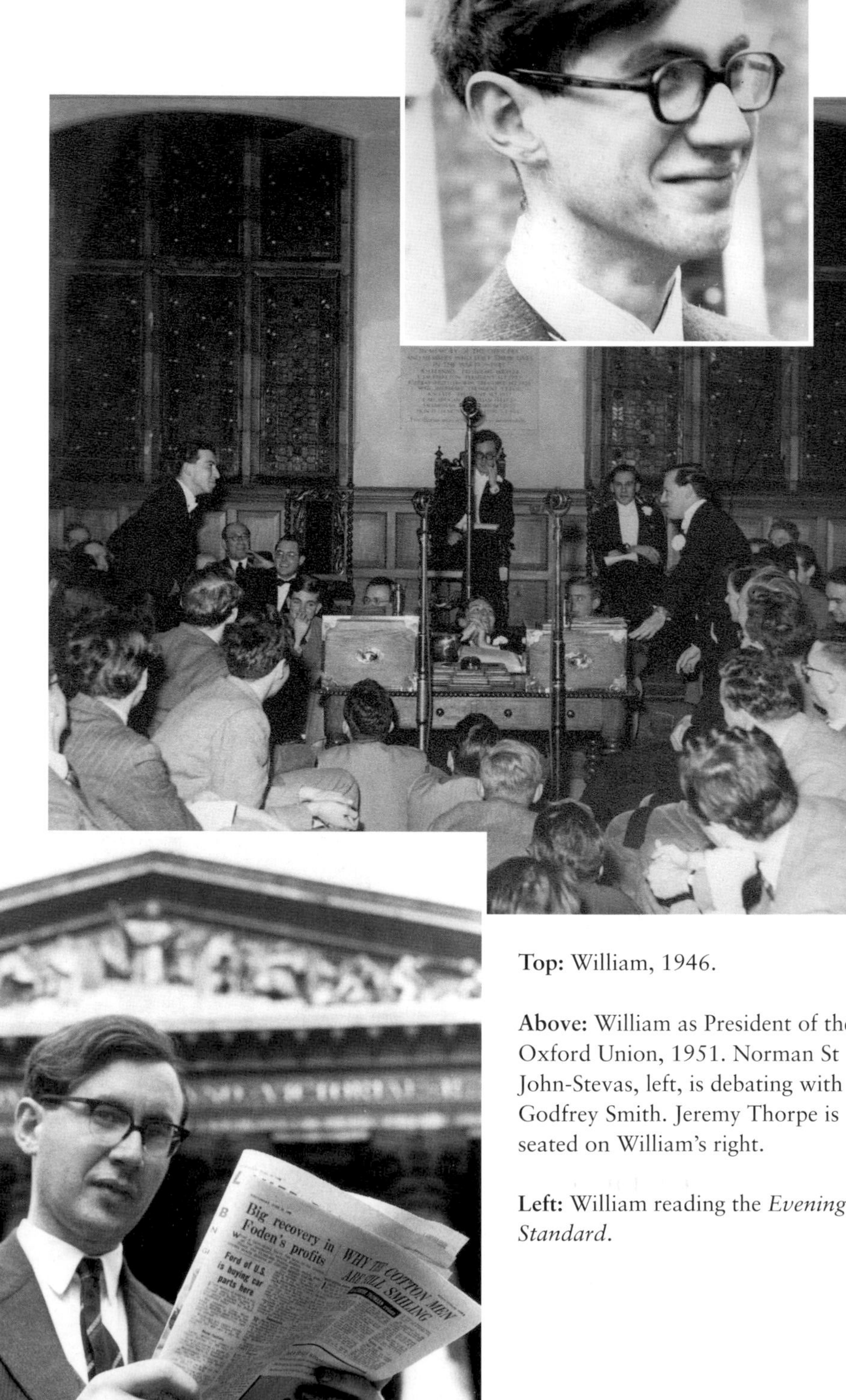

Top: William, 1946.

Above: William as President of the Oxford Union, 1951. Norman St John-Stevas, left, is debating with Godfrey Smith. Jeremy Thorpe is seated on William's right.

Left: William reading the *Evening Standard*.

Above: William and his family at Ston Easton. L-R: Beatrice, Thomas, William, Charlotte , Gillian, Jacob and Emma.

Above: William presenting Iverach McDonald, who joined *The Times* on 1 May 1935, with a salver after retiring from the paper in April 1973. This presentation was made in the Board Room on 3 May 1973.

Above: William and Roy Jenkins, Bath University, 1978.

Above: Harold Wilson talking to William while Wilson's secretary, Marcia Williams, opens telegrams, February 1963.

Right: William addressing editorial staff on Wednesday 22 October 1980, regarding the news that Lord Thomson of Fleet had decided to sell *The Times* and the *Sunday Times*.

Above: This image was taken at the press conference, at the Portman Hotel London, called by Thomson British Holdings to announce their choice of Rupert Murdoch as buyer of the Times Newspapers Ltd. L-R: Harry Evans, Rupert Murdoch and William.

Right: William and Margaret Thatcher in Hong Kong, 1999.

Right: William with Pope John Paul II. L-R: Pope John Paul II, Emma, Gillian and William.

Below: William, Father Alfonso de Zulueta, Shirley Williams holding Thomas, and Gillian, November 1966.

Above: William photographed in 1982.

Below: William and family on his eightieth birthday.

Right: Portrait of Alexander Pope by Sir Godfrey Kneller.

Below: The Mogg family, painted by Richard Phelps c. 1731. L-R: Dorothy Mogg (née Turner), Jacob, Francis, William, Elizabeth (later Mrs Season) and John.

Portrait of John Locke.

Self portrait by Joshua Reynolds.

William Pitt, Earl of Chatham,
by Richard Brompton, 1773.

Rhodesians. This was at best greatly exaggerated and more than slightly pathetic.

At last I went upstairs to bed and was shown to a four-poster in what had been Harold Macmillan's bedroom. There was a hot-water bottle in the bed. I woke about two hours later to discover that my hot-water bottle had burst. So the evening, punctuated with boastfulness, scheming and drinking by the Prime Minister, was finally rounded off sleeping in a sodden four-poster. All of us experienced a fundamental revision of our views of Wilson. Harold Wilson's belief that he could get us to dismiss a first-class Political Editor whom we all trusted and liked, as part of a deal, certainly left us thinking less of him; the bottle of brandy did not improve our opinion; nor did the boasting about how clever he was as a diplomat and how he had outsmarted Ian Smith, who, as we suspected, had outsmarted him.

Even before I was actually appointed to *The Times*, I had, therefore, had that disillusioning experience about Wilson. I had also reached the conclusion that all Wilson's talk about 'the white heat of technology' was not to be taken seriously. He claimed that modernization was necessary but he never put serious resources into his proposed technological modernization of Britain. As with New Labour in the 1990s, the promised modernization was indeed needed. In the 1960s all the comparisons between British and American or European productivity and research were extremely unfavourable to Britain. There was a so-called Brain Drain of our scientists to the United States. Almost everyone felt that the Conservative Government, which had been in power for thirteen years, had not grasped these issues. People felt that the Conservatives formed a very old-fashioned and upper-class Establishment, with a 'grouse moor' image, and that they did not understand science. Harold Wilson played on this effectively; he was very adroit at making the Labour Party appear to be the natural party of young scientists and of men in white coats.

That Wilson was not serious about modernization was clear from the outset of his first administration in 1964. He appointed Frank Cousins, an antediluvian trade union leader of the hard left, as the Minister for Industry. Nobody who wanted to modernize industry would have made such a reactionary appointment.

So, by the end of Wilson's first administration, I had already lost my sympathy for his talk of modernization, because I did not think he meant anything by it. But I was out of sympathy with the Conservatives also, since breaking most of my links with the party over the Alec Douglas-Home leadership affair in 1963, when I was still on the *Sunday Times*.

The *Times*' focus was not solely, of course, on domestic politics, although that was an abiding personal interest. *The Times* during this period had an extremely strong capacity to cover international affairs and wars. We had as many as eighteen foreign correspondents. We covered the 1968 Russian occupation of Czechoslovakia comprehensively. Our key war correspondent was Charles Douglas-Home, then the paper's defence correspondent, who covered both Czechoslovakia and the Six Day War. In the Six Day War, the *Sunday Times* lost their correspondent, Nicholas Tomalin; his car was hit by a missile on the Golan Heights. In this environment, Charles Douglas-Home was an outstandingly brave correspondent. At one point he was arrested for banging on the lid of a Soviet tank in Czechoslovakia, and asking the crew why they were there.

I had the pleasant duty of travelling around capital cities, which gave the foreign correspondents an extra opportunity to arrange interviews with senior Ministers and heads of government. These high-profile interviews helped me set the tone of the paper and retain control over and direct editorial policy in a personal way. Probably the most important international interview I ever conducted was with President Anwar Sadat, which I undertook in Cairo in November 1971. The interview was arranged through Denis Hamilton who had developed a good journalistic relationship with Sadat's predecessor, Nasser. No sooner had the interview begun than Sadat started to talk very freely about his desire to make peace. He said that, while he wanted to recover Egyptian territories, especially the Sinai, he also wanted to make peace with Israel. Peace between Israel and Egypt would, he hoped, be the prelude to a more general peace in Palestine. His ambition was that it would be perfectly natural for an Israeli to do his shopping in Cairo, or for an Egyptian to do his shopping in Tel Aviv. I was struck by his immediate candour.

This candour was matched only by his moderation. During our interview, I mentioned that my family and I were to spend Christmas in and around Jerusalem. We proposed to attend Christmas Mass in Bethlehem. During the interview, despite his repeated commitment to peace, Sadat had said that, if Israel did not agree a peace settlement within a given period, he would have to fight another war. He could not accept permanent Israeli occupation of Egyptian territory. I said that I did not want to take our family to Israel for their Christmas holidays if he was going to start a war while we there. Sadat then gave me this splendid assurance: 'I can assure you that I will not go to war with Israel during the period when the Rees-Mogg family are having their holiday.' So, with our four children, we went to Israel. I remember that when we took off from Heathrow, in an El Al plane, Jacob, who was two, said, in a loud two-year-old voice, 'I'm going to see Jesus.' That was not what the rest of the passengers were expecting. We stayed at the King David Hotel, where Jacob ate bananas covered in chocolate sauce, and were escorted by the Israeli defence department to midnight Mass in Bethlehem.

I offered to take the message Sadat had given me to Golda Meir, then Prime Minister of Israel. While in Israel, I spent a long evening – four or five hours – putting the case for a peace settlement to her. Sadat was offering terms which, after another war, became the basis of the Camp David Accord. Had Golda Meir then accepted them, the 1973 war of Yom Kippur would never have taken place. There would have been a return of territories to Egypt in 1972, peace between Israel and Egypt and an opening for a two-state solution for the Palestinian Arabs. The grounds on which Golda Meir refused were that she would have to confront issues inside Israel about the boundaries of the Palestinian lands which were under Israeli occupation. She pointed to the map and observed that the boundary issues would split both her party and Israeli politics. She did not feel justified in doing this when she could not be sure what the end result would be. In any case she did not trust Sadat, or any Arabs. Her attitudes made a negotiation impossible and war inevitable. I was not the only route by which she was receiving these messages. The American envoy, Mr Sisco, was taking much the same message between Sadat and Golda Meir. I think I had her confidence, and admired her tough character, but I failed to persuade her – not for want of trying.

In my last interview with Anwar Sadat he talked about his political philosophy. The politician he admired most was Bruno Kreisky, the Austrian leader. Sadat wanted to build a quiet social democracy in Egypt, rather like that of Austria. He even said that he hoped Cairo would become more like Vienna. He also talked about strategic issues. He observed that modern weapons such as tanks and strike aircraft were becoming increasingly vulnerable and could be regarded as 'high-cost targets'.

What I was doing was obviously important. As I had found in the Suez crisis, it is always fascinating to be involved in affairs which are part of history. No doubt, this excited me. However, I have always been somewhat uneasy about mixing the roles of journalism and diplomacy. It is sometimes inevitable but often risky. Journalists themselves fall into two groups: those who know more than they write and those who write more than they know. When you attempt to mix the two, you may be a bad diplomat because you are being a good journalist, or a bad journalist because you are being a good diplomat. It is sometimes hard to distinguish between messages politicians intend seriously, and those they merely want to see in the press. When I returned to London, I felt able to write about a large proportion, but not absolutely all, of the talks I had had with the two leaders. I think I retained the confidence of both of them, and I interviewed Sadat again some years later.

If I had known then what I know now, I think I would have tried to get in touch with the American State Department to find out exactly what they were doing (they might or might not have told me) and I would have told them more about what I was doing. As it was, I carried this message fresh and uncontaminated from Sadat to Golda Meir. That may have been more effective than if I had done more preliminary negotiation.

As I flew back from Cairo, I remember praying that my mission would succeed. It failed, and the consequences of the rejection have cost thousands of lives. Her mistrust of Sadat was, I think, Golda Meir's greatest mistake. My inability to unlock her mind was certainly the greatest failure of my life.

A journalist never knows which, if any, articles will be remembered thirty years later. In my case it proved to be a leader on the

Mick Jagger case, which I published on 1 July 1967. I criticized the judge for undue severity in a minor drugs case. Even now, from time to time people still ask me to speak about it on television. William Haley is remembered for his leader 'It is a moral issue' in which he took a moralizing view of the Profumo scandal. But I had merely argued that the Jagger prison sentence was bad justice. Justice, I argued, ought to be the same for the rich and the poor, for the famous and the unknown. Jagger was a first offender who was caught with a French seasickness pill in his pocket. It was on open sale in France but required a prescription in England. I took a line from Alexander Pope – 'who breaks a butterfly upon a wheel?' – as the title for the leading article.

I was aware, of course, that the Rolling Stones were a phenomenon, second only to the Beatles in youth culture; this made the Jagger case newsworthy. Moreover, I thought that a leader on Mick Jagger and the Rolling Stones fitted into our policy of appealing to a readership under thirty. It was, therefore, a good subject to be writing about for more than one reason. From that leader followed an interview on television between a panel representing the Establishment and Mick Jagger himself. I was accompanied, in an interview conducted in the garden of the Lord Lieutenant of Essex, by Lord Stowhill, a retired Labour Home Secretary, Father Corbishley, a Farm Street Jesuit, and Bishop Robinson, the suffragan Bishop of Woolwich. Jagger was a highly articulate and self-possessed interviewee. His remark, for instance, in another interview in *The Times*, that people of earlier generations (whose minds had been 'twisted by strikes, depressions and wars') had had 'a bigger trip than any of us – they've had the opportunity for danger and excitement' was particularly incisive. In the televised discussion, Jagger got the better of us, and certainly he got the better of Bishop Robinson. His views were perhaps more important than he or we then realized; he took a libertarian view of ethical and social issues which turned out to be one of the constituents, though only one of the constituents, of Thatcherism. It was not the soft-left Beatles but the libertarian Rolling Stones who best predicted the Anglo-American ideology of the 1980s, twenty years later. Mick Jagger was a Thatcherite before Thatcherism had been invented.

Specifically, I remember being struck by the fact that Jagger used the classic John Stuart Mill *On Liberty* argument: that you are entitled to do anything which does not affect somebody else adversely. He argued that that is the test of the permissibility of human action. The State has no right to interfere in anything merely because it may damage the person who chooses to do it. I did not believe, as some did, that Jagger's remarks were mere sloganeering. They represented, rather, a thought-out system of beliefs. When Jagger made these remarks in 1967, the British still made paternalist assumptions about government; the young were beginning to revolt against the limits put on liberty by Victorian tradition and wartime necessities, and, to a considerable extent, by socialist paternalism.

For me personally, the Jagger affair, although I could not have foreseen the extent to which my name would become associated with it, was important. I felt strongly that *The Times* should intervene on the issues which were of great interest to a generation which was taking a very different view of the world from its predecessors. Later that summer, Mick Jagger visited me at Cowley Street; my daughters Emma and Charlotte, then aged four and two, followed him up the stairs and were much struck by his red socks. He thanked me for my help, and asked me how to deal with some police blackmail he was facing. I have not met him since, but our youngest daughter, Annunziata, met him in the Caribbean. He told her: 'I have a lot to thank your father for. He saved my career.'

Newspapers should always stand up to official threats. One of the first such disputes of my time was in November 1967. It concerned a signed column in The Times Business News written by Peter Jay entitled 'Devaluation – who was to blame?' Peter had previously written a memorandum on devaluation while a principal at the Treasury and was, therefore, a master of the subject. He had been one of those in the Treasury who thought that Harold Wilson ought to devalue on coming into power in 1964. I accepted his view that devaluation was inevitable and, moreover, that once devaluation has become inevitable, any attempt to postpone it was bound to damage the national economy. But we were careful to write the leaders in such a way that we did not predict when devaluation would take place. That decision was for the Government, not for us.

As a result of Peter's article, and the possibility that he had relied, in the writing of it, on Treasury information, the Attorney General, Sir Elwyn Jones, considered bringing a charge against him. I did not think at the time that the risk was a serious one. My attitude was 'let them try it'. I thought that the publication was in the national interest. I also knew that a prosecution would have been very good news for us at the paper. It would have created a great deal of publicity. This publicity would have been largely favourable. Although some people would have enjoyed criticizing Peter, in the end the Attorney General, acting for the Government, would have had to drop the case.

An editor who is standing up for freedom of publication usually looks good. For Peter, however, it must have been a rough fortnight, though the paper would have defended him wholeheartedly, and most of Fleet Street would have been on his side. Certainly, throughout November 1967, there was some *froideur* between *The Times* and No. 10. There was *froideur*, also, between *The Times* and the civil service. Sir Laurence Helsby, the joint permanent secretary of the Treasury and head of the civil service, wrote to me asking for 'an informal talk'. Sir Laurence was, he stated, 'much troubled about some aspects of Peter Jay's article'. I took a call from him, with Peter in the room, and indicated that I would not be able to see him at all soon. Indeed, in a letter of 27 November, I defended Peter vigorously, writing that 'I have Peter Jay's assurance that none of the matters to which he referred in his article or in his broadcast were derived from his experience as a civil servant.' I did not feel, I explained to Sir Laurence, that 'I can come and see you without at any rate further clarification of the matters we should discuss'. We did meet on 14 December but, as National Archive documents show, Sir Laurence felt that he had got 'little change out of Rees-Mogg'. In Sir Laurence's 'Note for the Record' written on the day of our meeting, he observed that Rees-Mogg believed that Jay 'behaved honourably in deciding that he was justified in relying on the subsequent source of information that came to him as a journalist'. Sir Laurence went on to note that, in his belief, Rees-Mogg 'might take a different line if similar circumstances were to arise in the future'. In that he was mistaken.

Around the time of the stand-off between No. 10 and the paper, a sub-editor, questioning Peter about the content of a piece and asking for elucidation, received the reply from Jay that he was: 'writing for three people in the country and you are not one of them'. Certainly, there is an elitist element in Peter, possibly developed when he was a schoolboy at Winchester. There are two classes of Wykehamist. There is a very small group of Wykehamists who have measured up to Winchester's own idea of the intellectual life. They are treated as lions during their impressionable schooldays and they inevitably get a certain idea that it is a very special thing to be a clever Wykehamist. The other Wykehamists, the vast majority, leave Winchester not having measured up to these rarefied intellectual standards; they spend the rest of their lives thinking that they are rather stupider than they are.

Peter, without doubt, thinks of himself in the first category. And he is. I remember when I first had lunch to meet William Haley, he asked me – it was just after I had been appointed Editor – 'How are you going to handle members of your staff whom you realize are more intelligent than you are?' I regret to say, with the confidence of being the new Editor and thirty-eight, I thought that that was not very likely to happen. However, Peter was, in terms of economic analysis, streets ahead of me. I would not say that in every aspect of the human mind Peter's is greater than everybody else's, but when it came to lucid but penetrating economic analysis I had never worked with anybody like him. It is the same quality as one finds in Maynard Keynes (Keynes obviously had it to an even higher degree), and made it very stimulating to work with Peter as a colleague. *The Times* missed him when he went to Washington as Ambassador.

TEN

Rivers of Blood

Enoch Powell's 'Rivers of Blood' speech in April 1968 altered English politics. *The Times* saw the significance of the speech from the beginning. The topic of race had been used by minor figures, by individual members of Parliament, but it had not been taken up by anyone of Powell's stature before. Powell's choice of language on this topic came as a shock to everybody, particularly to his colleagues in the Shadow Cabinet.

I was down in Somerset when I heard the speech. I watched the television broadcast. It was obvious that it would create divisions in the Conservative Party. My reaction to the speech was that it was outrageous. It presented Enoch's typically rationalized points, some of which had some justification, but others of which were too extreme by any standards. He put the issues in an inflammatory way which could only encourage racial prejudice.

I had to develop *The Times*' response. I wrote the 22 April leading article myself and attacked the speech as a racist challenge to Ted Heath's leadership of the Conservative Party. I wrote: 'Mr Powell made an evil speech; it has to be repudiated, and he has to be repudiated with it.' Before I did so, I contacted three members of the Shadow Cabinet: Edward Boyle, Reggie Maudling and Ted Heath himself. Boyle made it perfectly clear that, unless the Conservative Party disassociated itself from Enoch's speech, he would resign from the Shadow Cabinet. Rather more surprisingly, Reggie Maudling, a more relaxed, practical politician than Edward, took the same view with equal firmness. When I rang Ted he had already decided to ask for Enoch's resignation. I thought this decision was correct and inevitable. Enoch at one point believed that I had tried to bully Ted, forcing him to sack Enoch by threatening to withdraw *The Times*' support. This was not true. It was not how it happened, nor how either Ted or I operated. I do not think that newspapers should try and take politicians' decisions for them. Certainly, I was favourably impressed by the anger which all three of the senior Conservatives openly expressed. I did not speak to Powell himself, though we became friends later in his life, and were in agreement on economic policy in the late 1970s and 1980s.

In Powell's career the speech was both a crime and a blunder. It did play on racial prejudice, but he had not fully foreseen the reaction. I believe that he did himself hold views that were basically racist. It cannot, I think, be doubted from what he said. He thought – and here he was proved right – that if he put them across in an effective, hard-hitting speech, he would strengthen the Conservative Party by winning over the more prejudiced part of the white working-class population in the West Midlands, and particularly in his own Wolverhampton constituency. Later on Enoch was even to win the respect of some of the immigrant communities. When I visited the Wolverhampton West constituency as a journalist in the election of 2001, I found the Sikh community was becoming a major source of Conservative recruits, and that Enoch was still admired, as much by the Sikhs as by the white working class.

Enoch was an emotional, as well as a logical, speaker, and a very effective one. As I wrote in a September 1968 leader 'Give the shares to the people', 'Mr Enoch Powell has three gears in which he operates, the wise, the exaggerated, the intolerable.' Enoch's 'Rivers of Blood' speech was both exaggerated and intolerable. It was very damaging to the right wing of the Conservative Party, of which he was the best speaker. Even Iain Macleod, regarded as a man of the Tory centre left, commented that he agreed with Enoch on many issues and often found himself travelling on the same train, but he got off before the terminus. On the issues of national sovereignty, Europe, monetarism, the use and abuse of price controls, Enoch was the best spokesman for the free-market position. The 1968 expulsion of Enoch from the Conservative Shadow Cabinet destabilized the Conservative leadership. With Powell removed, when Ted became Prime Minister in 1970 he was able to take the party sharply to the left. He did a U-turn over price controls and moved to an even less qualified Eurocentric position. All of this would have been different if Enoch had been in the Government.

A more distant effect may have been that the impact of Enoch later helped Margaret Thatcher to win what in America is called the hard-hat vote. In the West Midlands Enoch helped to win the 1970 election; he certainly damaged Ted in the 1974 election when he withdrew his support. This was a decisive factor in the Conservatives losing that election.

While *The Times* criticized Powell's exploitation of race, the main issues which made *The Times* criticize the early Wilson Government were financial and economic. In particular the delay in devaluing the pound seemed merely to be postponing the inevitable. We did, however, support Roy Jenkins' austere and effective chancellorship in the late 1960s. In addition to our criticisms of the failure of Wilson's policy of modernization of the economy, we also were pro-European. Wilson was neither a Europhile nor a Eurosceptic: his main concern was to avoid a split in the Labour Party. On *The Times* we thought he was missing opportunities to take forward what we regarded as the necessary cause of Britain's entry into the EEC.

In autumn 1969 *The Times* undertook, partly on my initiative, what was for us an innovative journalistic investigation; it might have seemed quite out of place to Sir William Haley. We unmasked corruption in the Metropolitan Police. It started by accident and ended with the gaining of the IPC Award.

I had had the idea that we should have a feature written on burglary. In order to provide our readers with advice about how to avoid being burgled, we decided to contact a professional burglar and interview him. We hoped he would tell us what burglars were looking out for and, in so doing, give our readers instructions on how to secure their houses more effectively. We put an advertisement in the Classified Columns to the effect that, if there was a *Times* reader who was a retired burglar who would like to come and speak to us, we would be keen to talk to him. Presently, a retired burglar contacted the paper, duly turned up at our offices and, with his cooperation, our Crime Squad wrote a useful piece.

Some months later, the burglar contacted us again. He was an elder statesman of the burglary trade; he stated that he had been asked for advice by a young, as it were apprentice, burglar. The young burglar, a small-time operator from south London called Michael Perry, had been walking along a London street when a police car stopped next to him. Two policemen jumped out. One of them, holding a stick of explosive, ordered Perry to open his hand. Perry obeyed the order. The policeman smacked this stick of explosive into Perry's hand and made sure that he got his fingerprints on it. The policeman then said that he knew that Perry was a burglar, and that, from now on, he should obey police orders. Specifically, he should continue to undertake burglaries but he should hand over part of the proceeds to the police. Michael Perry was alarmed. The policeman continued: 'Don't think there's any use complaining to anybody in the police about it, we're a little firm inside a firm and we can always get you.' This apposite phrase 'A little firm inside a firm' became the title of our exposé leader in late November 1969.

After his release by the police, Michael Perry, naturally very worried, approached our retired burglar for advice. The retired burglar, no doubt adding to the younger man's sense of surprise at these events, said: 'The only thing that can help you is the press. It's no good going to one of the popular papers, like the *People*, because the police will find it very easy to discredit their evidence. I would be happy to put you in touch with *The Times*. They treated me well.'

I re-entered the story at this point. Michael Cudlipp, at that time in charge of Home Affairs on the paper, was masterminding our response; he told me what had happened, and what he was thinking of doing. A young burglar's word would have no weight on its own against two experienced policemen. He was thinking of wiring the burglar to a microphone, and taping his conversation. I came to the conclusion, arguing from public interest, that this was the right course. The privacy laws, moreover, were even looser then than they are now. The young burglar would, of course, be under the supervision of two of our journalists. This, clearly, was a revolutionary step for *The Times*. It occasioned a great deal of surprise and comment and some criticism. We were later attacked for employing tabloid methods.

Having recorded a further conversation between the young burglar and the police, and written the story, the News Editor, Colin Webb, and Julian Mounter, a member of the news team, went to Scotland Yard an hour or so before the presses were due to roll. They offered the police the chance to comment. Naturally, their comment was 'no comment'. Our journalists were treated with a certain polite contempt and one of the officers mandated to investigate the matter was himself subsequently sentenced for police corruption. On 29 November 1969 the story was published under the headline 'Tapes reveal planted evidence. London police in bribe allegation'. Subsequently, this investigation led to the conviction of three policemen and a major reorganization of the Metropolitan Police.

In early July 1970, I received a letter stating that, as Editor, I had presided over a marked diminution in 'the authority, independence, accuracy, discrimination and seriousness of *The Times*'. The letter, with its aggressive set of accusations, was composed in a local public house, the White Swan, and signed by twenty-nine members of my editorial staff. Given that the signatories included senior writers of the paper I thought that, basically, they were criticizing themselves. They were certainly criticizing my editorship and the whole Thomson policy of modernization. In fact, they were particularly criticizing, on the one hand, Michael Cudlipp, a recruit from the *Sunday Times*, and, on the other, The Times Business News, whose work was initially marred by inaccuracy. Michael Cudlipp, who had made a great contribution to the modernization of *The Times*, was by no means as downmarket as some of his critics suggested. There was a certain unpleasant jealousy towards him – he was a nephew of Hugh Cudlipp, the leading tabloid journalist of his day. Michael Cudlipp was himself a first-rate journalist, a better one than most of the signatories and certainly more hard working.

My objection to the White Swan letter was not only the implicit criticism of Cudlipp. I had been running the paper on a collegiate basis, and had given the people who actually signed the White Swan letter a real measure of independence and authority. A blanket set of assertions signed collectively seemed to me less impressive than their particular criticisms of the paper would have been. Particular criticisms would have been open to particular answers.

I found it objectionable that the signatories, who had a duty to tell me if they were worried about aspects of the paper, had not come forward earlier and raised their concerns with me. I did not, therefore, have a great deal of sympathy with them. If they had been more junior members of the staff, without full access to me, then I would have been a good deal more sympathetic than I was. Owen Hickey, for instance, was one of the signatories – he saw me every day to discuss the leading articles. How would he ground a charge of my being inaccessible?

In response, I called a meeting for 10.00 in the morning in order to get all the twenty-nine into the office an hour earlier than their usual time. Instead of allowing them to accuse me, I accused them. I asked them whether any of them genuinely maintained that he did not have access to me, or that I had ever refused to listen to any criticisms of the paper that they had wanted to make. They all sat silent. It was easy to give them a brief rebuke, as they had behaved in what I regarded as an unnecessary and foolish way. Their intentions, no doubt, were good. They wanted to protect the old standards of *The Times*. I was, of course, as concerned to protect these standards as they were. Their error was to mistake bringing the newspaper up to date – which we were doing – with taking the newspaper down-market – which we were not doing.

The White Swan letter was the first open challenge to my authority as Editor. I had then served three years. At the time it was an incident of only modest importance. Subsequently, it has been seen as a dramatic event. On the whole, I was lucky to have such consistent support from the excellent staff I inherited. Of course, I never thought the paper was perfect. Still, I thought it, in general, an authoritative, independent, accurate, discriminating and serious newspaper. As it still is.

From the beginning of my editorship, I decided to delegate as far as I could in those areas in which I did not intend to take direct executive responsibility. However, there are some parts of editing which an editor neither can nor should delegate. The general thrust of the paper can only be decided by him. The editor, whether in terms of opinion or of news, must be close to the big news stories. He should discuss and take advice but he must decide the paper's attitude to big political issues, domestic and foreign. This was especially important for an Editor of *The Times*. The history of the newspaper is one of political information and political influence. Any editor must be concerned with developing the views and opinions of the paper. He has, clearly enough, to be concerned with establishing and maintaining good relations with his staff. I wanted to have a stable newspaper, particularly in the months after the original merger. I regarded *The Times* staff as a group of experienced professionals whom I had to lead, not as temporary staff who needed to be replaced.

Another reason for giving my main attention to areas where I could contribute directly was that I knew I did not have the capacity (as Haley and, in politics, Thatcher possessed) of doing highly intensive work for very long hours for a very long time. I recognized my own limitations; I wanted time to mix with people outside the paper and I wanted time to think. Gillian was a most important help in keeping me in touch with newsmakers and opinion formers outside *The Times*. I was not capable of regularly doing a fourteen-hour day; I had to husband my energy if I was to retain my ability to initiate projects and ideas.

An important editorial innovation of the early 1970s was the appointment of Clifford Longley to the new post of religious correspondent. Clifford was a great success, consistently writing thoughtful and sometimes profound pieces. Before we created this role for Clifford, religious matters occupied a less prominent position on the paper; they were covered by 'Our Ecclesiastical and Naval Correspondent', a byline which was an endearing quirk of the old *Times*. Clifford was interested in religious issues, in a very broad sense. He was interested in all the churches, and in inter-faith matters as well. In his personal religious development, he was a Catholic marked by the Second Vatican Council, as I had been. Cardinal Heenan, Archbishop of Westminster when Clifford was appointed, was bothered by this new concept of religious reporting. He complained to me about Clifford, and I defended my correspondent whom I admired. Eventually, Cardinal Heenan came to accept that Clifford Longley was a good correspondent, but he never became completely accustomed to ordinary press scrutiny of the workings of the Catholic hierarchy. This was the period when interdenominational religious reporting achieved its first prominence. The BBC appointed Gerald Priestland to a role similar to Clifford's. Priestland, brought up as a Quaker, had been a contemporary and friend of mine at Charterhouse and Oxford. He was a very thoughtful schoolboy and became an inspiring religious correspondent for the BBC.

In January 1971, *The Times* announced the appointment of Bernard Levin – the master of the long sentence – as a columnist. Levin was a great Whig soulmate for me on the newspaper. His office was next to mine; we shared, for a while, the same secretary – giving her dictation one day I said 'stop' at the end of a sentence and remarked to her 'I daresay you hear me say "stop" somewhat more often than you hear Bernard say it'.

Bernard added humour, companionship and his own wisdom to my time at the paper. His column rapidly acquired a very strong, even cult, following. And some of the columns were indeed classics. People still giggle about his account of the slippery stage at the Wexford Opera Festival. I found that, because, as a columnist, he was outside the paper, he had no professional interest to advance. He came in, wrote his column, had a chat and went away again. His advice was always sound and frequently excellent, even on trivial matters. For instance, I remember that when George Brown retired, I drafted the sentence 'Lord George-Brown is a better man drunk than the Prime Minister sober'. I then wanted to take it out, thinking it went a little far. Bernard, being a good columnist, thought that it was the best line in the leader, and persuaded me to retain it. We kept it in, and it became one of my most quoted lines.

The anxieties about inflation – which I shared – intensified between spring and autumn 1973. I am now sure I was wrong to give the qualified approval of the paper to Anthony Barber's first 1973 budget. In March 1973 I still hoped that economic expansion could be maintained. It was natural to want expansion. One of the British economy's problems was that, since the end of the war, competing countries had been able to maintain rates of expansion far higher than ours. We had been falling behind for fifteen years. In 1972 and 1973 the Heath Government proved to be too reckless about expansion; in 1973 their policy was overwhelmed by a succession of shocks. By the end of the year the first oil crisis and the Yom Kippur War had made the world into a different place. In a December 1973 piece, 'Not much of a budget', I signalled a change in *The Times*' view by calling for Barber's resignation.

During 1973 I was undergoing a process of conversion, coming gradually to the conclusion, perhaps not with complete consistency, that what *The Times* had believed economically, and what I had believed, at the beginning of the 1970s, simply did not, and could not, work. Perhaps I could have argued that it no longer worked because the situation had changed. Now, I prefer to think that I simply got it wrong. Like the Heath Government I took a far too expansionist view, in the hope that the economy would be operated near to flat out and that inflation could be checked by the direct governmental controls on prices and wages.

What impact did our championing of monetarism create? In a 1976 speech to the Labour Party conference Jim Callaghan as Prime Minister delivered what in retrospect was a funeral oration on 1970s Keynesianism: 'We used to think that you could just spend your way out of recession, and increase employment by cutting taxes and boosting government spending. I tell you in all candour that that option no longer exists.' *The Times*, and Peter Jay especially, had promoted the anti-Keynes, pro-Friedman argument for three or four years before Callaghan's speech. We had created the forum in which the Chicago school ideas could be propagated, challenged and accepted in Britain. Other journalists share the credit, particularly my old colleague and Peter's friend, Sam Brittan on the *Financial Times*.

The impact on the political right was no less striking. As Peter once stated in an interview with Carol Sarler for the *Sunday Times*, 'I don't know what I've done apart from being the first person to tell Mrs Thatcher about monetarism.' In September 1974 *The Times* published the full text of Keith Joseph's broadside on Keynes' legacy, our headline reading 'Sir Keith blames full employment for inflation'. We called it 'one of the most important political speeches of recent years'. Peter Jay reported it as the lead story and asked how far Ted Heath and his Shadow

Chancellor would be willing to give 'absolute priority to conquering inflation by controlling the budget deficit and the money supply at whatever temporary loss to employment, living standards, investment and political support'. Keith Joseph had told the press that this Preston speech was coming. Keith, whom I admired, had been a friend since the 1950s. We had both sat on a party policy committee under Rab Butler when we had failed to produce a policy of privatization of the nationalized industries. Shortly before the Preston speech, he had taken me out to lunch at the Savoy Hotel to explain what his argument would be. I had by then become convinced that the Government had to have a satisfactory answer to the inflationary problem; any party which came forward without having such an answer did not deserve to be elected. Keith had come to the same conclusion, so I was more than willing to publicize his message.

Subsequent events proved Keith right on the issues and proved *The Times* right to ascribe such importance to his speech. Keith's analysis of the need for conquering inflation by controlling the budget deficit was decidedly far-sighted. Control of the budget deficit is an essential part of developing a disciplined monetary policy; this was the deciding issue of British politics in the 1970s, when Denis Healey was Chancellor and again more recently, with Kenneth Clarke and Gordon Brown.

Keith's speech was immensely important because it was the first statement of what became the Thatcherite position. Margaret Thatcher herself has always retained a great affection and admiration for Keith Joseph's memory. I share that affection and admiration. He was an extremely able man, a man of intellectual responsibility and seriousness. He was the John the Baptist of Thatcherism. Keith would have been the right-wing nominee for the Conservative leadership when Margaret Thatcher won it. He would, quite likely, have become Leader of the Party in 1975, and perhaps Prime Minister in 1979, though he lacked her political decisiveness. However, Keith lost considerable credibility when he made an unfortunate speech of a speculative eugenics kind about the underprivileged having too many children. Eugenics is dangerous ground for politicians: in November 2010 a new Conservative peer, Howard Flight, made similar remarks about the poor having too many children. He embarrassed himself and his party and had to withdraw them. Naturally, Keith's speech did not go down well in the country. He was a man of ideas but not a politician. He would often express his ideas at quite the wrong moment. Or the ideas themselves would be over the top. But if one asks where the ideas which modernized Britain in the 1980s came from, they came, in large part, from Keith Joseph.

The Times supported Joseph's monetarist position in a leader I wrote published on Friday 6 September 1974:

> In our view the main lines of Sir Keith Joseph's argument are unquestionably right. Inflation is threatening to destroy our society. The threat is political as well as economic. Inflation cannot be cured without stabilization of the money supply ... There is now a much greater danger of mass unemployment if inflation is allowed to continue than there would be from such a stabilization policy, though the stabilization policy would cause some increase in unemployment.

In the ten days after reporting Sir Keith's speech, we published letters from Lord O'Brien, a previous Governor of the Bank of England, Reggie Maudling, Michael Foot, Lord Kahn and the economists Alan Walters, Wynne Godley and Phelps-Brown.

Reggie Maudling challenged Keith Joseph's position, and was rebutted by Alan Walters:

From Mr Reginald Maudling, Conservative MP for Barnet, Chipping Barnet

Sir, If Sir Keith Joseph's views on the relation between money supply, unemployment and inflation are sound, why have the recent sharp check in the growth of the money supply and the rising unemployment to which he refers been accompanied not only by failing confidence and investment but also by an increase both in the rate and the future expectations of inflation?

Yours faithfully,
Reginald Maudling,
House of Commons,
6 September

From Professor A. A. Walters, 10 September

Sir, Mr Maudling (7 September) asks why the monetary squeeze from December, 1973, has been accompanied by higher rates of inflation. I thought the answer was set out with clarity, conviction and honesty in Sir Keith's speech. There are lags. Few things happen, except election promises, 'at a stroke'. After initiating a monetary squeeze, the evidence is that there will first be an effect on employment and output – after a period of about nine months and persisting for many months.

Thus one should expect that over the period from August 1974 there would be a rise in unemployment and a reduction in the rate of growth of output. (Are there not signs?) During this period of 18 months to two years after the squeeze, that is up to the end of 1975, there would be no modification of the rate of inflation – indeed it usually gets slightly worse.

After two years however the rate of inflation begins to slow down and the rate of output growth to pick up. This attenuation of the rate of inflation will persist for perhaps a further two years until the effects of the initial monetary squeeze are fully worked out. The inflation is reduced, output will be growing at somewhere near its trend rate, and unemployment will be reduced to its normal level.

But it all takes time, and I believe that Sir Keith's 'three to four years' is about right. The evidence from the experience of the United Kingdom, the United States, and scores of other countries shows that the sequence of events and the time lags are consistent and similar in magnitude. One has to wait a long time for good effects.

But politicians' eyes are focused myopically on the next election. They want instant results and immediate euphoria. Mr Maudling's letter dramatically illustrates the politician's short-sight. When he was Chancellor in 1963/64, Mr Maudling pursued a policy of rapid expansion of the money supply. He produced instant euphoria – but at the cost of a large current balance of payments deficit and mounting inflationary pressure from 1965/66, which ended in the devaluation debacle of 1967.

Perhaps therefore one can understand Mr Maudling's anxiety to preserve the myth of instant effects.

Yours,
A. A. Walters
The London School of Economics

Looking back at this argument from the perspective of the 2008 banking crisis and subsequent recession, the gap between Maynard Keynes and Milton Friedman does not seem quite so wide. Both of them are essentially monetarist, both accept the need for expansion of the money supply to counter deflation. Keynes is more willing to expand the money supply in other circumstances. Nevertheless, the doctrine of monetary stabilization still seems to apply. I share the view that Alan Greenspan, as Chairman of the Federal Reserve Board, was too willing to expand the money supply in order to prevent what would have been minor recessions in the United States when bubbles collapsed. He was afraid to exercise appropriate monetary discipline. If a central banker is to have any control over monetary conditions he must be willing to accept periods of slow growth or even contraction. Central bankers should be stoics rather than epicureans.

ELEVEN

'The future of Europe is not a matter of the price of butter'

The Heath Government still seemed likely, in 1972, to secure a second term. Most governments which win one General Election have a second term. The general expectation was that Heath's would be the same, particularly as his major objective, of taking Britain into Europe, was likely to be achieved. It was only when oil prices started to escalate in 1973, following the Yom Kippur War, that Ted seemed likely to be ousted. His Government then began to show weakness in other areas. He had become too nervous, for instance, about the rise in unemployment. The money supply, during Tony Barber's chancellorship, had run out of control. After 1973 the Pay Board, and its sister body the Prices Commission, were flimsy dams against which a torrent raged. It was only a matter of time before they would in any case have been swept away. I strongly agree with John Grigg's assessment that, as 1973 ended, the public beheld 'the spectacle of a government defiant but scarcely, if at all, equal to the pressure of events'.

In the General Election of 1974 *The Times* advised the electorate to vote for the Government, believing that the manifestly excessive power of the trade unions was the key issue. The trade unions had gone beyond their proper function; they were no longer merely fighting for the economic interests of their members, but to destroy the Government. In this period, the trade union leadership politically included people who were not merely likeable old Labour figures, what you could call the genial pipe smokers of the trade union movement. Rather, they were militant Marxists, men like Arthur Scargill (strictly a Leninist and a man always with ambitions beyond trade unionism), who wanted to destroy the democratic basis of the Labour Party just as much as they wanted to overthrow the Government. Consequently, I felt strongly that this was an election in which the people ought to support their Government, even though there were plainly aspects of policy in which the Government had not performed particularly well. At some point Arthur Scargill would have to be taken on and beaten; though it wasn't to happen for ten years when he was beaten in the miners' strike of 1984 just after the militant print unions were defeated when Rupert Murdoch moved *The Times* to Wapping in 1983.

In the General Election of the spring of 1974, the Liberals obtained only fourteen seats in Parliament, but won 19.3 per cent of the poll and over six million votes. Under our 'first past the post' system the Conservatives lost the spring 1974 General Election and Harold Wilson was returned to power. In my leader of 5 March, 'The return of Mr Wilson', I concluded 'Mr Heath has gone. As a Prime Minister he was a man of serious purpose and absolute integrity of character. He lacks some of the qualities of a politician.' That still seems a fair enough judgement. Ted Heath, however, spoiled his own achievement by his thirty-year sulk at the loss of office. He lacked flexibility. He had little sense of what Rab Butler called 'the art of the possible'. He was not good with people. Indeed, he was very bad with his enemies. In political life, people have to rub along with those who are opposed to them, particularly inside their own party.

Strangely, Ted was even somewhat difficult with his friends, though he was capable of much kindliness. However, there was variability in his treatment of almost everyone. On one day, his temperament would be pleasant and warm and one would think, 'Oh, what a nice man Ted is'; on another day one would meet him, he would be abstracted, cold, distant. That inconsistency weakened his friendships, particularly with people in a subordinate position: those who worked for him did not know where they stood with him because of his alternation between friendliness and coolness. This variability affected Ted politically, too. He lacked political sensitivity. He once said '90 per cent of politics is administration'. This statement, which is in any case untrue, illustrates both Ted's character and his shortcomings. I would attribute some of Ted's outlook to his years as a staff officer in the war. When we first met in 1950, when he came to speak to the Oxford Conservative Association as a prospective parliamentary candidate, he was very obviously the young staff officer, fresh from his experiences of war. Later, he rose through the whips' office and became Chief Whip as though that was his natural destiny. Even as Prime Minister, he was always somewhat whip-like, expecting a degree of obedience which politics does not necessarily offer. He was quite a careerist himself, but was not always sympathetic to the ambitions of his colleagues.

I think he was jealous of Iain Macleod. The sudden and early death of Macleod, a few weeks after becoming Chancellor, was probably the reason why Heath's administration failed. Macleod was truly a brilliant speaker. Ted was never a brilliant speaker, though a perfectly capable one. Once, at the Blackpool conference Iain Macleod, as Shadow Chancellor, made a speech which won his usual standing ovation. It was a beautiful speech, in terms of phrasing and delivery rather than economic analysis.

As we came out of the hall Ted turned to me and said, 'Well, I hope you've learned a good deal about our economic policy' – a typical Ted putdown. A party leader should never put down his colleagues, particularly not to journalists.

One of my early judgement calls was also an early test of the Heath administration. In 1968, Rolls-Royce had committed itself to considerable expenditure on the development of a new engine for which it had contracts to deliver to aircraft manufacturers. These contracts contained punitive penalty clauses. In 1971, the Heath Government believed that these penalty clauses would run on indefinitely, leading inevitably to Rolls-Royce's insolvency. A few weeks too late, *The Times* discovered from Rolls-Royce's New York lawyers that these contracts had been drafted under New York State laws. They had an automatic cut-off. Under this type of contract, known as Murphy's Contract, because it had been developed to protect the Irish builders of skyscrapers, you pay a heavy penalty if you do not come in exactly on time, but the total penalty is capped. Had it been appreciated that this was the nature of the contract, it would also have been clear that Rolls-Royce was not threatened by insolvency. The required short-term financing could then have been provided. The Government should have known this and, *a fortiori*, the Directors of Rolls-Royce should have understood their own contract. Nevertheless, the Government panicked, and a Conservative Prime Minister found himself committing an unnecessary act of nationalization.

The Heath Government's decision to nationalize Rolls-Royce was reasonably regarded as a U-turn. It was taken as a sign of weakness. In their 1970 election manifesto the Conservatives had made a commitment not to bail out weak companies. They seemed to be reverting to old Labour policies of nationalization. Despite this, I still believe that the Government was right to save

Rolls-Royce. Britain had too few first-class industrial companies. To allow one of our few remaining globally competitive technological businesses to become insolvent and disappear would have been detrimental to Britain's interests. I was not very much concerned that this nationalization violated basic Conservative anti-interventionist principles. On *The Times* we wanted to see Britain preserved as a significant industrial power; that seemed to me worth defending whether or not it was compatible with the Conservative Party manifesto. In my leader of 15 February 1971, I stressed that Rolls-Royce aero engines were vital for national defence.

In the 1973 miners' strike a more flexible Prime Minister might have seen that, because he could not win the dispute, he would be advised to settle it. There was an opportunity to settle, the miners were prepared to do so and Scargill was not then strong enough to block it. However, Ted was not adroit enough to achieve a settlement. His absolute determination to see his policy prevail made it difficult for him to compromise. In the end, Ted's stubborn strength was his weakness.

The cornerstone of Heath's 1970 manifesto had been that Britain should again apply for entry to Europe. *The Times* supported this and, after 1970, I spent much of my time on European issues. I travelled regularly to Paris, Rome and Bonn and met successive Presidents and Prime Ministers and Chancellors. President Pompidou I particularly admired. He was the only French President who saw Europe as a cooperative enterprise rather than as a Franco-German monopoly. He had a lot of goodwill towards Britain. I have noticed – which was true of Pompidou – that Anglophile Frenchmen often speak no English. He saw Britain as a great European nation which was different and over there, not as similar and a rival. His successor, Giscard d'Estaing, spoke English very well, knew quite a lot about Britain, but retained an underlying jealousy towards us. I am not sure that Pompidou's predecessor, President de Gaulle, ever forgave Britain for having rescued France from Germany in the Second World War.

In early April 1971 I met Pompidou in the Elysée Palace. I was taken to the interview by our Paris correspondent, Charles Hargrove, who provided the British Ambassador with an account of its outcome, with my agreement. When I went in neither Ted nor I knew whether or not Pompidou was going to agree to Britain joining the Common Market. De Gaulle had refused twice. It was perfectly possible that France would either refuse again, or set terms which would be impossible for Britain to accept. I remember the sentence which made it clear what his position was. Pompidou said: 'the future of Europe is not a matter of the price of butter'. Charles Hargrove, in his memorandum of the meeting, stated: 'The Editor came away with the feeling that President Pompidou was absolutely sincere.' Charles went on to note that 'President Pompidou said "France is not trying to raise any obstacles, to spring any traps on Britain. But she wants things quite clear between Britain and her future partners."' Charles was right. I did come away with a strong sense of Pompidou's sincerity and his goodwill. I was right; Pompidou had decided to agree to British entry, partly because he, in his turn, was convinced of Ted Heath's sincerity.

An additional, and quite possibly unintended, consequence of my meeting with Pompidou was that Ted, going into a meeting with Willy Brandt in Bonn the following morning, was able to read Hargrove's story in *The Times*. It will have assisted Ted to have read our report that 'President Pompidou sincerely wants the negotiations for British entry to the EEC to succeed'.

Charles Hargrove's ability to arrange this meeting was characteristic of his being exceptionally well integrated into French society. A friend to whom he introduced me, Pompidou's *Chef de Cabinet*, Jean-René Bernard, told me that, when Charles visited, his children ran to him shouting 'The Ambassador has come'. Our two eldest daughters, Emma and Charlotte, improved their French by spending summer holidays with the Bernard family in Noirmoutier. Marie-Caroline, the Bernards' eldest daughter, who is now a successful television executive in Mexico City, spent a year in our family when she was at the London Lycée. No one could have been a more agreeable house guest, or a better representative of the calibre of her country.

President Pompidou and I subsequently met again. We had a long conversation at Chequers in the winter of 1973. Pompidou was already seriously ill and died a few months later. Ted sat me on the sofa next to Pompidou; Mme de Beaumarchais, the wife of the French Ambassador, acted as interpreter. We talked for more than an hour. Pompidou spoke as a dying man. He talked about the future of Europe, his continuing anxieties about the expansion of the Soviet Union and his feeling that he was the only person in France who could hold Western Europe together. He believed that his policy was essential to maintain the independence and security of Western Europe against the Russian threat.

In the early 1970s I was a 'good European', like Ted Heath himself, or my contemporaries, Geoffrey Howe and Douglas Hurd. They remained good Europeans. I did not. As with my conversion to monetarism, the process was a gradual one. I remained committed to the governmental pro-Europeanism of the Wilson and Callaghan administrations. I associate the beginning of my change of attitude with a dinner in Brussels early in 1981 with Roy Jenkins, then the President of the Commission. Roy and I were, by that time, friends of twenty years' standing. We had been allies in supporting the European policy, he as a politician and I as a journalist. When he was out of office in 1970, I had commissioned his series of essays on great contemporaries, later published in book form as *Nine Men of Power*. I supported him in the development of the Social Democratic project which emerged as the idea of the Gang of Four.

At our Brussels dinner, it became apparent to both of us that we were seeing the European issues from different perspectives. Perhaps, in retrospect, Roy had hoped to use the dinner to persuade me to support the idea of moving towards a single European currency through Britain joining the European Exchange Rate Mechanism. I was very interested in currency matters and put to him the difficulties which might arise from the differences between the European economies. I took the view that there were very great problems in adopting a single currency, or currencies tied to a single currency, because the economies of Europe were not in alignment, moved at different speeds, had different problems, different rates of inflation, and so on. They needed freedom to adopt appropriate interest rates. In short, I deployed the 'Lack of Convergence Argument'. Roy readily perceived that I was likely, therefore, to be opposed to his policy on the next stage of European development. Indeed, he saw it before I did; I thought that I was explaining the difficulties, but he saw that my doubts would lead to my opposing European Monetary Union. He proved to be right. From 1981 onwards, although we remained friendly throughout, we were increasingly divergent on the central issues of European policy. Inevitably, difference of fundamental beliefs affects one's relationships to a certain extent. With Roy, however, that was kept to a minimum.

My relationship with Ted, by contrast, was less able to withstand a divergence of political outlook. Much later he was very angry with me, though that was because I supported Chris

Patten's pro-democracy policy in Hong Kong. Our relations had remained close and friendly after his election defeat of 1974. Again, I remember a decisive meeting. William Waldegrave, who had been in the think tank under Lord Rothschild during the Heath premiership, invited Ted down to Chewton Mendip, Somerset, to stay with his parents. The Waldegraves gave a dinner party for Ted at Chewton House in the summer of 1974 after his first election defeat of that year. The party was arranged so that I should have a private conversation with Ted to put forward my monetarist views about inflation. Inflation was the central problem on which the Conservatives had lost the February 1974 election. I argued that inflation was a monetary disease and put the case for what one could call a hard-money policy. I went on to state that the Conservatives could not just go back to the incomes policy which had already proved disastrous. He had to create a new policy, whatever it was to be. Unfortunately, I could not get him to accept that he had to change the whole of his thinking towards inflation. So, although *The Times* still supported him in the second election of 1974 against Harold Wilson, when the Conservative leadership battle came in 1975 I had completely lost confidence in his ability to develop an economic policy. He failed to adapt to the reality of 1970s inflation. Writing a leader on 1 February 1975, I wrote: 'Mr Heath … cannot offer a future to the Conservative Party so long as he is the prisoner of his own past.'

After this, though I think we both had a residual goodwill for old times' sake, my relationship with Ted deteriorated. In addition to withdrawing *The Times*' support for him for his re-election as Leader of the Conservative Party, I moved increasingly to support Thatcher in the late 1970s and moved in the 1980s towards a specifically Eurosceptic position, which followed from my objections to the single currency and European Monetary

Union. We knew each other for over fifty years; difficult as he could be, I remained fond of him. He fought for what he believed to be right. I think he regarded me as a disappointment, as someone who shared the European truth, but was then a backslider.

My major reason for supporting Heath's application for Britain to join Europe in the 1970s was that I could not see how otherwise the Government could turn the British economy around. This problem obsessed all politically involved people of my generation. Britain had come out of the war very greatly impoverished, with a loss of markets, with obsolete industry, competing with the post-war industrial redevelopment of the US, Europe and Japan, and, even more important, with obsolete industrial practices. On some measures British productivity was only half that of European industry. Successive governments had tried and failed to bring this decline to an end. Germany, particularly, had surged ahead under the free-market policies of Adenauer and Erhard. Britain was very highly regulated and taxed, with income tax ranging up to 98 per cent. I saw the European Common Market as broadening the free-market area in which Britain could operate. I hoped that European competition would introduce higher standards of productivity and efficiency in industrial management. I knew that the British economy could not survive without radical change, though that change was not to come until the market reforms of Margaret Thatcher in the 1980s. If one believed in open markets and competition, Europe seemed the answer in 1970, but the obstacle in 1990.

A secondary, but important, argument for Britain joining the European Union was cultural. One of the strange things about the EU is that the European countries have tended to become more self-interested, more separate, less conscious of their common European culture than they were a generation ago. That may be a reaction to the intrusive bureaucracy of Brussels. It is most noticeable in the politics of France. The France of Pompidou was far more open than the France of Chirac or Sarkozy. There was in 1972 a feeling that we lived in the Europe of Dante, Goethe, Beethoven, Cervantes, Voltaire, and the other European cultural heroes, and that, in these terms, Britain was part of Europe. This feeling of cultural unity seems to me to have faded rather than to have strengthened in the last generation. There is little sympathy between Don Quixote and the Common Agricultural Policy, except that both are expressions of the absurd.

Economically and politically the last thirty-five years have been disappointing years for Europe. The great opportunity of the end of the Soviet Union has not been taken. This is partly because France has become more and more confined by the Franco-German alliance, under successive Presidents. Pompidou believed in a trilateral Europe in which the biggest decisions would be taken by agreement between Britain, France and Germany. Giscard, on becoming President, took these decisions back to a bilateral Europe of France and Germany. A bilateral Europe is, in the end, intolerable to Britain, and without Britain, Europe does not work very well. Bilateralism is not just intolerable for Britain, though it obviously puts us in the second rank, but for the smaller countries as well. One of the interesting weaknesses in the Lisbon Treaty is that the smaller powers recognize that their ability to influence events will be reduced rather than increased. It is a constitution which transfers power from the member state to the Commission and the Franco-German alliance.

In the early 1970s I was keen to establish contact with leaders of other European countries. I particularly enjoyed getting to know the Bavarian leader, Franz Josef Strauss. He was a European conservative but had been anti-Nazi. To those who thought that any German conservative must be suspect he seemed an alarming figure. I invited him to lunch at *The Times* where he told us that it made no more sense for Britain to have an air force than it would for Bavaria to do so. He saw the long-term future of Europe as being one in which the individual nations became local governments like the German *Lander*. I also remember being given a delicious breakfast in Munich by Frau Strauss who herself spoke excellent English and served a wide range of German sausages.

I was very impressed by Chancellor Schmidt, who became a friend of Ted Heath's. On only two occasions I took a group of senior members of *The Times* staff to examine particular areas of European opinion. One was a visit to Chancellor Kohl with Louis Heren and Charles Douglas-Home. I remember that I asked Helmut Kohl an opening question of an innocuous kind and received a reply which lasted for fifty-five minutes and effectively terminated the interview. More valuable was a comparable visit to Scotland in the late 1970s to discuss Scottish devolution. I became convinced that some form of Scottish devolution was inevitable but, not surprisingly, this aroused the unionist spirit of Charles. One of the Scottish leaders who took a cautious view about the form of devolution was Menzies Campbell, then seen as a leading Scottish lawyer, later to be leader of the Liberal Democrats.

In general during my editorship *The Times* took the liberal view of world events. We bitterly denounced the Soviet invasion of Czechoslovakia of 1968. We were consistently opposed to apartheid. We had no sympathy for the Cultural Revolution or for Chairman Mao. We also attacked Mrs Gandhi's suspension of Indian democracy. I only saw Mrs Gandhi once. She was insufferably arrogant, and very conscious of her image in the world. Our own correspondent in India, Peter Hazelhurst, had been ordered out of the country in the early seventies. *The Times*' stance was of a piece with the rest of the Western press. Because of consistent condemnation in the Western press, Indians were able to use the sense of moral outrage that existed in Western newspapers, rather in the same way as the anti-apartheid campaigners in South Africa were able to use the sense of moral outrage that apartheid caused. The liberal media of the West played a part in breaking the system both of apartheid and the Gandhi dictatorship.

Being half-American, I took an especially alert interest in American politics. I was almost the only journalist in the world who took a pro-Nixon line. Many of my colleagues on *The Times* thought it was my worst mistake, and they were probably right. Oddly enough, my attitude over Watergate was motivated by a concern for fair trials which was the basis of my argument in the Mick Jagger case. Did Mick Jagger take drugs? Of course he did. Did Richard Nixon send burglars in to steal Democrat papers? Of course he did. Did Mick Jagger get a fair trial? No, he did not. Did Nixon get fair coverage from the American press? No, he did not. My 5 June 1973 leader strongly defended him: 'It is perfectly possible for a wholly guilty man to be tried in a wholly unjust way.'

Fred Emery, the Washington correspondent, thought that I hadn't allowed him sufficient opportunity to cover the story in *The Times*. My memory is that we had published a whole series of his reports and feature articles. Certainly, I had no desire to stop our readers knowing fully how Fred, as our Washington correspondent, was seeing the Watergate issue. Fred took the anti-Nixon line in a relatively extreme way. My own view was that Nixon was basically a President on the defensive. His immediate predecessors, Kennedy and Lyndon Johnson, had played politics in an equally unscrupulous way, with the connivance of a largely Democratic press. After Watergate, Nixon was under fire from the American press, which was almost completely one-sided, particularly the most powerful newspapers, the *Washington Post* and the *New York Times*. In Washington there was a feeding frenzy, which extended to some members of the administration, including the odious Vice-President Spiro Agnew. Nixon was also under fire from Congress. I remember talking to one of Nixon's legal advisers in Washington, who said 'it's like being a little law firm out in the sticks, fighting every law firm in Wall Street'. My relative sympathy for Nixon was unduly influenced by my reaction to this hysterical frenzy. In the June 1973 leader, I wrote: 'The President of the United States is in the unenviable position of being tried by his fellow countrymen in three different forums, each of which has its own particular deficiencies ... That is not to say that the President is innocent ...'

I still think that Nixon was treated by the English language press in a very different way from their treatment of Presidents who were Democrats. Nixon was an able though flawed President. One needs to remember that Nixon had had the experience of losing the 1960 election to Kennedy on a fraudulent ballot.

TWELVE

Palladio on Mendip

One of the people I admired in the Labour Government of 1974 was Denis Healey. I first met him during the Suez crisis in 1956. We were both invited to discuss the Suez invasion on the BBC World Service and went to a small studio in Bush House. I defended the Government's policy and Denis Healey criticized them. I have never taken part in a debate in which I was more thoroughly worsted. Denis became Chancellor of the Exchequer in the Harold Wilson Government and remained Chancellor under Jim Callaghan.

He was sensitive about his knowledge of economics. I remember him saying that he, too, had read Joseph Schumpeter on business cycles. In fact, he went through much the same process of conversion to a monetarist explanation of the inflation crisis as I did. He was persuaded by Peter Jay that Milton Friedman provided the best explanation of the inflation of the 1970s.

He came into office with that desire which incoming Labour Governments usually have: to remedy defects of the previous Government which they attribute to spending too little money on the social services. He inherited an economy in crisis which he was unable to control, resulting in the International Monetary Fund visit in 1975, perhaps the most humiliating time in British financial history. The IMF came and told us that they were not prepared to provide continued support to sterling unless the Government cut back on expenditure. Healey, a very decisive man, a 'full-speed-ahead, damn-the-torpedoes' type of man, when required to do a U-turn, does it in style. I have always found him delightful, highly intelligent, aggressive, very tough-minded, amusing company, with strong views on almost every subject but with the strong views clustering round a moderate political position. He possesses unusually wide cultural interests.

At the same time as Healey was becoming convinced by the monetarist argument, Margaret Thatcher was immersing herself in monetarist philosophy. With Keith Joseph and Enoch Powell no longer credible as candidates of the right, Margaret Thatcher was elected Leader of the Conservative Party in February 1975. I did not foresee this outcome, although I had been told that it would happen. The preceding summer, Jerry Wiggin, the Conservative Member of Parliament for Weston-super-Mare and an active member of the right-wing group who were planning to pick their own candidate, came to tea at Ston Easton with his children. He said that there were three possible candidates whom the right might support: Keith Joseph, Edward Du Cann and Margaret Thatcher. Joseph's eugenics speech counted strongly against him. Du Cann, Jerry said, was unpopular in the City, and not, therefore, a viable candidate. Jerry went on to say that it was going to have to be Margaret Thatcher because she was the only one of the three who was, as it were, still standing up as a candidate. I should have taken more note of his forecast.

Following Margaret's election as Leader of the Conservative Party, Bernard Levin, in an excellent piece of 28 January 1975, stated that 'Mrs T is clever; she has stamina; she can mix it with the best, not to mention the worst. It is a pity that she apparently has no vices … and a greater pity that she has no interests either.' In retrospect, I do not agree with the final reservation, knowing that Margaret is a much more interesting and thoughtful person than she was then (or even later) recognized as being. Bernard missed the fact that she was genuinely interested in the ideas. Keith may have had some of the ideas of Thatcherism first, but it was she who thought that the Conservative Party should commit itself to a Hayekian philosophy of politics, and she had read *The Road to Serfdom* in 1945, as I had. I vividly remember Margaret, in about 1976, sitting on the floor in the Conservative Philosophy Group looking up at Hayek as a disciple looking at the master. She was then Leader of the Opposition, and few party leaders pay such reverence to living philosophers. Historians, such as John Grigg, may have been right to point out that Margaret Thatcher's gifts were the gifts of a politician rather than the gifts of a political theorist. Yet, for her, Hayek's defence of liberty and free markets had been a formative influence. Reading Hayek's work validated some of her own beliefs and gave her the confidence to speak out. In the Heath years Hayek had not been fashionable in the Conservative Party. In the 1970s Margaret suddenly discovered, to her delight, that she did not need to be guarded about what she really thought. As a young woman at Oxford, she had already formed her belief in what was then seen as a very old-fashioned type of Conservatism. This was the Conservatism of personal responsibility, of fiscal responsibility, of two and two making four, which she sometimes described in a housewife's terms. This had been the Conservatism of her family and of her father. It is a Conservatism which comes very naturally from trying to make a small business work.

Conservatives of this kind have always believed that those same disciplines, which govern a family and its finances or a small business and its finances, are disciplines which have, or can and should have, a very important application in running the policies of a state. This outlook was, even among Conservatives, extremely unfashionable in the post-war period. We all thought that we had to be Keynesians. We all thought that Keynes had comprehensively demonstrated that economics was counter-intuitive; that these simple disciplines were misleading when the economics of a state were to be managed. State-level economics were not merely quantitatively but also qualitatively different from the economics of small businesses and family. Heath's more inflationary policies were a good example of Conservatism which had adopted Keynesianism, without perhaps fully understanding Keynes. Indeed, Keynes' *General Theory*, published in 1936, was arguably appropriate for the conditions of the 1930s, but certainly not for the conditions of the 1970s. Margaret saw that what she believed in the first place – what Rudyard Kipling called 'The gods of the copybook maxims' – could still apply, could still be useful in the inflationary circumstances in which she found herself. Thatcherism is based on the copybook maxims. It is deeply conservative, in the sense that it is based on the accumulated practical experience of human affairs.

Margaret was a successful politician partly because she was a great simplifier, an invaluable political quality she shared with Ronald Reagan 'the great communicator'. In contrast to, say, Keith Joseph, she always had a very clear sense of which ideas she could put to use. She was not a pure intellectual but she was an intellectual politician and a pragmatist. She was using ideas in order to provide herself with a clear set of political rules which she could put forward to the country.

This, perhaps under-recognized, strain of intellectuality could be more clearly seen in the period after she left office. She became extremely interested in the Anglo–American relationship, in the joint tradition of the English Common Law, and particularly in the way in which the American Constitution provides for liberty under the law. She chose to become the Chairman of the Institute of American Studies at London University. I sat on that body with her and it was obvious that she thoroughly enjoyed the subject, eagerly joining in the conversations and often speaking herself. Clearly, the idea of liberty under law took her back to her own training as a lawyer. She was proud to be a barrister of the Middle Temple. Despite the example of Tony Blair, who was a master of spin, many lawyers make indifferent politicians, too glib at making arguments. She did not suffer from that defect.

Margaret Thatcher's philosophy of life was a very interesting combination. She possessed a clear sense that liberty only works if you have strong moral rules guiding you. This related to her childhood and to the non-conformist religion in which she was brought up. Margaret was a believer in liberty; no one ever could call her a libertarian.

It was one of my larger editorial mistakes that I did not support Margaret in the 1975 Conservative leadership election. In my leading article of 5 February, I came out strongly in favour of Willie Whitelaw, stating 'Mr Whitelaw's gifts are those of a chairman, and it is a chairman's gifts which are at present wanted'. I thought it was quite likely that Margaret Thatcher would be a failure. I underrated her. Perhaps I underrated her because, when I had known her at Oxford, she had been narrower and more of a party professional than a politician. I did not appreciate her capacity for development. She seemed at Oxford, and in the years immediately afterwards, purely a Conservative Party politician, limited by the concepts of her party. She was then, and has remained, passionately loyal to her party. Excepting Margaret, most party leaders I have known have either actively disliked their parties or, at any rate, had considerable reserve about them. She was totally a Conservative and that usually implies a narrowness of view. Many of the best politicians – like Tony Blair – tend to sit a little bit uneasily with their parties because they have ideas which do not fit that party's framework. Margaret was different in the early years. She loved her party and her party loved her.

The Margaret Thatcher of her years as Leader of the Conservative Party was a much broader and a much more interesting person than the Margaret Thatcher of even ten years before she became Leader. For all that Margaret had broadened, she was still a zealot. This turned out to be an extremely good thing. In the economic conditions of the early 1980s, the Conservative Party needed a zealot. Britain needed a zealot. Anybody who was not a zealot would not have been able to do what she did.

In the spring of 1976, Wilson resigned as Prime Minister and was succeeded by Callaghan. It was said that MI5 had plotted Wilson's downfall. I do not believe there was an MI5 plot; but there was certainly a plot of some kind. I am fairly sure that it came from the dissident group within the security services. This opinion is confirmed by Peter Wright's *Spycatcher*, which described how a group of officers in MI5 became convinced that Harold Wilson was a Soviet agent. Of course, Harold Wilson was certainly not a Soviet agent.

In 1975 I was sent a dossier at *The Times* which purported to be a facsimile of a Swiss bank account held in Harold Wilson's name. This would then have been illegal. The document seemed to me to be a clumsy forgery, merely a doctored photocopy. I never discovered the origin of this document nor who sent it to me. Still, I reported it to the Special Branch. That was the last I heard of it. I was satisfied, and so were colleagues on the paper, that it was a forgery because the typewriter used to put in Harold Wilson's name had a different font from the typewriter that had been used to fill in the rest of the document. I concluded, therefore, that the document related to some genuine Swiss bank account with a balance of £20,000 or thereabouts, and that the connection with Wilson was non-existent. After I had read *Spycatcher* I thought that it had probably been sent by the MI5 dissidents.

By mid June 1976, it became clear that in the United States Jimmy Carter was to receive the Democratic nomination. *The Times* supported Carter's incoming administration. I never met Carter but I started with a friendly attitude towards the administration, based on a feeling that Carter's was a moderate Democrat administration in contrast to the left-wing Democrats who had taken over the party after 1968. Carter was a sincere man, with a detailed knowledge of the business of government, a naturally detailed mind and a certain idealism. I also thought Carter, unlike any American President for the previous twenty years, was honest. Indeed, his administration was one of the straightest American administrations of the post-war period.

On the other hand, I felt that Carter probably was not tough enough or experienced enough to deal with the real world of American politics. Specifically, the mildly puritan Protestantism of the Georgia Southern tradition was not likely to work for the United States taken as a whole. I did not, therefore, feel terribly optimistic about the administration although I felt fairly sympathetic to it.

I may have been influenced by my mother's response to his election. My mother, born and brought up in America, a lifelong Democrat, who had voted in the first presidential election in which women were enfranchised, said that Carter was the first Democrat running for President whom she thought she would not have voted for. Looking at it from the point of view of the culture and attitudes of, at any rate, New York State, her home state, she saw Carter as a goody-goody.

My mother's analysis proved entirely correct. Americans became more and more bored with Carter; he was the least exciting President, with the possible exception of President Ford, of my lifetime. Americans do not feel that their President should be an innocent in a wicked world. This was the impression that Carter left. And the world did turn wicked. Carter had no response to the Iran hostage affair, which lasted from 1979 to 1981. He was dealing there with forces stronger than himself and, in the Ayatollah Khomeini, a leader much tougher than himself. Perhaps the tougher foreign policy of, say, Henry Kissinger would have been better suited to that kind of crisis.

If you are leading the strongest power on earth, a substantial element of realpolitik is unavoidable. It cannot all be done by kindness. It cannot all be done without taking responsibility for decisions and actions which I am thoroughly glad that I have never had to take. People with that particular combination of purpose and realism are few and far between. They are unenviable, taking a terrible moral responsibility onto themselves.

Carter, interestingly, has been far more effective as an ex-President than he was as a President. Indeed, more effective as an ex-President than perhaps any other ex-President of my lifetime: a reflection on the way in which world sympathies have been moving. His championing of a human rights-based approach to foreign policy has achieved considerable support. It is easier for a good man to be an ex-President.

Jim Callaghan became Prime Minister shortly before Carter was elected President. They became close friends. They were both moderate leaders of left-wing parties. The decision to send

Callaghan's son-in-law, Peter Jay, as Ambassador to Washington strengthened the personal link. Peter became very close to the young White House team, Jimmy Carter's equivalent of 'the brightest and best' of the Kennedy White House. Callaghan and Carter were also influenced by the coincidence that they had the same initials, initials they happened to share with Jesus Christ. Jim Callaghan had a suit made from cloth with these initials woven into it. He apparently offered the left-over cloth to Jimmy Carter for him to make a matching suit. Carter replied that he was not able to accept gifts, so he paid £5 for the material and had his own suit made.

My own dealing with Callaghan during his premiership was influenced by my having caused him considerable offence a long time before he became Prime Minister. He was then trying to become Leader of the Labour Party after the death of Hugh Gaitskell in 1963. I was one of those, of whom there were many, who saw Jim Callaghan as a nice chap but not one equal to the job of Labour Party Leader. I set this out frequently in the *Sunday Times*. Callaghan thereafter viewed me with a degree of suspicion and as a supercilious intellectual snob. Matters did not improve with time.

On the other hand, I never felt that our relationship was a particularly bad one either. I respected him as a man of basically good intentions with a good character. I came, over time, to see that he had quite formidable political skills, if of a rather run-of-the-mill kind. He had been Prime Minister, Chancellor, Foreign Secretary and Home Secretary without holding any of the posts with marked distinction. Perhaps he was the only man to hold all four roles. Churchill, for instance, was never Foreign Secretary, nor John Major Home Secretary. Callaghan held these roles because he was the archetypal safe pair of hands, very good at transacting business, and he did not get his party or himself into trouble. His weaknesses were strategic rather than tactical. He rarely possessed any clear view of his long-term objectives, possessing, for instance, no ambition in European policy, which divided men of a different temperament from himself. Personally, he had a rather bad temper. I remember his ringing me up in my office once, and giving me a furious telling off for some fairly minor thing that *The Times* had done, to which I listened politely. Naturally, I was rather surprised that a Prime Minister should ring up an editor in such an oversensitive way. Otherwise, he was an agreeable man to relate to; normally calm, friendly and businesslike. Gordon Brown seems to have behaved far worse, but I was never close enough to him to be insulted.

In the round, Callaghan's prime ministership was rather like John Major's. You had a basically amiable man, of considerable political skills, who was Prime Minister at a time when the tide was going out. At the end of the Callaghan period the Labour Party went out of office for eighteen years; at the end of the Major period the Conservative Party suffered their biggest defeat since 1906, only to suffer another one at the following General Election, and were to be out of office for thirteen years. It is intriguing to wonder whether another figure of different temperament, promoting different policies, could have prevented these profound setbacks. I very much doubt it. In both cases, the public had lost confidence in the party in power but were looking for continuity. It became natural that the party should look to somebody who was going to risk making things worse.

* * *

Very few of the dreams of the 1960s survived the chill of the 1970s. The grand gesture of my life had been the purchase of Ston Easton Park in 1964. It turned out to be a decision I could neither regret nor wholly justify.

Ston Easton Park, which is midway between Bath and Wells, is one of the finest Palladian houses in England. It was probably designed by the Woods family of Bath. There are drawings of the house by Wood the Younger. It was based on a seventeenth-century house, but the main building seems to have been done between the 1740s and 1760s. It has an eleven-bay front which looks out across a lawn and a ha-ha towards the parish church. The downstairs rooms include the saloon, the library, a print room and a plunge bath, as well as the old parlour of the seventeenth-century house, which became my mother's sitting room in her last years. The grounds lead down, at the back of the house, to a cascaded stream designed by Humphry Repton in the 1790s. His 'Red Book', in which he drew up a new plan for the garden, still survives.

The Ston Easton house and estate originally belonged to the old Somerset family of Hippisley, who originally acquired their wealth from a successful Elizabethan lawyer. In the eighteenth century, the family which built the present house was the Hippisley Coxes, though the estate reverted to the Hippisleys in the nineteenth century. The Moggs and Rees-Moggs had repeatedly intermarried with the Hippisleys. There were two Mogg–Hippisley marriages in the seventeenth century, and, in the late nineteenth century, another Miss Hippisley married my great-grandfather, Henry Stiles Savory. At the time of her engagement to my Rees-Mogg grandfather, my grandmother Lily Savory was staying with her Hippisley cousins at Ston Easton.

Commander Hippisley, the last member of his family to live in the house, died in 1956. There was a sale of the furniture, at which my sister Anne and I bought one or two small pieces, and the house itself was sold to a local timber merchant. Subsequently the rest of the estate was sold to the tenant farmers. The house then passed through several hands, becoming more or less derelict. Lead was stolen from the roof and the house became riddled with dry rot.

In 1962, I heard that the house was for sale, but I was too late to buy it. It had in fact been bought by Stephen Clark, a member of the Quaker family which had created the thriving Somerset company of Clark's shoes. Stephen had started the process of restoration, established contact with the Government department which then dealt with heritage issues, chosen a Bath architect, Peter Tew, who had had vast experience of derelict Georgian houses after the Bath bombing, and employed Hayward and Wooster, a specialist firm of Bath builders. Stephen did not want to live in the house, so when he heard that I was interested, and would make it a family house, he offered to sell it to me for what he had paid – £7500. We took on the commitment of restoration, with the aid of a grant.

This was to put a considerable strain on my finances. Not surprisingly, the actual cost of restoration proved a problem manageable in the first ten years, but less and less manageable in the inflationary crises of the 1970s. I remember my bank manager at the NatWest, a kindly man, telling me in 1977 that I would have to sell the house. It is the only time I have shed a tear over a business decision. I knew he was right, and we sold Ston Easton Park in 1978 – in every way a bad year: not only did we have to sell a much-loved house, but it was also the year in which my mother died, *The Times* was shut down and the country was ravaged by inflation. It was also the year of my fiftieth birthday.

Nevertheless, we had fourteen years at Ston Easton, and they were golden years. Gillian was very young; she had been twenty-two when we married and was only twenty-four when we moved to the Park. I was quite young myself; I was only thirty-five when we moved in. Our four older children had their childhood there, which they remember with great pleasure. Even Jacob, the youngest of these four, was nine when we left. In 1970, my mother moved into the old parlour; she had her own suite of rooms and was looked after by a succession of housekeepers. In her late seventies and early eighties she enjoyed independence but she also enjoyed the family company and was wonderfully good with her grandchildren. There was also a small flat for my sister Anne. When I became Editor of *The Times* in 1967, Ston Easton was a splendid, if somewhat over the top, setting for editorial entertaining. We had leading figures to stay, including Roy Thomson and Ted Heath, as well as our friends, and we had a conference weekend for the senior *Times* staff. Gillian was an extremely good hostess and a wonderful mother. It was a life of much pleasure and at the right age for us when we were young enough to enjoy it to the full. I do not think it greatly mattered that it came to an end when I was fifty – all good things pass, and a later parting might have been more painful, when we had less energy with which to establish the next stage.

THIRTEEN

The Times' *Lost Year*

I obviously owe a great debt to Roy Thomson, the proprietor of Times Newspapers who died in 1976. His successor, Ken Thomson, continued his father's policy of editorial independence but he was a man of very different temperament and interests. His heart was in Canada, whereas Roy regarded his achievements in Britain as central. I think I had a good relationship with both men but my relationship with Roy was undoubtedly closer. Roy Thomson was a great proprietor, but one who had no interest in being Editor-in-Chief. He was born in Toronto in the 1890s. His mother, who had been born in Somerset, was a hard-working and capable woman with a very strong influence on him. His father was a drunken Toronto barber. The little boy had extremely bad eyesight, in later life always wearing thick pebble glasses. From the beginning he was quite determined to extricate his family from poverty and from the bottom of the pile. He achieved this in business. His first business venture was to become a farmer. There could have been nobody less suited to farming and he went bust.

Not to be brought down by such a blow, he set up a general store in Timmings, in the north of Canada, and bought a consignment of radio sets. He soon discovered that because there was no radio station near enough to be received there was consequently no market for the radio sets. He thought the only way he could sell his radio sets was to establish a radio station. From there, he developed a network of profitable small-town operations in radio and in newspapers. The banks became very fond of his low-cost formula because it always worked. He recognized that the world was in a long-term inflationary period and that therefore if one bought something and held it, one would be able to sell it later for more money than one originally paid for it. This inflationary period added to his existing ability to make money.

By the age of sixty he was a wealthy man, worth about $9 million. He decided to leave Canada, and get out of his son Ken's way, so that Ken could continue to run the Thomson business in Canada. Roy was torn between buying a bank in Florida or the *Scotsman* newspaper. He bought the latter in 1953, and from there, very rapidly, had the opportunity to be the first proprietor of Scottish Television when commercial television was launched in Scotland. His timing was fortunate; the start of Scottish Television coincided with the breakthrough of British commercial television into profit. He called it 'a licence to print money'. In 1957, he consulted Warburg, who recommended him to buy the Kemsley Group newspapers which included both regional newspapers and the *Sunday Times*. This purchase, completed in 1959, put him in the big league and made him a newspaper proprietor of considerable importance. His next venture was the purchase of *The Times* in 1966.

In June 1974, *The Times* moved from Printing House Square to Gray's Inn Road. I argued against the move. It was nevertheless decided at the Thomson Organization level. The whole thing was botched. The offices were sold. The financial deal on the side building with the *Observer* was very favourable to the *Observer*. In all, *The Times* failed to get a good price for its offices. Furthermore, it proved a damaging policy because it brought to an end, by housing them in the same building in the Gray's Inn Road, the separation between *The Times*' and the *Sunday Times*' printers. These printers were made in quite different moulds. *The Times*' printers possessed an absolute loyalty to *The Times*; they were proud of being *Times*' printers. By contrast, the *Sunday Times*' printers were contractors; their loyalty was to the print unions not to the newspaper. Furthermore, it was already known that there was a good deal of perfectly understandable institutional rivalry between the two papers. Consequently, the printers themselves did not like working in the same place. This caused unnecessary friction and it made them more difficult to manage. The print unions were organized in branches called chapels. The printers believed that this derived from the fact that Caxton had originally printed in a chapel at Westminster Abbey. Some of the *Sunday Times* printing chapels were particularly militant, including the crucial NATSOPA chapel. This increased contact between the printers on *The Times* and the *Sunday Times* led to a general worsening of industrial relations on the former. *The Times* itself had 1970s militancy creeping in even among journalists. Jake Ecclestone, a figure of the far left, was eventually to cause the sale of the paper by bringing his journalists out. It was an irony that a journalist with Maoist sympathies should have been responsible for persuading Ken Thomson, the mildest of proprietors, to sell to Rupert Murdoch, who was to show in the Wapping move that he was the toughest of the lot.

I had welcomed the appointment of Marmaduke Hussey as Chief Executive of Times Newspapers in 1971. By then I had reached the conclusion that Denis Hamilton, though a very good Editor and an even better Editorial Director, was not a particularly good manager: his experience had not made him think like a businessman. Duke Hussey, who came from the Daily Mail Group, was a straightforward newspaper manager and a very good one. He was also a man of great personal courage, who had been seriously wounded in the war. I found him a very congenial personality. There was never any conflict between us in over thirty years of working together at *The Times* or in the House of Lords. Duke had a professional understanding of the separation of functions between the Chief Executive and the Editors of the two papers. He immediately provided proper business management; the losses were rapidly reduced to a manageable level. It helped our relationship that Duke had a Somerset connection: he was married to Lady Susan Waldegrave and they soon acquired a house close to us in Somerset. From 1971 until his death in 2006, we were regularly in touch at weekends and on holidays; we became close personal friends.

During the 1970s both Duke Hussey and I became progressively more concerned about the effect of militant trade unionism inside and outside *The Times*. Outside it, the events of 1973 to 1974, when the miners' strike led to the downfall of the Government, convinced me that the use of militant picketing by the trade unions was intolerable. I believed this menace would have to be dealt with both by a future Government introducing new trade union laws, and by employers, becoming more united and tougher in their resistance. There were several union practices which lowered productivity. The worst was the practice of closed shops – union monopolies in which particular jobs were reserved for members of particular unions. I strongly supported the view that secondary picketing, the closed shop, which was universal in the print unions, and the nihilist militancy of shop stewards, were destroying British business.

The general view was that it was impossible to impose laws on trade union power. I did not agree. Between the repeal of the

1927 Trade Union Act by Atlee's administration, and 1979, there had been only one attempt to introduce any kind of limit to the powers of the trade unions. This was Geoffrey Howe's unsuccessful attempt during the Ted Heath Government, which Wilson had repealed. I saw the relationship with the unions as being the immediate threat to press freedom. We were under pressure, which we resisted very strongly and, for the most part, successfully, from attempts at union censorship. Some other newspapers, regrettably, withdrew articles because their unions told them they would not print them. The furthest we ever went was to say that we would take an article representing the print union's point of view. Throughout, I was prepared to have the paper not come out rather than allow the unions to censor it. A good many of the unions refused to adopt modern working practices. They frequently failed to provide a reliable service. Some of them were undoubtedly corrupt. Their actions limited the number of newspapers which could be published in London because they pushed the costs to a level which no new newspaper could afford. On the closed shop issue, I believed that people have a right not to belong to a union, and that it should never be a condition of employment. The trade unions' strike power meant that any and all attempts to break the unions would fail. This created one of those political moods in which something which is absolutely necessary is, at the same time, thought to be outside practical politics. I agreed absolutely with Hayek's statement in his op-ed piece of 10 October 1978: 'I can say with conviction that so long as the general opinion makes it politically impossible to deprive the trade unions of their coercive power, an economic recovery of Great Britain is also impossible.' I was, naturally, rather pleased to get Hayek to write for *The Times*.

Times Newspapers was destined to become the battle ground on which the issue of press freedom as against the print unions was fought. The struggle had two phases under two proprietors. The first battle, which was over the introduction of computer technology, led to the stoppage from 1 December 1978 to 12 November 1979. During this phase Ken Thomson was the proprietor though Roy Thomson, before he died, had been wholly committed to the introduction of computer technology. This first phase of the battle was won by the trade unions. The second phase was the transfer of printing to Wapping in 1986. By then the proprietor was Rupert Murdoch and the print unions were defeated.

The primary reason why we felt we had to shut the paper in 1978–9 was because our attempts to introduce new computer technology, then being introduced all round the world, were resisted by the print unions. A secondary reason was that the increasingly militant unions were also simply refusing to print *The Times* or the *Sunday Times* whenever they felt like it. Additionally, we were overmanned, and the unions were seriously overpaid, especially in relation to their productivity.

By the time of Roy Thomson's death in 1976 the British economy was coming out of recession. In 1975 *The Times* had made a loss of almost £1.5 million. By 1976 the loss had decreased to under £900,000 and in 1977 the loss had dwindled to £60,000. *The Times* would actually have been making a profit if it had not been for the costs of unofficial stoppages. The story has been best told by John Grigg in *The History of The Times*.

As the economy improved, labour relations worsened. Throughout the newspaper industry inflation had made the trade unions increasingly militant as workers saw the real value of their pay reduced by rising prices. According to Grigg, 'trade union militancy and anarchy were growing while newspapers were no longer able to plead, as they could two years previously, that their financial circumstances were grave, or in some cases, desperate'.

In an attempt to curb inflation the Government had introduced a policy of wage controls which, alone in the industry, the Thomson management adhered to.

> The motive for this was not exceptional civic virtue, but fear that the group's other interests might suffer if it failed to give the government total support in its anti-inflation policy. The Thomson Organization had a contract to fly British troops to and from Germany; it also published the Yellow Pages directories for the Post Office. Above all its stake in North Sea oil was subject to government regulation. While other managements were finding ways of breaking the government's rules and paying the traditional print union's blackmail, Times Newspapers Ltd was being forced, for reasons extraneous to the newspaper industry, to allow its employees' earnings to drop to the bottom of the league table.

According to the pay control rules, increased pay was only permissible where there was increased productivity. In order to increase productivity the Thomson board wanted to take advantage of the photocomposition and computer technologies which were now widely used in America. But the introduction of new technologies required the agreement of the print unions.

Before Roy Thomson died he had installed a new printing system known as SDC. SDC used photocomposition rather than hot metal setting and was a much quicker process which halved labour requirements. The company promised that there would be no compulsory redundancies and that the financial savings made would be spent on the pay and conditions of the workers who remained. The National Graphical Association

(NGA) was not convinced. When Ken Thomson took over from his father the equipment was still lying unused on the third floor of Gray's Inn Road.

Behind the unions' fears lay the threat of computers. It was now technically possible for journalists and telesales people to set their copy directly onto a computer terminal, a practice known as 'single keystroking'. The NGA was determined that only its members should ever access computer terminals for keystroke setting. It was an issue which they were not prepared to discuss.

It was not only the archaic technology which made the production of *Times* newspapers inefficient. As John Grigg records:

> Even for the existing machinery and methods of production Gray's Inn Road was grossly overmanned. As in other London newspaper plants, the union chapels controlled recruitment and did so in such a way as to ensure that as many names as possible were on the payroll. Moreover, since not all the names necessarily corresponded to real people, there was all the more money to be shared between those who were genuine employees. The function of management had been largely abdicated to the chapels, whose threats of instant disruption – at a potential cost of thousands in lost copies and millions in lost advertisement revenue – were usually enough to produce instant ad hoc pay concessions. The ascendancy of union power on the shop floor was enhanced by the fact that so called managers at the lower levels were themselves obliged to be union members. The system that had evolved over the years left management facing a monopoly on the production side that was, within itself, fragmented and anarchic: an extraordinary combination of evils.

In March 1978 the Thomson Executive Management Committee declared that industrial relations had become 'intolerable'. It was time for a showdown. Marmaduke Hussey, as Chief Executive of Times Newspapers, Harold Evans as Editor of the *Sunday Times* and myself travelled to Birmingham on 13 April for a meeting with the general secretaries of the print unions in the Metropole Hotel. My main recollection of this meeting is the dreariness of the hotel and the insipid taste of the coffee. There was a follow-up meeting in the Waldorf Hotel in London on 24 April. Duke Hussey then wrote to each of the general secretaries summarizing the company's position, and setting out a list of proposals for discussion.

1. The common purpose will be the absolute continuity of production … No unofficial action will be taken. Dispute procedures and current agreements will be honoured … Overtime will be worked as necessary …
2. We negotiate a fast-acting and effective disputes procedure.
3. We negotiate, in consultation with union representatives, a general wage restructuring. This will be based on new technology systems, and on efficient manning levels in all departments. A considerable improvement in earnings and conditions could accrue.
4. We have already stated, and confirm now, that no compulsory redundancy will arise from the introduction of the new technology systems.
5. All these negotiations shall be concluded by 30 November 1978.

The letter ended with an ultimatum:

> I have to tell you that it is the firm decision of the Board of Times Newspapers that, if it is not possible to negotiate a joint approach to resolve these problems and if disruption continues, publication of all our newspapers will be suspended. Suspension will last until we are wholly satisfied that publication can be re-started on a basis of reasonable staffing, efficient working and uninterrupted production.
>
> We earnestly hope that you can join us in a final endeavour to avoid this inevitably painful measure.*

Not many of the general secretaries replied to Hussey's letter. Owen O'Brien of NATSOPA shared the company's concern about the loss of production but was unhappy that 'we're being asked to negotiate under duress'. Joe Wade of the NGA took three months to reply that his union would not negotiate anything under the threat of suspension.

Shortly afterwards, Hussey received a response from a group of the eleven fathers of the NATSOPA chapels. They asked for a meeting and made it clear that they would not be bound by any agreement between their national union leaders and the company in which they were not involved. Hussey's reply was that it would not be 'appropriate' for him to negotiate with the chapels while discussions with the general secretaries were ongoing, but a management team was set up to negotiate with fifty-six union units on fifty-four detailed proposals.

In John Grigg's view,

> The dispute was essentially about power. The company's proposals threatened the interests of many individual members of the

* 26 April 1978, quoted by John Grigg in *The History of The Times*, vol. VI, *1966–1981*.

> print unions, who did well out of the existing corrupt system, and who might not be employed at all if it were replaced. But above all it was a threat to the entrenched power of the chapel bosses, whose little empires would disappear if the newspapers were produced efficiently, rationally and honestly. Some of these men exercised their power as genuine class warriors, seeing the trade unions as the means whereby capitalism could be overthrown and workers' control established. Others were at heart neither socialists nor syndicalists but cryptocapitalists. Others again were confused in their motivation, working the system by instinct and living in a fog of ideological cliché. But all knew that they had positions of more or less independent authority to defend.

The threat of suspension did nothing to limit unofficial action. By October 1978 *The Times* had lost 3.9 million copies that year. None of the negotiations – with the general secretaries or the chapel fathers – made any progress. Nor was there any intention to make progress on the union side. Of the ninety meetings held with the NATSOPA chapels during the autumn, Barry Fitzpatrick, father of the *Sunday Times* clerical chapel, turned up on only four occasions and R. A. Brady, father of the *Sunday Times* machine chapel, put in three appearances. On 1 December 1978 *The Times* was suspended.

I went daily, of course, into the office. There were endless discussions about how to deal with the situation, and we were planning for what we would do when we came back. The planning was secondary. We did not know when we were going to be coming back. There was a danger that we would not come back at all.

The House of Commons was broadly sympathetic towards us. The Labour Party, by the time our stoppage began, had come belatedly to realize that militant trade unions and low productivity were damaging the country. Actually, although they were unable to do anything very effective, the Labour Government was more useful to us than the incoming Thatcher Government in its early months. There was a high level of governmental interest in, and concern about, the situation at *The Times*. The Labour Party was interested in the trade union question from two points of view. One was that they had by 1979 realized that the whole of national productivity was damaged by trade union militancy. They recognized the need to defeat militants especially where the militants were refusing to install advanced equipment. They were totally sympathetic to us on that. The Labour Government also preferred the national leadership of the trade unions to the militants, believing the former wanted to raise productivity and implement the initiatives of the Callaghan Government. So I think that the TUC itself, and the Government, were both trying to find ways to put some pressure on the unions to make a reasonable settlement. However, the Government initiative of March and April 1979 came to nothing. Following the General Election of May 1979, Margaret Thatcher's Employment Secretary, Jim Prior, who had been a contemporary of mine at Charterhouse, favoured, in John Grigg's phrase, 'the softly-softly approach'.

He apparently thought it foolish of any employer to fight the unions, any attempt being unlikely to succeed, and that the balance of power was such that we were merely spitting into the wind. His policy was to appease the militants.

Margaret Thatcher was probably a good deal more personally sympathetic to us. She saw, and later dealt with, the problem of trade union militancy as a problem that her Government would have to tackle if it were not to go the way of Ted Heath's. However, this problem came perhaps too early in her administration and Margaret could not do much to assist us.

There was a similar split on the Board of Times Newspapers and it was a split along the lines stated by Michael Leapman in the *New Statesman* on 8 June 1979: 'the hawks are led by Duke Hussey, flanked by their spiritual adviser Rees-Mogg. The moderate camp seems now to be headed by Gordon Brunton ... backed by Denis Hamilton ... who has kept a low profile throughout.' Positions varied. Duke Hussey and I were convinced, and remained convinced, that you could not run *The Times* as a proper business unless you could develop and control efficient methods of composition for the paper. Our failing was that we did not have an adequate plan if the unions could not be induced to settle. Duke Hussey had previously developed a very sensible plan which would have led to several papers producing together. This might have worked but we could not get the agreement of the rest of Fleet Street.

Duke and I certainly were the hawks. Gordon Brunton was a bluffer. Initially, he pressed for *The Times*' board to grasp the nettle. He strongly supported a shutdown in order to force a settlement. But, as a bluffer whose bluff was called, he thought 'well, the right thing to do when your bluff is called is to stop bluffing'. So, he swung from being the hawkiest of the hawks to be the doviest of the doves. Ken Thomson and his adviser, John Tory, wanted to beat the unions, but Ken was not at all keen on the battle when the battle emerged. Denis Hamilton was a dove, more or less from the beginning. He was extremely doubtful. He was very uneasy that what he regarded as his life's work, which was the merger of *The Times* and the *Sunday Times*, might not survive the dispute. He saw that the dispute would lead to the sale of the newspapers by the Thomson Organization. Denis was more than happy when Gordon Brunton decided that the bluff was not working, and became, as Michael Leapman says, an ally of Gordon Brunton in bringing the thing to an end.

I did remain a hawk to the end, stating that we would only get even a reasonable settlement if the trade unions remained convinced of our willingness to continue the battle. Even when, therefore, I had come to the conclusion that we were not going to win, I still wanted us to follow an aggressive line. I now see our battle as being essentially one of those first battles that you have to have if you are going to prevail at all. In this, to compare small to big, it was like Dunkirk. You start off a war underprepared, you underestimate the strength of the enemy, the enemy then wins the first battle and you are lucky to escape with your skin. It all looks very bad. Then later, the same situation, the same confrontation in some form or another re-emerges because the logic has not been settled, and the second time round you win. If you take our stoppage and what Rupert Murdoch did at Wapping, that fits exactly into this pattern. Indeed, when the decision was being taken as to whom the newspaper should be sold, I was in favour of Rupert Murdoch, because he was the only potential purchaser who seemed to have the toughness to recognize the battle that would have to be fought, and the toughness to win it.

Eric Jacobs, analysing *The Times*' shutdown, made the statement in his Stop Press that the real victor was 'not the company, the unions or the staff, but the fact of chapel power' and that 'the chapel stood revealed as the dominating force ... and the chapels dictated the pace of the protracted negotiations which led to the newspapers' return'. That is again correct, but it only takes you up to the actual return. The chapels were not under the control of the union leadership. At the beginning the union leadership hoped to use the dispute as a weapon with which to discipline the chapels. Before the stoppage, one of the union leaders told Duke Hussey: 'you've got to hold a pistol to my head', meaning that unless a pistol was held to his head he himself would not be able to get an agreement through his chapel. The union leaders naturally wanted to pull back power from the leaders of the individual chapels. They failed to do so. We were frequently dealing with militant leaders of the chapel who, being able to control their chapel, were therefore able to control events. Rupert Murdoch analysed absolutely correctly where the power lay and was therefore able to destroy chapel, and indeed print union, power at Wapping. He was then able to bring in the new technology. Journalists were now allowed to use computers. Fleet Street was revolutionized.

Looking back, different members of Times Newspapers took different lessons from it. I felt that you should not get into a situation which you could not win. We should have worked out earlier how we could see off the unions. We should have waited until we had a viable plan like printing on a different site. We tried this by going to Frankfurt in April 1979. This was an extremely important development. Frankfurt was a declaration that some of us were prepared to do what Rupert Murdoch successfully did later at Wapping. However, as we had not prepared it properly beforehand, and acted hurriedly, we were then faced by the obstruction of the German unions threatening violence. A further mistake was our belief that we could beat the chapel power essentially by bluff.

Our negotiating position proved to be totally unsatisfactory because we relied, mistakenly, on the power of the national officers of the union as against the chapels. The national officers were as anxious as we were to break chapel power if they could. Chapel power not only made our lives extremely difficult but made the national officers' lives extremely difficult as well. Yet further problems arose because we thought we had an agreement that the national officers would behave as national officers in the print union used to behave, for instance when I was on the *Financial Times* in the 1950s. In that period, if there was a threat of a chapel stoppage, the national officer of the print union came in and just told his people that he would tear up their cards if they refused to return to work, whereupon they went back to work. All of us, consequently, had memories of the real power of the print unions resting with the national officers and not with the chapel officials. We failed, however, to realize how far that had changed. We failed to realize that the national officials, although they would have liked to recover their power, had in fact lost it.

In retrospect, I have no doubt that the Board of the Thomson Organization was responsible. They decided to accept the risks of the stoppage, they decided when the stoppage should be brought to an end and they decided to sell the newspapers. The ultimate decisions inevitably came from Canada.

Throughout the journalists' strike, Ken Thomson was worried about the losses of *The Times* and by the print unions' failure to cooperate in the introduction of the new machinery. The year's stoppage must have seemed to him to have been a year wasted. I do not know whether, if the striking and shutdown had not occurred, he would have continued with the ownership of *The Times*.

As John Grigg records, Ken's decision to sell Times Newspapers was announced on 23 October 1980 under the headline 'Lord Thomson to sever connexion with *The Times*'. The paper published the full text of an announcement by Thomson British Holdings which stated that 'with the utmost reluctance' and 'despite strenuous efforts of management at all levels, and the expenditure of massive sums of money', the company would be 'withdrawing from the publication' of *The Times*, the *Sunday Times* and their supplements. The announcement cited 'the continuing troubled history of industrial relations' as one reason for the decision.

Even before the stoppage The Times Newspapers' losses went far beyond the investment that the Thomsons ever contemplated. One could not possibly criticize any commercial concern for not pouring more money into what seemed to be a bottomless pit. The early assurances of investment made by the Thomsons were by and large followed. Nevertheless, the Thomson family bore substantial losses and continued to give substantial support. The Thomson family's capacity to invest more money in *The Times* may have been affected by their need to fund their developing North Sea oil interests.

In October 1980 I wrote an article called 'Now *The Times* is going to fight for herself', setting out my plans to raise funds in America and Canada to purchase *The Times*. The plan had the support of the staff. *The Times*' journalists formed themselves into a group to create what would now be called a management buyout. Linklaters and Barings advised us *pro bono* and provided first-class service. I recruited a board which included John Baring and Arnold Weinstock. We possessed strong City support but the question was how our bid compared to other bids. I wanted throughout to maintain a sense of reality about this bid, but I saw it primarily as a fallback if the Thomson Organization failed to make a satisfactory sale of Times Newspapers together, without splitting them up.

Following the Thomson announcement on 23 October, Warburg put out an invitation to people to enter tenders to buy *The Times*. The Thomson Organization set up a committee, on which I served, which had the responsibility of satisfying itself of the suitability of the people making the bids. Ken Thomson wanted to sell the paper but he did not want to sell the paper in such a way as would be damaging or destructive to it. The only two substantial bids came from the Daily Mail Group and from Rupert Murdoch. The Mail Group only wanted the *Sunday Times*; it was never clear that they would take on *The Times*. It was clear that if they did, they would do so with extreme reluctance. We were faced, therefore, with a single serious bidder. Our consortium was only interested in protecting the future of *The Times* – two consequences followed from that. The first was that we could not be competitive with any bidder who was seriously interested in both papers; the second was that we would have become serious bidders in the event that the only other bids were for the *Sunday Times* on its own. The Thomson Organization wanted to sell both newspapers together and were very doubtful whether *The Times* could survive on its own.

I had seen Rupert Murdoch in New York when I was canvassing support for my buyout syndicate. He had not then decided what he was going to do. Rupert had been a contemporary of mine at Oxford, but I did not know him well – I was in my last year when he was in his first year. I did, however, meet him a couple of times. He was a vigorous, rather left-wing member of the Labour Club, with a radical reputation. I came across him first at the Union. Even then his energy was his most striking characteristic.

One day in the summer of 1951, I was walking along The Turl in Oxford. Rupert stopped me and said that he had heard that *Cherwell*, an undergraduate magazine, was for sale. He was thinking of buying it. He wondered whether I would like to join in. So long as I could remember *Cherwell* had lost money – it was one of those undergraduate magazines which are always on their last legs. I said that I thought it was bound to continue to lose money. Rupert replied that it should be possible to sell more advertising. I had tried selling advertising for the Conservative magazine the *Oxford Tory* at one time and knew how reluctant the Oxford shopkeepers were to put their good money into buying space in undergraduate magazines. I did not become an investor; Rupert did not buy *Cherwell*. Nevertheless, that abortive effort may have been his first attempt to become a media proprietor. The opportunity to enter into a partnership with Rupert Murdoch on whatever basis, and however apparently unsound, was probably one I should not have turned down!

The next time I met Rupert, he *was* a proprietor. He had built up his Australian group, founded the *Australian*, and bought the *News of the World*. There was a grand lunch given by the Press Club some time in the early 1970s. The lunch was to celebrate a new building, or an anniversary or both. I found myself at the top table. I think it may have been a circular table; at any rate we were all able to join in the conversation. The guest of honour was the Queen. All three of us would then have been in our forties, with the Queen as the eldest and Rupert as the youngest. I am sometimes slow to join in the conversation on those grand occasions. My conversational powers resemble the performance of an old-fashioned steam engine, which requires a period of grumbling and gassing before it starts to drive its pistons. I cannot remember that I found anything to say. I was like Samuel Johnson meeting King George III, on which he afterwards commented: 'It was not for me to bandy words with my sovereign.' I did not need to exert myself. Rupert set out to amuse the Queen and chatted with her in the easiest of styles. She was amused. I cannot remember a word that was said, and I suspect that nothing was said that was not trivia. I simply remember the lunch as an occasion where we were all still quite young, on which I was happy, the Queen was happy, and, I imagine, Rupert was happy as well.

Rupert is often criticized for his alleged republicanism. It seems to me to be exaggerated or misunderstood in many people's minds. The root of his attitude is to be found in his father's experience of Gallipoli. His father, Sir Keith Murdoch, wrote a report on the Gallipoli campaign for the Australian Government. He concluded, no doubt correctly, that the amateurishness of English generals had cost the lives of young Australian soldiers. Almost all Australians believe that to be true, but Rupert was influenced by the personal experience of his father. This left him with an underlying view that the British Establishment was amateur, indecisive and out of date. In business terms he saw the Establishment as uncompetitive. He had, however, a great respect for those English businessmen whom he found to be as competitive as himself. He had an admiration, fully reciprocated, for Arnold Weinstock – but one could hardly have seen Arnold as a typical member of the British Establishment.

This did not make Rupert a republican in British terms – he probably thinks that a matter for the British – though he may well be a republican in Australian terms. He would, I think, tend to judge the Royal Family in the way he judges the world at large. Do they do their job well or badly?

I did not meet Rupert again until the period of the sale of *The Times*. My great concern in 1980 and 1981 was that *The Times* should survive. Whatever else happened, I did not want to be the last Editor of *The Times*. When Rupert put in his bid for Times Newspapers it seemed to me that he had a much better chance of saving *The Times* than did our syndicate.

As a member of the vetting committee, I was influenced by the fact that I had liked Rupert on the three occasions when our paths had crossed. The real question was one of trust. When Rupert gave the assurance that he would run *The Times* in a commercially efficient way but respecting editorial independence, would he keep his word? Far less able proprietors than he would have found ways of evading such assurances. The decision had to depend on trusting him.

Looking back, he has been an excellent proprietor for *The Times*, but also for Fleet Street. He has given *The Times* first-class commercial management. The number of titles has increased; there are more and better paid journalists than could be afforded in the old days. Above all, the power of the print unions was broken, and the new technology of 1980 is now itself archaic. As I had fervently hoped, I was not the last Editor, but have been succeeded by seven others, to date only one of whom, Harry Evans, fell out with his proprietor. In that dispute, I thought Rupert Murdoch was in the right. In addition to those benefits for Times Newspapers, Rupert has built up a huge worldwide media business, one of the big entrepreneurial achievements of his generation.

In my personal life, he has had an entirely benign effect. I left *The Times* in 1981, because I thought that it was time, after fourteen years, to get out of the way. I had the delightful experience of writing a column for Andreas Whittam-Smith's *Independent* from 1986 to 1991. I had a couple of invitations to write a column for *The Times* which I accepted in 1992. I have had good relations with all my successors as Editor, and with Rupert as proprietor. It took me eleven years to go back to *The Times*, but the period since then has been one of my happiest periods in journalism.

Although Rupert Murdoch was the clear front-runner to purchase Times Newspapers, people were divided on Rupert Murdoch himself. As the owner of the *Sun* and the *News of the World* he was seen at that point as a tabloid proprietor. He had some commercial enemies and among journalists he had critics from the left. On the other hand, his appointment reunited the top tier at *The Times*. Denis Hamilton, Duke Hussey and I had not been in complete agreement during *The Times* strike, but all three of us saw Rupert Murdoch as the best option to save the newspapers.

Both Rupert Murdoch and Roy Thomson were 100 per cent dedicated to making their newspapers a business success. Roy Thomson was not in the least interested in the editorial line being taken by his newspapers, so long as he was satisfied that it was responsible. Rupert Murdoch was intensely interested in everything about newspapers. He was, and is, a newspaper addict. He is devoted to, and is fascinated by, newspapers. He enjoys every minute of dealing with them. However, there has never been credible evidence that Rupert pressures Editors of *The Times* and the *Sunday Times* to take one editorial line or another.

Rupert takes a rather similar view of Prime Ministers as he does of editors. He admired Margaret Thatcher because he thought she was effective. He likes politicians who have an entrepreneurial quality and particularly the virtues of energy and decision. He also likes winners. In the period before the 1997 General Election Tony Blair courted Rupert assiduously. Obviously, from Blair's point of view, he would have liked to have had the support of all the Murdoch newspapers. Crucially, Murdoch gave him the support of the *Sun*, but *The Times* did not support the Labour Party in 1997, on the grounds of their European policy.

I wanted Charles Douglas-Home to succeed me. I had consulted an inner group of ten colleagues about the succession. The majority of them thought that Louis Heren, though a great journalist, was too old. Charles Douglas-Home was widely thought to be the right answer. He was then Home Affairs Editor and the number three on the paper, with Louis as the number two. Both Louis and Charlie had been absolutely staunch and helpful supporters to me during the stoppage.

I let Rupert Murdoch know what the view of the senior staff was. I recommended Charlie. He was an extremely good *Times*' journalist, had lots of courage, had been a brilliant and brave war correspondent, and possessed a deep knowledge of international affairs and British politics. Oddly, he had been one of the signatories of the White Swan letter. Nevertheless, I had great admiration for his work.

Rupert Murdoch had already formed the notion that what Harry Evans had achieved on the *Sunday Times*, which was to make it a very successful paper, poised between the tabloids on the one hand and the more austere broadsheets on the other, could be replicated on *The Times*. I never thought this would work. I knew *The Times*' staff would be worried. I also knew, which was more, I think, to the point, that Harry was a wonderful editor but not a good budget manager. Rupert decided to give the editorship to Harry. He held it for less than a year.

In all human terms the period of *The Times*' closure was a depressing business. We were all condemned to turn from our proper work of writing or editing to mitigating the damage done by the strike and trying to overcome it. However, I had the happiness of family life, and the delight of a new baby, Annunziata. She was born on 25 March 1979, the Feast of the Annunciation, which is the subject of half of the most beautiful pictures of the Italian Renaissance. When she was born, I was fifty, Gillian forty and her nearest sibling, Jacob, was coming up to ten. He was a devoted older brother. When Annunziata was three, Jacob went to Eton, and he made her part of his school life and friendships. I was surprised to see how willing his contemporaries were to play with a toddler. Annunziata, however, stood up for herself – she was always determined to be an equal to her brothers and sisters. Of course, Jacob was a great influence on her, particularly in drawing her towards the political life. At the election of 2010 Jacob won the seat of North East Somerset, while Annunziata was unsuccessful as the Conservative candidate for the neighbouring constituency of Somerton and Frome.

FOURTEEN

My Life as a Quangocrat

I signed off from *The Times* in March 1981, not with a formal leader but with a signed op-ed piece, in which I struck a suitably more personal note. I wanted to express some personal things which would have been slightly confusing in a leader. It became a farewell piece written in a leader style. This was in keeping with the style I had aimed for as Editor. My editorship was, I still feel, more personalized than most. In *Supping with the Devils*, Hugo Young recalls my statement that when I was on the *Sunday Times* I was writing for an 'overworked doctor in Leamington Spa'. I took this outlook across to *The Times*. Similarly, on *The Times* I aimed to present the personality of the Editor as something the readership could relate to. I do believe that personality in newspapers – personalities of the columnists, of the particularly strong correspondents and of the Editor – give a newspaper at best a crackle which it cannot have if it is all written in an impersonal way.

In the farewell op-ed piece, 'My resumption of liberty', I stated that I was looking forward to 'a second adolescence, full of freedom, impertinence and hope'. This never came my way and I remained to some degree constrained and institutionalized.

After I left *The Times*, the next stage of my career was involved in publishing, antiquarian bookselling, helping to run quasi-autonomous non-governmental organizations (quangos), and acting as a non-executive director or chairman of various companies. This was followed by a return to journalism as a columnist. I never solicited any of my quango positions and, indeed, I received them by different routes. There was, however, one common, core factor and that was Margaret Thatcher. Margaret, for whatever reason, having known me at Oxford, and having met me around, had confidence that I would do a reasonably good job. This meant that people making recommendations for quango jobs felt that she would probably say yes to my name, when they thought she would probably say no to others.

Rab Butler once predicted, when Gillian and I were having lunch with him at Whitehall Court, that I would never find any work as important as that of Editor of *The Times*. I do not think my subsequent career altogether proved him wrong, though I held some interesting offices. I do not feel, in retrospect, that I did a good job as Vice-Chairman of the BBC. I did a better job as the Chairman of the Arts Council and at least a competent, but a much less important one, in being the first Chairman of the Broadcasting Standards Council.

The BBC is a creative bureaucracy. I admired its creative work. Its bureaucracy, however, I found devious and stifling. I did not like the atmosphere at all and the BBC did not like me. The senior staff regarded me as a meddling amateur, but they thought that of almost all the Governors. For me being a Governor of the BBC was like swimming through porridge. There was continuous intrigue, including the use of leaks to the newspapers, to advance personal careers and policies inside the BBC. People used their patronage in a highly politicized way. The contribution the Governors were supposed to make was resented. As the management controlled the levers of power, battles between the Governors and the senior managers were normally won by the managers, though the Board of Management was itself usually divided.

The Governors were there to look after the public interest. They were also the ultimate source of governance of the BBC. They were non-executive directors of the BBC, and were supposed to see that the BBC's finances were properly regulated. Their goal was to protect the independence of the BBC, to ensure that the BBC was doing its job as well as it could and that the management was effective. The Governors were answerable to nobody except Parliament. They were not answerable to the Prime Minister of the day, but they had to bear in mind that the BBC's finances depended on the licence fee. Therefore, if they got into too hostile a relationship with Government, it could be damaging to the next licensing negotiation, though the BBC is so powerful an institution that politicians seldom want to keep up a quarrel. Since my time the BBC has been reorganized, the management board has the ultimate executive authority and there is a board of trustees which partly replaces the function of the Governors. The Chairman of the Trustees does not seem to know whether he is supposed to be a loyal supporter of the institution or its chief critic. The old system of Governors and a Director General lasted for three-quarters of a century. I do not believe that the new constitution will last for a comparable period. So far, it seems less able to deal with the BBC's problems than we were.

In the spring of 1981, shortly after I had resigned as Editor of *The Times*, Ian Trethowan, who was the Director General at the time, invited me to lunch at the Travellers Club, and asked me whether I would like to become the Vice-Chairman of the BBC. I had worked with Ian on three previous occasions: in the parliamentary lobby in 1954; in the early 1960s, on current affairs programmes for Independent Television News, on which he was a presenter, and when I was first Editor of *The Times* he wrote a weekly political column for me. So, we were old friends and colleagues. We shared broadly similar political views: liberal Conservative views, pro-European. The appointment would be in the gift of the Home Office; at that time the Home Secretary was Willie Whitelaw, whom I also knew. The appointment would obviously have to be approved by Margaret Thatcher, who was the Prime Minister.

I told Ian that I would not be interested in becoming the Vice-Chairman of the BBC unless it was with a view to succeeding as Chairman, when George Howard's term would run out. In my view the BBC needed significant change and reform. A Chairman could do that but a Vice-Chairman could not. Ian said he would take my conditional acceptance back to Willie Whitelaw and the Government. Margaret Thatcher agreed that I should have the succession, though such an agreement would obviously be unenforceable.

Subsequently, about a year later, I was offered the chairmanship of the Arts Council. I had realized by then that the job of reforming the BBC was even more difficult than I had supposed and ideally required more financial experience than I felt myself to possess. I had by then spent a year as a non-executive director of GEC, and began, as a result of seeing Arnold Weinstock's work, to have an idea of just how hard it was to make major changes in an institution of that size. So, when I accepted the chairmanship of the Arts Council, I sent a message that I was doing it on the assumption that I could continue as Vice-Chairman of the BBC, but that I would not go beyond my five-year term. It was not possible to be both the Chairman of the Arts Council and the Chairman of the BBC. Nor would it have been desirable.

I was in any case in favour of the succession of Stuart Young to the chairmanship. Later, I went to the Prime Minister when the succession had to be decided to state that I had been very impressed by Stuart Young as a colleague and fellow Governor of the BBC. His experience and skill as a successful chartered accountant made him most suitable to combat the substantial business and financial problems of the BBC.

Throughout my time, the Governors met as a board every fortnight. There was in 1981 no Board of Management. That was created shortly after I became a Governor. The Director General reported to the Governors. They raised questions with him about problems, complaints and conflicts that the BBC was having. One of the biggest struggles in my time came when Stuart Young was the Chairman. It concerned a fly-on-the-wall documentary on Martin McGuinness. The Home Secretary, then Leon Brittan, heard that this documentary was to be screened and made a complaint on the grounds that this was neither a proper nor desirable way to interview terrorists. It would give a terrorist the 'oxygen of publicity'.

We, as Governors, had to consider Leon Brittan's complaint. I was concerned that the BBC had broken all its own rules, especially the producers' code, which had a paragraph covering interviews with terrorists. The code ruled that no interview should be arranged with a terrorist without reference upwards, right up to the Director General. If the Director General gave his approval the interview was to be conducted on a tough basis. The natural question: 'Why have you played a part in killing innocent people?', should be put to the terrorist. Certainly, it should never be a simple, soft interview which presented the terrorist in a favourable light, without challenge.

For the McGuinness programme, approval had been given at a considerably lower level by the National Director for Northern

Ireland, who, though an excellent person, had failed to consult Lucy Faulkner, BBC Governor for Northern Ireland. She would not have agreed to the form of the interview. The decision not to refer the documentary upwards was to my mind quite probably deliberate, not a mere oversight, though I never knew who had decided not to refer either to Lucy Faulkner or to the Director General, Alasdair Milne. The chosen method of interview, simply to turn the camera towards the person being interviewed and let him speak freely, was unsatisfactory. To display him in a friendly, family light, as though he were an ordinary family man, was an abdication of normal journalistic standards.

Should the Governors view the interview before transmission? This was not customary because that was felt to involve censorship by the Governors. The Charter gave the Governors absolute powers and absolute responsibility. However, the convention was that they should not use their powers until after the event. Of course, by that time it would be too late. At the board meeting, I moved that we should view this interview; it had broken the rules laid down in the BBC producers' guide, and was not, therefore, covered by the normal convention. Stuart Young was already ill; he died about a year later of lung cancer. Because, throughout a greater part of his chairmanship, he was suffering from lung cancer, we were all reluctant to put too much pressure on him. Alasdair Milne was out of contact on a ferry in the Baltic.

We proceeded to view the programme. As I had feared, it showed McGuinness, who was at the time the leader of the Provisional IRA, as a genial Irish father of a family. He faced no questions about why he had assisted in procuring terrorist acts. It seemed to me to amount to propaganda for the IRA. I therefore felt that the Government were making an entirely legitimate complaint. We then ran into a staff problem. The staff of the BBC believed that the Governors should defend the BBC against the Government, right or wrong. They did not believe that the Governors were there to adjudicate on a complaint by the Government. They believed the Governors were there to reject all such complaints, in order to retain the BBC's absolute creative autonomy. This view, while understandable, conflicted with the BBC's constitution. Having viewed the programme, we did take the judgement that it should not be shown. I have continued to believe that this was justified both by the character of the interview and by the breaches of the BBC's own guidelines.

A huge outcry arose inside the BBC; the news refused even to show an interview with the Chairman, Stuart Young, explaining the Governors' decision. After about a fortnight of tension between the Governors and the Board of Management, and following Alasdair Milne's return from his Baltic holiday, Stuart Young wanted to quieten the situation down by showing the programme. I did not wish to hold out against this decision. I felt the point had been made. We had either to remove the Board of Management and Alasdair Milne or, alternatively, to allow the Director General to show a programme he wanted to show. Alasdair maintained that he would have approved the programme if he had been asked beforehand. So, with considerable remaining reluctance, I agreed to it going ahead.

Complaints by the Government were quite rare and when they came up they were always difficult. In practice, the BBC is not only excessively defensive about complaints by the Government, it is also excessively defensive about complaints by ordinary individuals. During my time as a Governor, we lost a couple of entirely unnecessary libel actions where the BBC had too little evidence but had refused to climb down. I found the

BBC's attitude to complaints arrogant. As Vice-Chairman, I was frequently required, during the illnesses of Stuart Young and George Howard, to sign replies to complaints. I repeatedly refused to sign them in their existing self-justifying form, and asked for them to be redrafted; this added to my reputation as a bolshie Governor who did not stand up for the BBC.

The most difficult board meeting I ever had concerned the late Dick Francis, not the novelist but later the Director General of the British Council. Dick Francis was the Managing Director of BBC Radio during Alasdair Milne's period as Director General. Alasdair decided to make a change in the top echelon of managers, and told Dick Francis that he would have to give up his job. I think he offered him the post of Managing Director of the World Service. Dick felt that he was being fired, without reason, from his position as Managing Director of Radio. Alasdair decided to persist. Dick then made a formal complaint to the Board of Governors. He asked the Governors to give him a hearing, to which he was entitled under the BBC rules. A very painful board meeting then followed. Stuart Young was in the Chair, but was suffering what turned out to be his final relapse, but, nevertheless, he was sitting there in the Chair, looking extremely ill and distressed, and finding it very difficult to manage such a tense meeting.

Dick Francis, an honest and active executive, made an eloquent statement of his case, saying that he had been given no reasons for being dismissed from his post and that he was not conscious of having done anything wrong. Alasdair Milne gave what I regarded as a very feeble account of his own reasons. He left the impression that he thought the Director General was entitled to make changes in his senior staff without being required to state his reasons. The Board of Governors were left in an extremely difficult situation. We were not at all satisfied by

Alasdair Milne's explanation. We felt that Dick Francis had a strong case. However, we saw that, if we decided in favour of Dick Francis, the only possible conclusion was that we would have to say that we had no confidence in Alasdair Milne. We would, therefore, in effect be firing the Director General. The next Chairman, Marmaduke Hussey, did later fire Alasdair Milne, but it is a very major decision for a Board of Governors to take. Apart from one wartime instance, no previous Director General had ever been fired. We all felt extremely sympathetic to Stuart; we knew that he was, in all probability, in the last stages of a fatal illness. We did not feel, rightly or wrongly, that we could simply allow justice to prevail, that would have meant finding in favour of Dick Francis and against Alasdair. I felt that we were behaving very badly. However, I also felt that we were behaving in the only way we could behave. The situation was one in which it would not have been in the interest of the BBC to ask a dying Chairman to handle the crisis caused by firing the Director General.

Stuart and I then had to go out to the Chairman's office in Broadcasting House and tell Dick Francis that we were not able to uphold his appeal to us. Dick Francis burst into tears. Stuart Young was himself extremely distressed. So was I. At that point I believe the conviction crystallized in Stuart Young's mind, and in mine, that Alasdair Milne would in the end have to go.

When I joined the BBC I discussed the need to modernize the institution with Arnold Weinstock. He warned me that the reform of a big institution was only possible for a team, and the team had to have power. Stuart and I were genuine modernizers and there were other Governors and managers who shared our ambition; in particular, there was a group of women Governors who wanted more women to be promoted to senior jobs in management, but power, in the BBC, rested with the Director

General and Alasdair Milne was not sympathetic to our modernizing policies. Stuart Young and I put on pressure to raise the commercial energy of the corporation. Not with great success. Very often the elephant just turned over in its sleep.

I admired several of my fellow Governors, particularly Jocelyn Barrow, who later served as my Deputy Chairman at the Broadcasting Standards Council. I worked with Jocelyn with great pleasure. She was one of the very few Afro-Caribbean women to rise on their merits to Establishment positions.

I have always enjoyed television, as a viewer and an occasional performer, but I have never been much good at it. My appointment as a BBC Governor came after a good deal of involvement with television. I first appeared on television in 1951 in America. In the early 1960s I played a part in interesting developments at ITN in, for instance, the first budget broadcasts and the first computer-aided General Election broadcast in 1964. Needless to say, the computer's forecast proved to be wrong. The computer thought that the Conservatives, under Alec Douglas-Home, had won the election. As the resident expert I told the computer it was mistaken.

Shortly after I gave up the editorship of *The Times* in 1981, I was taken out to lunch by John Fairbairn, who invited me to join the trustees of the Esmée Fairbairn Foundation. The Esmée Fairbairn Foundation had been set up in the late 1960s by the Fairbairn family to protect their family holding in M & G, the unit trust group, from having to be sold in the event of the deaths of the founders. Esmée Fairbairn herself, after whom it was named, had been killed by a flying bomb during the Second World War. The holding in M & G was a controlling holding, but it had originally only small value, I think about £70,000. By 1981, the trust had grown very substantially but it was still a small trust with a limited range of objectives. It was run by the trustees with a secretary. The first objectives of the trust were to promote the cause of popular capitalism, to strengthen public understanding and awareness of the benefits of consumer investment and to help develop think tanks, like the Institute for Economic Affairs, which took an open-market view.

The trust did not spend money on overseas projects. It did not spend money on medical purposes, believing that both were better financed by larger and wealthier charities.

I remained an Esmée Fairbairn Foundation trustee until I reached the age of seventy-five, the trustees' retirement age. My most important contribution turned out to be in the Arts, where I had the experience of the Arts Council, and in the area of investment. The shares in M & G appreciated in value very substantially during the period I was a trustee. I was on the Board of M & G itself for a few years, leaving at their retirement age of sixty-five, so I got to know not only the Foundation and its needs, but also the M & G business and its potential.

In 1999, after I had left the Board of M & G, the shares were sold to the Prudential. The Chairman of M & G who negotiated the sale, for a very good price, was Rod Kent, also at that time Chairman of Close Bros. He is an extremely good and capable businessman, with whom I found it a particular pleasure to work. Good businessmen, unlike most journalists or politicians, deal in reality. That is intellectually very attractive. The result of this advantageous sale was that the Esmée Fairbairn Foundation had £650 million to invest, a huge increase on the original £70,000. I was very conscious that this large sum would, but for their generosity, have belonged to the Fairbairn family.

We reorganized the Foundation into four separate sector groups. One was for the Arts and Heritage, of which I took the Chair; one for the Environment; one for Social purposes; and one for Education. John Fairbairn was the Chairman while this was taking place, and had also been Chairman while the sale of our holding in M & G was completed. I took some part in the process of the sale, as a member of the Investment Committee. I had for some time been concerned about the concentration of the assets of the Esmée Fairbairn Foundation in a single investment, but fortunately we did not sell too early or for too low a price.

I was then asked to be the Chairman of the Investment Committee during the period in which the £650 million had to be invested. After a year or so we appointed Rod Kent himself as a trustee. He came onto the Investment Committee to join myself, John Fairbairn and Ashley Downs. Investing a billion dollars is obviously a big responsibility, particularly difficult as we received the money early in 2000, at the top of the dot.com bull market on Wall Street. We set ourselves a target of 4 per cent return which would be used for the charitable expenditures of the Fund. When I left the chairmanship three years later, we had found the 4 per cent and we still had our original capital intact. We had done well in a very volatile market in which we had started at the top. This was a collective effort, with a collectively agreed strategy receiving advice from the American charity advisers Cambridge Associates.

My work with the Esmée Fairbairn Foundation pleased me a good deal. I became a trustee because I thought it a useful Foundation. I had no idea it would grow as much as it did. That enabled it to do as much good as it has done, partly because it was willing to take on the funding of charitable purposes which other foundations thought were too far out, or too difficult, for one reason or another. It took, on the whole, a businesslike view of its function because it was a charity emerging out of business, and all the early trustees were from the business community. It was trying to get a good return on its investment. It was looking for results.

I would single out as a particular success the original investment of the Foundation in free-market think tanks. Undoubtedly in the 1970s the ideas of the Institute for Economic Affairs were extremely influential, not only on the Conservative Party, where they formed the intellectual background to the economic theories of Thatcherism, but also on the Labour Party. Even by the later 1970s the Labour Party had become much more an open-market party than it had been earlier. That was a major success. There were other specific successes, especially in the development of distance learning, which was one of our major themes.

In 1982, Paul Channon, then Minister for the Arts, asked me whether I would take on the chairmanship of the Arts Council. In one sense it was an unenviable job, since the Chairman was almost always criticized for failing to get enough money out of the Government. In another sense it was a quite delightful job since it was part of the function to visit as many as possible of the arts companies which were receiving Arts Council support. The Arts Council even had its own box at the Royal Opera House at Covent Garden. Gillian came with me to most events and was a great help. She is very interested in the arts, has a much better ear for music than I have and is much better at creating immediately friendly relations with strangers.

Paul Channon never admitted how many other people he had asked before me. However, I am fairly clear that at least one or two people had already refused the job. Chairman of the Arts Council is an unpaid job, taking up quite a bit of time. I spent about three days a week on it for a six-month period, when I was getting to know it and getting control of the system. Thereafter, I averaged one or two days a week. On the other hand, the Arts Council is an organization in which, because of its size and structure, it is quite possible to make a difference. When I went to the Arts Council in 1982 it was still very much in the tradition which had been established by Arnold Goodman, in Jennie Lee's years as Minister for the Arts in the late 1960s.

I found that the Council was run by the officers rather than by the members of the Council itself; at the first Council meeting I attended it was the officers who expected to be called on each item of the agenda. I called the chairmen of the various Arts Council committees who were all members of the Council. The Secretary General seemed to take the view, which the management of the BBC took in their case, that he and his officers were the executive directors of the Arts Council. The members of the Council, by implication, were the non-executives who should leave the decisions largely in the hands of the executives. However, the Secretary General was due to retire in the ordinary course of events. I believed that the Arts Council was itself the responsible body. If we were to make any changes one would have to empower the Council. This would mean making various officers act as the servants of the Council rather than the Council as the servant of its officers. So far as I can tell, the conflict of jurisdiction between Council members and officers applies in every quango and most charities and can never be permanently resolved. The outcome of this tug of war depends on the personalities involved.

In the first six months I had not only to learn the business of the Council but also to take a lot of decisions myself. With experience, I developed various policies. The most important change was to maximize funding for the arts from all sources. In the late 1960s Jennie Lee, as Minister for the Arts, had been able to get a great deal of money from the Treasury because of her status as the widow of Nye Bevan, of whom Harold Wilson's Labour Party still stood in awe. She had taken the view, shared by the left wing of the Labour Party but not, I believe, by Arnold Goodman, that private funding of the arts was not compatible with public funding. I saw it as complementary.

I believed that the arts needed to raise money from all the possible sources of revenue, indeed to cultivate the Government as only one source of funds. At the beginning of my chairmanship, the Arts Council was focused on its own funding and rather unsympathetic to all the other forms of funding; by the end, the Arts Council was successfully devoting energies to maximizing all the sources of funds.

There were very exaggerated criticisms of Mrs Thatcher's financial impact on the arts. We managed each year, as far as I can remember, to secure at least an inflation-weighted increase for arts funding from the Government. We were successful in encouraging local authorities, which at that time had some money, to increase their own arts funding. We established schemes to encourage business sponsorship. We encouraged ballet and theatre companies to market their seats in an effective way and to improve the efficiency of their business administration. The result was that the 1980s was a comparatively good decade for arts revenues, if less good for new capital projects. We did particularly well when Grey Gowrie was the Minister for the Arts. Grey and I managed to persuade the Treasury to replace the money that was liable to be lost by the closing of the Greater London Council. We secured considerably more money than we had actually lost. In this, the Arts Council of the 1980s worked with, rather than against, the Government machine and the Thatcherite ideology. I did not scruple to remain on good terms with our paymasters.

Naturally, the arts institutions always wanted more money and we received a lot of criticism, particularly from Peter Hall who climbed on a desk at the National Theatre in order to denounce us. This criticism was helpful because it gave extra publicity to the need for arts funding. People in the arts were liable to behave imprudently because they had become accustomed to relying on grants. I remember very early in my time as Chairman, a board member of one national company said to me 'but of course it's our duty to overspend, because unless we overspend and get into a really difficult budget situation, we won't get any more money from you'. This was representative of widely held beliefs. I had to persuade the arts bodies that they would not get more money from us if they got themselves into avoidable difficulties. Our policy would be businesslike. This was the best way to get them to act in their own interests. As a result, we did not lose a single company which was a client of the Arts Council in the seven years, from 1982 to 1989, that I was there. We had a 100 per cent record in keeping them solvent. Most of them received more money and the revenue side of the arts went along surprisingly successfully.

Despite the hostility of the arts world, Margaret Thatcher herself was in fact usually very helpful. Her position on the arts was interesting. She thought the arts were a part of the national apparatus which maintained the prestige of the country. What she wanted was that foreign visitors should come to London and be immensely impressed by the quality of the best available arts in the major London venues. It was partly a matter of encouraging tourism but it was even more one of diplomatic prestige. About every eighteen months she would call me in to Downing Street and explain what she thought we ought to be doing. In short, we should be giving more money to the Royal Opera House. I would explain to her that the money came from the taxpayers, that the taxpayers were distributed throughout the country and that they did not all live in London. Our policy, I would continue, was to strengthen the arts throughout the regions, so that if somebody lived in Lancashire or in Durham they would have as good access to the arts as we could manage. She would always listen to my explanation and see that it was a perfectly reasonable view of a matter which was not at the centre of her thoughts. We would part on the friendliest of terms. Eighteen months later she would repeat her views to me. I would repeat my views to her and we would again reach a happy agreement and would go on doing what we were doing. I enjoyed my meetings. This was the arms' length policy in action.

In 1983 we published a document called *The Glory of the Garden*, which followed a conference in Yorkshire. I took the Arts Council up there to conduct a weekend strategic review, away from the London atmosphere. The document that emerged was essentially regional. Most of what *The Glory of the Garden* spelled out had been achieved long before the end of my period. This, despite Margaret's view that arts funding should be London-, if not Royal Opera House-, based.

I was enormously helped in achieving change at the Arts Council by Luke Rittner, who became the Secretary General in 1983. He was then in his early thirties. He had been the Secretary General of ABSA, the Association for Business Sponsorship of the Arts, having previously been the Director of the Bath Festival. I selected Luke, partly because I knew the work he had done at the Bath Festival had been very good and partly because business sponsorship was exactly the kind of additional funding I wanted to encourage. The very fact that he had been Secretary General of ABSA was held against him by some of the senior staff and members, who tried to block his appointment when it came forward as a recommendation from the Selection Committee to the full Council in the December 1982 meeting. It was argued by some members of the Council that he was too young, by others that he only had two O levels, by yet others that he was too keen on business sponsorship. I was not at all sure that there was a majority in his favour. I did not in the least wish to expose Luke to the humiliation of being the recommended candidate for the job of Secretary General, and then being turned down. The Director of the Welsh Arts Council, who had been the Permanent Secretary of the Welsh Office, saved me. He passed a little note across the table saying 'Why don't you postpone it for a month?' I immediately saw that, if given a month, we could be sure of a majority, whereas if we took the vote now we might lose it. So I put the vote off for a month, over Christmas, and told Luke (to his natural distress) that I did not think there had been a majority in that meeting, but that we could make sure of it for the January one. By the next meeting, there were another couple of members on the Council whose views on the matter I had managed to ascertain in advance of their appointments and Luke was chosen, as far as I remember, with nobody voting against him. How valuable it is to have experienced ex-Permanent Secretaries around in such a situation!

I worked with three Ministers for the Arts, Paul Channon, Grey Gowrie and Richard Luce. All of them respected our independence. Indeed, there was no attempt by any Minister in my time to tell us how to conduct our business. Obviously, we had to satisfy the Minister that we were doing a good job, because the Minister provided funds from the Treasury. To this end, we had a monthly meeting with the Minister and his Permanent Secretary. These meetings were actually very valuable. The Minister asked sensible questions, the Permanent Secretaries knew what they were talking about, and Luke Rittner and I enjoyed what was essentially a helpful conversation.

I enjoyed being Chairman of the Arts Council but it was not a job for which one should expect any thanks. In fact, only one person ever did thank me for Arts Council support – that was Simon Rattle, who invited us to a concert and a dinner afterwards. I felt very grateful to him.

It is one thing to expect no thanks, but another to have death threats, which one does not expect at the Arts Council. One day in September 1990 our telephone rang, and Thomas, our elder son, answered it. The caller asked for Lord Rees-Mogg, and Tom explained that he was the son rather than the father. The caller said – in an Irish accent – 'tell your father we're going to kill him'. Tom replied, 'you must be mad', and put the telephone down. I assume that this was intended as a warning rather than a threat; if you really want to kill somebody, you are unlikely to tell them so in advance.

In the 1970s and 1980s I had been aware of the threat from the IRA. The Governors of the BBC had at least one meeting in Belfast, staying in a heavily protected hotel; we were entertained to dinner at Hillsborough Castle by Douglas Hurd, then Secretary of State for Northern Ireland. Gillian and I became friends with Lucy Faulkner, the BBC Governor for Northern Ireland, and visited her home. Lucy was the widow of Brian Faulkner, the Prime Minister of Northern Ireland in the early 1970s.

Several of our friends were murdered by the IRA, or the INLA, including Airey Neave, who was killed as he left the House of Commons car park, Norris McWhirter and Tony Berry, MP, who was a contemporary of mine at the Oxford University Conservative Association.

Many others were threatened or injured, some of them gravely. In 1983 a young journalist, Philip Geddes, came to our house to interview our fourteen-year-old son Jacob for the *Daily Express*. A few months later he was killed by a car bomb outside Harrods.

In 1988, I was invited to join the committee to celebrate the bicentenary of the revolution of 1688–9 which brought William of Orange to the throne. The celebration was Anglo-Dutch, and I was invited as Chairman of the Arts Council, in case there should be any artistic celebrations. It was a strange committee; so far as I know, it never met. At any rate I never attended a meeting. The Chairman, whom I never met either, was a well-known brewer who lived in Hampshire. I was never invited to any of the Anglo-Dutch celebrations which we were supposed to organize. Unfortunately, the IRA assumed that the committee must exist not to celebrate the Anglo-Dutch relationship, but to celebrate the Battle of the Boyne, and that it had therefore some sinister Unionist purpose.

I already knew that some people, presumably sympathizers with the IRA, regarded me with hostility, perhaps because they saw me as a member of the British Establishment, and perhaps because of my opposition to the BBC documentary about Martin McGuinness. As a Catholic of Irish descent I was, in fact, not oversympathetic to Protestant Unionism. One summer evening in the early 1980s, I had received a package, postmarked Cork. Annunziata was about four years old, and I was reading to her in the sitting room at the Old Rectory, Hinton Blewitt. I started to open the package. It contained a dummy bomb, including a detonator which was a Jew's harp, such as we had played with as children, a battery and some sticks of Plasticine, which, for all I knew, might have been Semtex. I sprang to my feet and threw the package into the garden. We spent the evening with the Uphills, who were our next-door neighbours, and the bomb squad brought their remote-controlled robot, which worked like a toy dog, to blow up the bomb. Bits of Plasticine were scattered over the garden.

My association with the 1689 Committee led to a more serious threat. We first knew that there might be a problem in early September 1990. Mr Leakey, our gardener, who lived a few doors away, was having trouble sleeping. One night, at about three o'clock in the morning, he heard a car draw up and stop outside the Old Rectory. He saw two men get out and inspect our premises.

A few days later, we had another report. A lady from Hinton Blewitt was out riding. She met a friend of hers who worked in an estate agency in Chew Magna. They chatted, and the friend mentioned a strange occurrence which had happened at her office a day or two before. Three men had drawn up in a large car; two of them had come into the estate agents and enquired whether there was a cottage available in Hinton Blewitt. They spoke in strong Irish accents. The agency had no such cottage on their books, but they thought it odd that the Irishmen should specify Hinton Blewitt, which is a little-known village even by local standards. The Hinton Blewitt lady knew Mr Leakey, or knew a friend of his. At any rate, the Hinton Blewitt defence system worked, and we were soon told.

It was a day or two later that Thomas received the call. We telephoned the police, and were put on to Special Branch. The response was very impressive. We were given a twenty-four-hour guard of armed police, complete with flak jackets and sub-machine guns. They worked in three eight-hour shifts of four men each. In all, twenty-eight signed our visitors' book. For much of the time we were in London, but Tom was at home, and they taught him how to assemble a machine gun and put on a flak jacket. They stayed in our drawing room from 29 September until 12 November.

My unfortunate Chairman, the brewer, had a similar guard. The Irishmen, presumably the same ones, did come up his drive, in the middle of the night. The police tried to catch them, but they escaped, only to be caught at Stonehenge. They were imprisoned in Brixton, but escaped again. I believe they are still alive, living in Ireland.

I remember that the police gave us a code word to use on the telephone in case we had been kidnapped. It was 'Dickens'. We thought out ways of bringing the word 'Dickens' into an apparently innocent conversation in such a way as to deceive an IRA guard. Not with much success.

We never heard anything more from the IRA. The 1689 Committee must hold a record for achieving nothing at considerable expense.

FIFTEEN

The Best of Business

Whilst I was Chairman of the Arts Council Jacob Rothschild was the Chairman of the Board of Trustees of the National Gallery. I had first met Jacob in the early 1970s and had had an account with Rothschild's bank while he was still there, to help deal with my mother's estate duty. In 1987, I joined the Board of J. Rothschild Holdings plc as a non-executive director. I was invited to do so by Nils Taube, whom I had known since the early 1950s. Nils was widely admired in the City as one of the most brilliant and successful investors of his time. Indeed, he was a fund manager's guru. Nils had come to England after the war, his family were Baltic barons in Estonia with historic connections going back to the Swedish Empire and the period of the tsars. His mother was English. He had spent the war in Germany, where at high school he was known to the German children as the Englander, and had survived that experience. He had then joined the stockbroking firm of Kitkat & Aitken and become its senior partner at a relatively early age. I had met him through Arthur Winspear, who was writing the Lex column for the *Financial Times*; Arthur was later recruited by Siegmund Warburg.

Jacob Rothschild, who was establishing his own financial group, had brought Nils Taube into his business at St James's

Place as the principal fund manager. There was also Gilbert de Botton who was building his investment company. I served from 1987 to 1990 on the Board of J. Rothschild Holdings plc and on the Board of J. Rothschild Investment Management from 1987 to 1996. Jacob has a remarkable combination of experience and skills in banking. He applied his entrepreneurial energy to rescuing three great buildings: Spencer House and Somerset House, in London, and one of the Rothschild homes, Waddesdon Manor, in Buckinghamshire.

I had always made fairly frequent visits to the United States as a journalist, and after leaving *The Times* decided to explore the possibilities of developing professional work in America. My first step was to propose to an American publisher that I should write a book on the Republican Party. Despite the fact that I had been in the United States at least once or twice a year for twenty years, I found that I was overreaching myself. I simply did not know enough about the inner workings of the Republicans to write a satisfactory book. However, I had one interesting encounter which arose from this failed attempt. I had an interview with President Nixon, ten years after Watergate. I had met him once before, in London, and had then been impressed by his strategic sense of American politics.

I arrived a little early at his New York apartment, and can remember the sadness and sense of failure in his expression. I can also remember his observations about Republican canvassing. 'There comes a time in every Republican campaign when someone says "let's go the other side of the tracks". The trouble is that the Democrats already are the other side of the tracks.'

In that early visit I decided that I would want to live in Boston, founded by my Winthrop forebears, if my American work took off, and we decided to have an American as well as an English home. That never materialized, but we did have one excellent holiday in Plymouth, Massachusetts, the family home of Muffy Brandon, who had married the *Sunday Times* correspondent, Henry. Browsing in their bookshelves I came across the 1910 Year Book of Harvard University, which included Muffy's father's entry, and the entry for T. S. Eliot. However, my seventeenth-century ancestor had gone to Harvard much earlier than that. Samuel Winthrop was in the Harvard class of 1643.

My conscious plan to develop an American career never reached the stage that would have justified the purchase of a home there. My successor as Editor of *The Times*, Harold Evans, had a much more substantial American career, with his wife, Tina Brown, and has become an American citizen.

It was a chance meeting in Oxford which resulted in my first major business contact with the United States. In the summer of 1982, we paid a family visit to White Barn, the home of Philip and Valerie Goodhart. A year before they had let their cottage to a visiting American, Jim Davidson. Jim happened to be spending a short holiday in England and had come to lunch with the Goodharts. I went for a walk with him after lunch, and we talked about our interest in the development of a newsletter, with an investment theme. We took the optimistic view that investors would be interested in a newsletter written from an American and an English point of view. In fact, it was not our different angles that proved of interest, but our agreement on the themes of low taxation, sound money and personal independence. We were also both interested in using economic history as part of the basis of economic forecasting. Jim already had a particular interest in the Great Slump of the United States, then only fifty years behind us. Fifty years was the approximate term of the major economic cycle named after the Russian economist Nikolai Kondratiev. I later published a translation of Kondratiev's works with Pickering & Chatto (Publishers).

Jim Davidson and I agreed to publish an investment letter, which would develop these ideas. Initially, it was called 'London and Washington'. In 1983 we organized a small company of which I gave a small percentage to each of our children.

Later on, the opportunity arose to buy another newsletter, Strategic Investment, which had a disagreement with the American regulator, SEC. At that period SEC was claiming to regulate investment letters, a claim which has been overruled in the courts on constitutional grounds. I went to the SEC office with Jim Davidson and found that SEC required that all the shareholders should be registered. Annunziata was registered as a fit and proper person to give investment advice. She had no criminal record. Her infant school was accepted as an educational qualification, she had the minimum shareholding. She was duly registered with SEC at the age of four. We changed the name of the London and Washington to Strategic Investment, under which name the newsletter flourished.

Two developments were helpful to what was now called Strategic Investment. We transferred the commercial end to Bill Bonner, a long-term friend of Jim. His company, Agora, operated out of Baltimore. He was very successful in raising the sales. Bill and I also formed a partnership in London; I am still the Chairman of Fleet Street Holdings, which is his company. He also bought an equal interest with me in Pickering & Chatto (Publishers), when Pickerings had sold its antiquarian side and needed money to expand in academic publishing.

In the meantime, Jim Davidson and I published three books, each of which had an English as well as an American edition. They were works of futurology: *Blood in the Streets*, *The Great Reckoning* and *The Sovereign Individual*. All three forecast a return to conditions of recession, which occurred in Japan, temporarily in the rest of Asia and belatedly in the dot.com world in the United States. Those forecasts of doom were surprisingly popular in the United States. Rupert Murdoch said that one of them, probably *The Great Reckoning*, had kept him awake all night, which was, no doubt, why they sold so well.

In all explorations of the projected future there will be misjudgements. However, our three books and Strategic Investment got more right than wrong, including the earlier stages of the growth of China, the decline of Japan after 1989, the disintegration of the Soviet Union, the fall of the Berlin Wall. We also foresaw the growth of terrorism and, specifically, the vulnerability of the World Trade Center. In 1993, I wrote in the preface of the English edition of *The Sovereign Individual*: 'For the individual, explosive power is cheap, for the state, the power to counter terrorism is expensive and usually ineffective. Society is vulnerable, like the plate glass skyscrapers of the World Trade Center.'

A very interesting friend whom I met through Strategic Investment was Chris Ruddy, who founded his own magazine, *NewsMax*, in the late nineties. That is now a very successful conservative magazine. Chris asked me to be the Chairman in its early days, which I enjoyed.

Other parts of my working life also took me to America. When I was Chairman of the Investment Committee of the Esmée Fairbairn Foundation, the Cambridge Associates, whose head office is in Boston, were, as I have said, our investment advisers. I arranged for an annual meeting in Boston, to keep the committee in touch with US investment. It helped to know, for better or worse, what the US market was thinking or expecting.

Since a heart attack in 2002, my trips to the United States have been less frequent. However, as I write this I have just returned from a visit to San Francisco with Gillian, which took in talking to a class at Stanford, a university I much admire, on *The Sovereign Individual*, and a visit to the Greek Theatre at Berkeley, where my mother had started her theatrical career in 1913.

My most important business experience was on the Board of GEC when Arnold Weinstock was the Managing Director. I served on the board from 1982 to 1997. I had first met Arnold at a *Times* lunch in 1968. He was making a bid for Associated Electrical Industries, a large and stultified electrical business, which had been run on grouse moors and premier cru claret – I was once served Mouton Rothschild at an AEI business lunch – by Lord Chandos, who had been a wartime Minister and a friend of Brendan Bracken and Churchill. Tony Vice, who was editing The Times Business News, suggested that we should invite Arnold to lunch at the new *Times* building in Blackfriars.

At that stage, Arnold had a ferocious reputation as a cost-cutting businessman, a reputation he did nothing to discourage. He had become the Managing Director of the General Electric Company in 1961, as a result of a reverse takeover by the much smaller Radio and Allied. I had covered that takeover as City Editor of the *Sunday Times*, but somehow – perhaps professional incompetence – I had never met Arnold, though I had commented sympathetically on his restructuring at GEC. Because of his ruthless reputation, I was cautious about supporting his bid for AEI, and I began the lunch in a sceptical mood. He had a quickness and amusement that was extremely charming. As Tony Vice had expected, during the lunch I became convinced that AEI would benefit from being reconstructed by Arnold. Lord Hanson, himself both a successful manager and a trainer of managers, once said to me that he regarded Arnold as the best manager in post-war British industry.

Arnold came from a Jewish-Polish family. He grew up in Stoke Newington, was orphaned at the age of nine and brought up by a much older brother. Arnold did not himself believe that he had any particular management method. He thought that making business decisions was usually a matter of common sense. He was distrustful of what he called the 'conceptual' approach to business, which makes it the more ironic that GEC was destroyed by a conceptual extravagance in its approach to telecoms within a few years of his retirement. He did not believe that you should subordinate the ordinary rules of sound business to broadly framed strategic ideas. You should not pay more than a transaction was worth, simply because it fitted into some strategic scheme.

I had known both GEC and AEI as a journalist for many years and had seen how Arnold had transformed the old GEC. Economy, attention to detail, efficient reporting and personal responsibility were the four pillars of his management style. Arnold hated committee decisions and held his executives to account for the outcomes of their own decisions. Hard work was essential, and no one worked harder than he did.

This approach came across at the lunch, as did Arnold's sardonic humour. I remember a later lunch at GEC when a pompous South African supporter of apartheid was a principal guest. The South African was explaining how impossible it would be to have equal pay for both white and black workers. Arnold intervened to say that he believed in equal pay – the white workers in South Africa should be paid the same as the blacks. Politicians sometimes found this aspect of Arnold's humour a little uncomfortable.

Arnold was the opposite of many 'business leaders'. He never spent a penny of GEC's money carelessly, but he was very generous with his own, giving to charities, willing to lend it to help his friends, extremely hospitable, both at home and on the race course. On the whole he preferred his own hospitality to other people's; he seldom went to receptions, which in later years he found tiring.

The weekend after that first lunch, I was going down to Ston Easton for the weekend, on the Bath Pullman. As I got off the train I again met Arnold, who had recently bought a Georgian house, Bowden Park, near Lacock in Wiltshire. We had a brief conversation, and agreed that we should exchange visits in the country. From that time until Arnold's death in 2002, we saw each other almost continuously; our two families became friends, and we have remained friends after Arnold's death. Netta Weinstock still lives at Bowden.

Arnold and Netta came to our son Jacob's christening in 1969, and Arnold saw himself as a quasi godparent. We enjoyed each other's successes, such as Arnold's victory with his horse, Troy, in the 100th Derby. When I had business problems, I discussed them with him, and always received excellent advice. Arnold joined the syndicate which in 1981 was ready to make an offer for *The Times* if no joint bidder for the newspapers came forward.

With Rab Butler I had always felt that he had a much deeper understanding of British politics than anyone else I knew – certainly deeper than mine. It was the same with Arnold in the analysis of any business question. We never had a discussion of any business problem, without Arnold pointing to some relevant issue that I had not seen.

In 1981, when I had decided to leave *The Times*, Arnold invited me to join the Board of GEC, then still at the height of its success; GEC was the most valuable industrial business on the London Stock Exchange. I actually joined the board a few weeks before I left *The Times*. In those days there was no distinction between executive and non-executive directors. All directors were expected to help the company succeed in its business; some were full-time and some, in varying degrees, part-time. The idea of separate corporate governance by the non-executive director, which tends to split the board into two camps, had not yet arisen. To the end of my service at GEC, fifteen years later, I held the view that all directors have an equal responsibility in company law to the staff, the business and the shareholders.

Arnold had a complete open-door policy for all directors, though we did not all make equal use of it. He usually lunched upstairs in the GEC offices, and I kept in touch with the business by lunching there most weeks, as well as by attending the largely impromptu meetings which flowed through his office. At a crisis period, such as the final takeover of Plessey, which might involve the press and public issues of which I had experience, I would work almost full-time for a week or so. Otherwise I was merely part-time.

One role which I saw as useful was to be an independent auditor of debates. From below, Arnold could be seen as an autocratic leader, though he was anything but that. His method was that of Socratic questioning, at budget meetings or at board-level discussions, which he preferred to formal board meetings. He was interested in establishing the truth by enquiring into the arguments. He did not come to such discussions with unshakeable preconceptions, and was prepared to accept arguments, even from junior staff, which convinced him. His authority was real enough, but it was based on his detailed and meticulous knowledge and his superior business judgement. He usually won the argument after a process of open debate on policy.

People tend to think that the role of a business leader is a relatively simple matter of giving orders and bullying people, and there are indeed business leaders of that type. Like a general, a businessman employing 100,000 people generates a certain awe, without resorting to bullying. What has struck me most about the most creative business figures I have worked for is their intellectual grasp of the businesses they were running. They know in detail what they are doing and why. That was true of Roy Thomson, of Rupert Murdoch and of Arnold Weinstock. I am not particularly modest, but I realized that they understood their businesses not only better than I did – that was obvious – but better than I ever could.

I once did a calculation of Arnold's intellectual grasp on GEC. At the time, with the main groups and their subsidiaries, we had about a hundred operating companies. Arnold had a detailed understanding of all of them, and could detect variations from their expected performance within a very short time of them arising. He operated quite largely by spotting, and seeking to eliminate, negative deviations from the planned budget.

I reckoned, and I may have been flattering myself, that I could have handled about ten of these hundred businesses, but that I would only have had about a tenth of Arnold's understanding of the way they were developing. That would have made me, on a rather favourable estimate, 1 per cent as effective as a manager of the 100,000 staff of GEC as Arnold was. I feel much the same about my experience of the Thomson Organization or Newscorp. I can cope with the interplay of general ideas, but it is not just general ideas, but details, which determine success in business.

However, my general ideas were sometimes good. Naturally, I remember the advice that Arnold did not take, particularly when it proved correct. There were two points at which it was important. I advised Arnold to set up a full-scale Treasury operation to maximize the return on GEC's cash. Modern Treasury operations are not infallible, but by the use of different currency exposures and derivatives they can increase yield and reduce risk. I never managed to persuade Arnold that this complexity would benefit the company. He stuck with the fact that GEC was a manufacturing company, not a bank, and that sterling was the currency in which most of its costs were incurred, and, indeed, in which its dividends were paid. I have little doubt that I was right; we had a cash mountain; given more modern management it could have been considerably larger. I must admit that with hindsight Arnold's judgement looks a good deal better than when we first discussed the issue.

The other occasion on which my advice was not taken was over the chairmanship. Lord Carrington had been made Chairman in 1983, a couple of years after I joined the board. He was an excellent Chairman, popular in the company and a great asset in the defence world and, indeed, with the British Government. Unfortunately, he was then offered the job of Secretary General of NATO. It was a case of the old Punch joke 'She was a good cook as cooks go, and as cooks go, she went'. What happened then was that Arnold asked Lord Aldington, who had been the Chairman in the 1960s, and was then the Deputy Chairman, to sound out the board about a possible successor. The candidate Aldington, and, I think, Carrington, had in mind, was Jim Prior.

Aldington duly sounded out the board, but until five minutes past midnight he did not sound me out. I had known Jim since we entered Charterhouse together in 1941. Arnold was a highly intellectual Jewish businessman; Jim was a solid-minded East Anglian politician. The problem, as I saw it, was that they were far too dissimilar to make a satisfactory partnership.

When Toby Aldington finally did tell me the plan, I objected, on the grounds that Jim was not a suitable Chairman for Arnold.

I also felt that Jim had been a weak Secretary of State for Employment in 1979; certainly he had done nothing to help us during *The Times* stoppage. A further problem for GEC would be that Jim had been forced out by Margaret Thatcher, who, despite his good work in Northern Ireland, saw him as a Tory wet and 'not one of us', which he was not. It did not seem to me to make much sense to appoint as Chairman of a major defence contractor someone whom the Prime Minister rightly saw as a political enemy.

I went to Arnold and expostulated. He was surprised, as Toby Aldington had not told him my views. He said that he was sorry, but that it was now too late to go back. The job had been offered and accepted. I wrote a note to Jim, saying that I had been opposed to his appointment, that I thought it better I should let him know, but that I would no doubt prove to be one of the least of his problems. That proved to be true.

My relationship with Jim was a very English one. There were aspects of our characters which allowed there to be some friendship. But there were also aspects of our characters which naturally clashed, and had done so since we were thirteen. On economic issues, he was an anti-Thatcher wet, and I was a pro-Thatcher dry. He had made a most distinguished career as a politician, and I had made my career as a journalist. For more than ten years at GEC we jogged along together, and Arnold and Jim jogged along together. Jim proved to be a useful high-level salesman for the company. Senior politicians give access to other senior politicians. Jim took skilful advantage of such openings.

It was only at the end that the difficulties emerged, and they affected the succession to Arnold as Managing Director. Arnold had originally wanted to be succeeded by his son, Simon. I am not sure that was a wise idea, nor am I sure that Simon wanted it. He was totally loyal to his father and was himself highly intelligent, but he did not have his father's executive temperament. He would, in my view, have made a better, indeed a very good, Chairman, rather than a Managing Director.

Arnold was in his early seventies. He seems to have come to the conclusion that Simon could not succeed immediately, but that an interim appointment would allow an eventual succession. That became the plan. Jim Prior wanted Arnold to go. He thought GEC needed new leadership. The relationship between Arnold and Jim had never been a close one. Arnold had never really respected Jim and Jim had, so far as I could tell, always resented that. Jim seemed to be using a politician's methods to persuade the City and the press that Arnold should go. That judgement was a legitimate view for a Chairman to take, but the fact that Jim appeared to be briefing against Arnold did nothing to improve their relationship.

Arnold and Jim settled for an outside candidate for the succession, George Simpson, a Scottish accountant with something of a track record for doing deals. Arnold still saw Simpson as a temporary Managing Director. Jim saw Simpson as the man to make the radical changes he had come to regard as necessary. He wanted not only to get Arnold to retire, but also – as it seemed – to get rid of Arnold's influence altogether.

I had the misfortune to be Chairman of the GEC Remuneration Committee, and therefore had to negotiate Simpson's salary, but I was not a member of the Nominations Committee, and therefore had no part in the decision to appoint him. I cannot tell whether I would have seen through his bluff and trustworthy Scottish manner.

I first met George Simpson at an introductory meeting when all the directors lunched with him in the office. By then his appointment was settled. He did make rather a good impression, expressing his admiration for Arnold's work and, more importantly, his expectation of continuing to work with Arnold's staff, and his desire to consult Arnold himself as a valued elder statesman. It is natural enough for new appointees to say these things, and they should always be taken with a pinch of salt. In this case a bucket of salt would have been more appropriate.

As soon as the handover took place, the very able team that had worked with Arnold began to be dismissed. I remember a meeting I had with Jim Prior in which he explained that George Simpson wanted to have his own team. Jim suggested that I might choose to retire six months before the end of my current three-year appointment, to allow Simpson to have his own team of non-executive directors. Non-executive directors are not there to protect or obey the chief executive. I served out my time, as I could see no reason not to do so. Several first-class executive directors were then eased out, and Arnold himself became *persona non grata*. He still had an office in the building, but the executive directors were not encouraged to talk to him.

Simpson wanted to do a deal with the company. His first proposal was to merge with British Aerospace. I remember a stormy board meeting in which some of the non-executive directors questioned the merits of the proposals, which did not seem to be in the shareholders' interests. With the help of my son Jacob, whom I relied on for a much greater financial expertise than my own, I asked some pointed questions. Those did not go down at all well. George Simpson went red in the face, said that he could not be expected to deal with amateurs, and left the room in a huff. The unattractive British Aerospace proposals did not proceed, which turned out to be bad news for the shareholders. They were unsatisfactory, but what actually followed was far worse.

So far as I can make out, the departure of Arnold and his key colleagues brought to an end the existing financial control systems of the company. From some time in 1997, GEC seems to have been flying blind, with little knowledge of the growing risks of the business. I left the board in the autumn of 1997, and never met Mr Mayo, the new Finance Director. When I left, nothing irrevocable had happened. The company still had good businesses and an extremely strong balance sheet. Jim Prior left shortly afterwards, and was not responsible, as Chairman, for the disastrous decisions which followed. However, many of my non-executive colleagues remained to the end, and share the responsibility for the catastrophe. I sold my shares on leaving the board, because I thought Simpson was not a man to invest in.

Simpson and Mayo decided to change the name of GEC to Marconi, partly, I suppose, to repudiate the Weinstock legacy. They realized the cash and borrowed further billions to buy telecoms manufacturing companies. They did this at the top of the Wall Street boom, but Marconi's shares also rose. They had little or no personal knowledge of the telecoms business. Even after this buying spree, Marconi was by no means a market leader. Telecoms orders turned down. Marconi responded more slowly than its competitors. It had to sell good assets to raise cash to repay the loans. The company ended up in the hands of the banks; the shareholders, including many members of the old GEC staff, lost almost every penny. A great business was destroyed by business decisions that were totally reckless.

Obviously it was a tragedy for Arnold. After reaching the age of seventy, and after a life of extraordinary and hard-earned success in business, he had lost his son Simon by illness. He had always hoped that Simon would be his successor. He had lost his business through stupid decisions on which he had never been consulted, and lost a large sum of the money he had made. Yet he was remarkably resilient and peaceful under these blows of fate. He knew that it was the loss of Simon which mattered most. His own health was failing, and he bore that with equanimity. When I had a heart attack in April of 2002, he rang St Thomas' Hospital to give me support. We met again at Bowden, after I had recovered, and he invited us to stay on holiday in France in August. Before August he was dead. It was like the Book of Job. I have the happiest memories of his friendship.

SIXTEEN

My Road to Bibliomania

My psychology, and a significant part of my life, has been bookish. The first antiquarian book I bought came from George's of Bristol. I was eleven. It was the start of a lifetime of collecting old books. For ten years, in my fifties and early sixties, I also dealt in them. My first purchase reflected the last sunset of my childish interest in the horrors of state executions, but it turned out to throw a light on a strange historic episode in my ancestry.

The title page reads '*The Dying Speeches and Behaviour of the several State Prisoners that have been Executed the last three hundred years ... London 1720*'. It was not until 1998, nearly sixty years later, that I discovered that Thomas Walcot, one of the prisoners who suffered that most barbarous form of execution, was a direct ancestor of my grandmother, Emily Walcot Savory. He was executed for his part in the Rye House Plot, an amateurish attempt to kidnap and murder King Charles II, together with his brother, the Duke of York, later James II. His part in the plot amounted to little more than joining in alehouse gossip. Walcot was drawn to Tyburn on a hurdle and there hanged, drawn and quartered on 20 July 1683, and his head was displayed at Aldersgate in the City of London.

Book collecting provided me with a second and independent education. Every book collector is aware of what Horace

Walpole, a great eighteenth-century collector, termed 'serendipity', the way in which a relevant book or passage comes to hand, almost by chance. In those early years, I collected almost entirely eighteenth-century books, which were still available at second-hand prices.

Throughout my life I have been reading like this, buying books which had at first only a collector's interest, and finding passages which enlarged my knowledge or stimulated my imagination. This has been how I have read poetry, history, economics and religion. Like Samuel Johnson, I have seldom read books through. I dip, I skim, I use the index. I am not a good reader from the beginning to the end, except for occasional novels. I am aware that this does not make me a critic, an historian, an economist or a theologian. It is not a systematic study of any subject. It has, however, been useful to me as a journalist, has given me a large range of perhaps superficial knowledge, has given life to my imagination and, in terms of religion, strength to my faith. It has provided over seventy years of interest and pleasure. My books have been my education and often my friendships.

As a book collector I was initially funded by my father. In 1942, when I was fourteen, seeing how my interest was developing, he gave me a generous allowance for books, starting with a cheque for £15, the equivalent of some £450 in modern money. I made my first use of these funds, at Bayntun's Bookshop in Bath – they are famous for their bookbindings – and I was later to become a friend of Hylton Bayntun-Coward, who took on the family business after the war. During the war the shop was run by a manager, who sold me a very fair copy of the First Edition of Boswell's *Life of Johnson* for £8 10s, perhaps now the equivalent of £250. Such a copy would now fetch about £2000 in an antiquarian bookshop.

It was on my journeys to and from Charterhouse that I made my vital connection with serious book collecting. I gave myself a few hours in London; time for some shopping, time for lunch, which could be obtained for five shillings, under wartime price control, at the Savoy Hotel, time for getting from Paddington to Waterloo. By 1942, when I was first making these journeys, there was no daytime bombing. By 1944, when there were rockets and flying bombs, I enjoyed my hours in London so much that I disregarded the bombs, though I still have a memory of ducking for cover as a buzz bomb's engine cut out over Oxford Street.

Sometime in 1942, I took a cab from Paddington to the British Museum, because I had heard that there were good bookshops in that area. I wandered around and found McLeish and Sons, at 22 Little Russell Street. There were then two brothers, George, who kept the shop, and Charles, who did the binding and went to buy at auctions. George was my tutor in book collecting. He taught me the basis of valuing a book, its rarity, condition, associations if any, intrinsic interest and fashion. He was very patient, as I now see, a cautious, kindly, thoughtful, shrewd Scot.

In those days, a good bookseller could build an excellent stock for very little money. When he retired, George McLeish gave me one of the two surviving sets of the firm's catalogues. The stock at the time of my first visit is reflected in the catalogue for December 1942; that year would have been near the low point of wartime prices. It includes First Editions of Blackstone's *Commentaries*, 1765–9 (£48), Boswell's *Johnson*, 1791 (£20), Butler's *Hudibras*, 1663, 1664, 1678 (£35), Chesterfield's *Letters*, 1774 (£14), Defoe's *Plague Year*, 1722 (£10), Dodoens' *Nieve Herball*, 1578 (£40), Goldsmith's *Traveller*, 1765 (£18), Harcourt's *Voyage to Guiana*, 1613 (£20), Harding's *Chronicle*, 1543 (£20), Pope's *Rape of the Lock*, 1712 (£15), Priestley's *Essay on Government*, 1768 (£2 10s), Raleigh's *Discovery of Guiana*, 1596 (£28), Rousseau's *The Confessions*, 1783 (£3), Mary Shelley's *Frankenstein*, 1818 (£28), The Pope–Swift *Miscellanies*, 1727–32 (£8), Tennyson's *Poems by Two Brothers*, 1827 (£15) and Voltaire's *Letters Concerning the English Nation*, 1733 (£1). I bought, and still have, the Pope–Swift *Miscellanies*, but the range of the McLeish stock at that time meant that I was seeing really good and important books and being taught what values they then had. Now the prices seem amazingly low, even when adjusted for inflation.

If I had spent £100 on McLeish's December 1942 catalogue, I could probably get £15,000 to £20,000 at auction for my purchases now, even after paying the seller's commission. Such a purchase would not have made me rich – the real rate of return after inflation is about 3 per cent – but it would have provided a reliable store of value. Book prices taught me how inflation works; that proved to be a useful lesson for the late twentieth century. Book buying also taught me that it is markets which determine prices; supply and demand decides.

Later I went to many other bookshops, including Robinson, Quaritch and Maggs in London, Blackwells in Oxford, Flemings in New York. I had particularly close associations with Martin Hamlyn, both at Robinson's in Pall Mall and at Murray Hill in Sloane Avenue. After my friend Dudley Massey died in the early 1980s, I bought his business of Pickering & Chatto.

My love for the eighteenth century and the influence of my painter sister Anne led to collecting paintings as well as books. We had a number of family portraits at Cholwell, including a Somerset conversation piece of the early 1730s, painted at Cholwell by the local Somerset painter Richard Phelps, which shows the then widow Mogg with her five children, including my direct ancestor John Mogg, Elizabeth, Francis, William and

Jacob, who was born posthumously. There were also the oil paintings of my grandparents, and the pastels of my father and aunt as children. So we had some paintings, but only a family portrait collection. Even the conversation piece only came back to Cholwell from my great-aunts when I was six or seven.

I have bought four seventeenth- or eighteenth-century portraits in oils, which represent people I greatly admire. In terms of my admiration, they would rank as Alexander Pope (1688–1744), the greatest English poet of the classical period; William Pitt, first Earl of Chatham (1708–88), the greatest English Minister of the first British Empire; John Locke (1632–1704), the greatest English liberal philosopher; and Joshua Reynolds (1723–92), the greatest English classical portrait painter. I bought the portraits of Pope and Chatham in the 1960s, each for about £100 at Christie's; the Reynolds at a Bath auction in the early 1980s for £450, and the Locke, from our own stock at Pickering & Chatto, in the early 1990s for £2500. I also bought another portrait of Pope, in pastel, privately for £500 in about 1980, when I remember that I was feeling particularly short of funds, and was reluctant to part with the money. In all, I acquired six major English historical portraits, which have given me enduring pleasure, for about £3500, over a period of some thirty years.

In total I now have about six portraits of Pope, two of which are by Kneller, the leading portrait painter in the reign of William and Mary and Queen Anne. The oil painting is particularly moving. Kneller's reputation has always been obscured by the large number of hack portraits of the aristocracy he turned out as though on a production line. He had a facile ability to catch a likeness, and painted the faces himself, but often he employed others, some of them good artists in their own right, to paint in the clothes. So, after all, did most of the busiest portrait painters, including Van Dyck, Lely and Reynolds himself.

This painting shows Pope with a pen in his hands; there is a Kneller drawing which shows the same pose of the hands, and the general pose is similar to that of his excellent portrait of Dr Mendoza, the Spanish physician, which was in the Walpole collection and is now in St Petersburg. The Pope portrait is inscribed, under the paint, '*Alexander Pope, at the age of XVI*', and is the second youngest surviving portrait, dating from 1704 when he was being introduced to London as the boy poet. His body already shows the warping of his spine, which stunted his growth. The face is astonishingly intelligent, luminously so.

The other Kneller is a pastel, relating closely to the portrait owned by Pope's friend Lord Harcourt, and seems to be the original pastel drawing from which the Harcourt oil painting was taken. It is more fully coloured than most of the other Kneller drawings. The pastel is unfinished, and has various differences from the oil painting and from subsequent engravings.

One of my children recently remarked that I was an easy person to deal with in the home because all my aggression ran out into my pen. That may be true of my journalism, but it is certainly true of Pope's poetry; he was a sweet man with a vicious pen. I do not necessarily think that one should be like Pope; I admire the character of some other eighteenth-century figures more than I admire his. Samuel Johnson was a nobler character; George Berkeley was more spiritual. But Pope himself knew all that. Much as I have learned from both Johnson and Berkeley – and intellectually, as I have observed, Johnson was a second father to me – Pope has been much more like a brother, what T. S. Eliot called '*mon semblable, mon frère*'. I have felt like that about at least two of my friends on earth, Clive Wigram and Arnold Weinstock, both Jewish. I was probably also drawn to Pope by his Roman Catholicism. That does resemble my own – a strong faith, but little dogma. And, since I have owned his youthful portrait, I have felt compassion for the young genius, deprived, by an illness in adolescence, of so much he would have enjoyed in life. I pray for him; perhaps he prays for me.

That was my 'elective affinity' to Pope, and I do not have anything like the same intuitive sympathy with my other heroes. They have also played a large part in my education, but they have not, in the same way, entered my inner mind. It occurs to me, as I write, that all four have two qualities I admire very much, qualities which I have recognized in other people I admire: energy and fertility of intellect.

Pitt the Elder's widow lived to see Pitt the Younger become Prime Minister. She told someone that she greatly admired her son – who was the man who saved Britain and Europe from the tyranny of Napoleon, just as Winston Churchill saved Britain and Europe from the tyranny of Hitler. She added that, having known the two men, it was her husband who had the more extraordinary genius. From a comparatively weak political base, Pitt the Elder organized victory in the Seven Years War, which made the British Empire the controlling power in North America and India. The English language, and to a large extent English culture, permeates the modern world because of his work: 1759, 'the year of victories', was the turning point, and those victories decided that it would be England rather than France which would do much to shape the modern world.

Pitt the Elder was a manic depressive; he suffered from bipolar disorder. To some extent, it may be a positive condition for great men; certainly Winston Churchill also suffered from these mood swings, though not to the degree of Pitt.

My portrait of Pitt the Elder is the original sketch in oils from which all the state portraits, and even some statues, were copied in Chatham's later years. It is unfinished, with the clothes painted in a rust-red. It is inscribed '*Will. Pitt, Earl of Chatham etca 1773. Richd Brompton*'. The unfortunate Richard Brompton made a good market in portraits of Chatham derived from this original, but later sought to advance his career by going to paint for Catherine the Great in St Petersburg, where he died of pneumonia. This portrait shows Chatham looking like a dominant eagle, in his own long white hair; he also looks, as he did, more than a little crazy. The state portraits show him sanitized, in a proper wig. There is no doubt that Brompton's sketch is the most revealing surviving portrait.

Certainly Chatham meets the test I set for my heroes of energy and fertility of resources. He was able to bring superior force to bear against the French challenge, in Europe with his ally Frederick the Great, in India with Clive and the East India Company, in Canada with the young British hero General Wolfe. He was able to dominate Parliament – his colleagues were in awe of him. If his advice had been taken, the American colonies, which he had defended in the Seven Years War, would have been able to live in a good relationship with the English crown. Bute, North and George III threw away Chatham's legacy. He understood America, and he understood freedom. Along with Churchill, he is the greatest Prime Minister in English history. When one looks at his portrait, one can have a faint glimpse of the energy which dominated his contemporaries. It is, in its way, a terrifying energy, such as one might have seen also in the face of Julius Caesar at the Capitol, or Lenin in 1917.

If Pitt the Elder is the supreme English example of the man of power, John Locke is the supreme example of the English philosopher. His doctrine of liberty justified the British

Revolution of 1688, and inspired the American Revolution of 1776 and, to a lesser extent, the French Revolution of 1789. Tolerance, independence, the rule of law, freedom of choice, liberty, the rights of the citizen, are essential to the idea of a free society. Locke provides the basic historic argument for all of them. When Jefferson drafted the Declaration of Independence, he took two phrases of Locke, 'Life, Liberty and Estate' and 'the pursuit of happiness' and moulded them together. Ever since I first studied Locke under Marcus Dick at Balliol, I had been gripped by his political ideas, all the more so as I have always lived within a few miles of Locke's house in Pensford, Somerset, and of Wrington, where he was born.

The portrait is not a great one. Locke is shown by the unknown, perhaps Dutch, artist, sitting in a library. He is reading what appears to be a book of maps; the portrait may belong to that period, around 1673, when Locke, under his patron the first Earl of Shaftesbury, was Secretary of the Council of Trade. The portrait includes a bleeding bowl, the sign of his profession as a doctor. In the late 1660s, at the start of his friendship with Shaftesbury, he acted as Shaftesbury's surgeon, draining an ulcer. I have not been able to trace a provenance for the painting, though the firm of Dawson's of Pall Mall, from whose stock it originally came, were very active at the time of the Shaftesbury book sales in the 1970s.

My portrait of Joshua Reynolds is an example of his last great self-portrait. An inscription on the back states that it was given to William Mason, the poet, who was a close friend and became Reynolds' literary executor. Reynolds gave his friends several copies of this portrait. No doubt they are studio copies, but they would have been done under his supervision and conceivably been touched by his brush. The frame of this portrait is identical with that of another copy, which hangs in the oval dining room at Brooks's Club in St James's Street. Presumably, therefore, both were framed for Reynolds, before he gave them to his friends.

In 1980, my old friend the bookseller Dudley Massey had died. The Masseys had become the proprietors of the antiquarian booksellers Pickering & Chatto, in succession to William Pickering, who founded the business in 1820; Basil Montagu Pickering, who refounded the business after his father's death; and old Mr Chatto, who bought the business after Basil Montagu Pickering's death in the late 1870s. I brought in the Rees-Mogg family as the fourth family to have controlled the business.

Antiquarian bookselling is a good deal more difficult than people think, or than I imagined in 1981 when I bought Pickerings. It is indeed the attractive life which one might imagine. Rare books are fascinating objects. They have a scholarship of their own and a devoted community of book lovers. The greatest collector in England in my time was Sir Paul Getty, a very sweet-natured man. The book trade is full of interesting people; the dealers compete and cooperate. They buy much of their stock from each other. In Pickerings we had, in the ten years I was the proprietor, an expert and interesting staff, whom it was a delight to work with. Gillian helped me a great deal. I am very grateful to Roger Gaskell and Christopher Edwards, who were the Managing Directors.

The trouble with antiquarian bookselling is that every sale is a 'one-off'. I was fortunate in that Dudley Massey had been a book miser. His stock, then held in a modern shop in Bloomsbury, which closely resembled an underground car park, contained a dozen imperfect copies of the Second Folio of Shakespeare, which I suppose the firm had held for a century in the hope they would be able to complete them. One can have a wonderful stock if one does not sell too many books. The trouble is that one's best books do sell, usually rather quickly, and the stock tends to consist of the books which sell slowly.

After a couple of years we moved out of the concrete basement and into a very attractive shop in Pall Mall. Our new shop had been occupied by two leading antiquarian booksellers: the Robinson brothers and Dawson's of Pall Mall. We had our great coups. Christopher Edwards knew of the whereabouts of a very fair copy of the First Folio, in an eighteenth-century binding. We had it authenticated by an elderly professor from the United States, who arrived on 17 April 1984, the day of the shooting at the Libyan Embassy, which was just around the corner. Christopher sold it to the Dallas Public Library. We would never have another First Folio.

My own greatest find was the Blake rummer. A 'rummer' is an early nineteenth-century pub glass, with a characteristic stem and bowl. They are quite common and can usually be picked up at a sale or in an antique shop for about £50. One day in the late 1980s I was walking up St James's Street. As I reached the corner of King Street, I was thinking about Geoffrey Keynes, the brother of Maynard, himself a great book collector, particularly of William Blake. I was not intending to go to Christie's, but had the idea that I might look in at their King Street rooms.

There was a glass sale on view, which was to be sold a couple of days later. One lot was a rummer which had been broken and repaired. Such glasses would normally have no commercial value. The catalogue said that it was inscribed 'Blake in Anguish. Felpham. August 1803' – it also had a couple of lines of poetry engraved on the bowl:

THOU HOLDER OF IMMORAL DRINK
I GIVE THEE PURPOSE NOW I THINK

and on the opposite side a faint but very Blakean angel. It looked perfectly genuine to me. Christie's estimate was only about £50.

It was obvious that the antiquarian glass market did not share the values of the rare-book market. Had the rummer been in a book sale, the estimate would have had to be in the thousands. I went back to our shop and looked up the relevant facts. In August 1804, a drunken soldier named John Schofield had stumbled into Blake's garden in Felpham, and Blake had turned him out. Schofield had threatened Blake in the King's name, and Blake had replied 'Damn the king. The soldiers are all slaves.' He was then arrested and charged with assault and high treason, a capital offence. Fortunately he was acquitted of all charges at the Chichester Assizes.

I asked Roger Gaskell to go and bid for us – he agreed that the glass must be genuine, and, as I remember it, he bought the lot for £54. It is now in the most eminent glass museum in the United States, and the two lines have been added to Blake's collected poetry. But like Shakespeare First Folios, Blake rummers cannot be replaced. In fact, I wish I had kept it.

From the point at which I first thought of buying Pickering & Chatto, I felt that it would be interesting to take the firm back into publishing. William Pickering himself had been one of the major publishers of the first half of the nineteenth century. He founded his publishing business in 1820, developed an impressive list of authors, including Samuel Taylor Coleridge, was the first posthumous publisher of William Blake, and the first publisher to use cloth as his standard binding. He was also a patron of excellent printing. He ran his antiquarian bookshop in tandem with his publishing, and was a pioneer of collected editions in English literature. From my earliest dealings with Pickering & Chatto, I had felt that Pickering's type of publishing could have a place in the modern age.

In 1983, I took the first step and set up a company, Pickering & Chatto (Publishers). I relied on our experience in antiquarian bookselling to identify authors who merited a collected critical edition. Roger Gaskell is an expert in antiquarian scientific books; Pickering also had a specialization in English literature and in economics, an area of special interest to me. We had, therefore, three areas in which we had sufficient knowledge of the literature. I sent out a letter to Pickering's customers, asking if they would be interested in scholarly edited editions of a possible list of major figures. I received encouraging replies. Thomas Malthus, the English economist and the founder of modern population studies, received the most votes. Roger was already Managing Director of Pickering & Chatto and he took on the additional work of being Managing Director of our new publishing company. I liked the idea of restarting William Pickering's work, and of restarting publishing in the eighteenth-century style, from a bookshop. My eighteenth-century ancestor Andrew Henderson had been a publisher (not a very successful one), and had kept a bookstall in Westminster Hall, so I felt that I was also reviving a family tradition.

Roger found two excellent editors for Malthus: E. A. Wrigley and David Souden. Our planned edition was parallel to the excellent edition of David Ricardo, which Piero Sraffa had edited for the Cambridge University Press. We adopted a uniform style, based on William Pickering's. Malthus came out in 1986, in eight volumes, and received excellent reviews. It was the first collected edition of Malthus's work. An attraction for me was that William Pickering had published the second edition of Malthus's *Principles* in 1834.

I had some other experience in publishing in the 1980s. Lord Forte, who had created the Trust House Forte hotel group, was Chairman of Sidgwick & Jackson, an excellent trade publisher with William Armstrong as Managing Director. Charles Forte had taken on the chairmanship of Sidgwick in succession to Lord Longford. He asked me to take over the chairmanship from him. We found it very difficult to make a profit, despite William Armstrong's work, and despite having Nigel Newton, who was to go on to be the founder of the successful publishers Bloomsbury, as the Marketing Director.

The trouble was a matter of simple commercial arithmetic, which still makes ordinary trade publishing an exceptionally difficult business, even for the best publishers. Put roughly, if we sold a book for £10, about 10 per cent would be taken by the author's royalty; as much as 52 per cent would be taken by the bookseller; the cost of printing would be about 15 per cent. That left about 23 per cent, or £2.30, for the publisher. The books would be distributed on a sale or return basis, and anything from 20 to 35 per cent might actually be returned. In those days, a respectable non-fiction book might only sell 1000 copies, which would produce £3000 for the publishers, to cover the cost of distribution, including representatives who had to visit all the bookshops to place books and take orders. Almost all Sidgwick & Jackson's books did make some contribution to the overhead, but it took a bestseller to make a profit, and bestsellers usually required a large speculative investment in an advance which might never be recovered. William Armstrong managed to create some bestsellers for us, including books by Ted Heath on music and yachting and General Hackett's book on the Third World War. I also learned that books on Marilyn Monroe always made a profit. But I was impressed by my experience with Sidgwick & Jackson that publishing would only turn a profit if one could find an edge. Nigel Newton was to find his edge in Harry Potter, though he had already established Bloomsbury by his marketing skills.

One of the most interesting books we published was *Seeds of Change* by Henry (Tom) Hobhouse who has been both intellectual company and a close friend to our family. The book is a classic of what might be called vegetable Marxism. Somerset, with John Locke and Friar Bacon, and brainy aristocratic families like the Waldegraves, the Hobhouses, the Asquiths and the Trevelyans, is more of an intellectual than a field sports county.

I decided that the revived Pickering's should be an academic publisher. We would not seek to sell through the bookshops, thus saving part of the 52 per cent discount. We would not publish authors still in copyright – though we later broke that rule for *The Letters of H. G. Wells* – thus saving the author's royalty. We did, of course, employ live academic editors, who have done excellent work. We even decided against dust jackets. Our main customers were to be the 2000 great libraries of the world – they throw away the dust jacket when they receive the book. These decisions allowed us to spend more on the product, producing high-quality books with an archival life in small editions, but they still left the publisher with a much higher proportion of the gross receipts than in trade publishing.

Even so, I underestimated the difficulty of establishing a small and independent publisher. From the start, we were helped by having the existing organization and overhead of the bookshop. We had an existing system for marketing and selling books, which was also capable of dealing with editors. We did not have to set up a book business from scratch. We also had worldwide contacts in the book trade. Two major Japanese booksellers, Kinokuniya and Maruzen, to whom we had already been selling antiquarian books, were essential to the sales of our early titles. We paid our printing bills for Malthus from Kinokuniya's order for the sets that they took.

Now Pickering & Chatto has published about 500 titles, amounting to more than 1000 volumes, all of which are effectively in print. We publish over 50 new titles, or about 130 volumes a year. Following Malthus and Darwin, we have published editions of Boyle, Defoe, De Quincey, Mary Shelley, Mary Wollstonecraft, Kondratiev, Irving Fisher, Hazlitt, Playfair's *Adam Smith*, Rowe's *Shakespeare*, Godwin, Swift, and so on. We helped the Trollope Society to produce the first complete edition of Trollope's novels; our own Darwin was in 29 volumes, Defoe 44 volumes. Well over half our titles have been purchased by Harvard University Library, which I regard as an ultimate test of their quality and academic importance. By now, we have a backlist which provides more than half our cash flow. I have remained as a non-executive chairman. With the backing of our American partner, Bill Bonner, the business has expanded with considerable success, under our Managing Director, James Powell, and our Publishing Director, Mark Pollard, who have developed a valuable list of academic monographs. Though a publisher whose business model is influenced by early nineteenth-century publishing, we are also successful in selling e-books, where appropriate.

In 1992, I felt that I had to make a choice. I could either concentrate on bookselling or on publishing. Both required capital, and were in competition with each other for funds. In the end I sold the bookshop to an American investor, William Leas. I am glad to say that it is now flourishing, from premises near Sotheby's. There were two attractions in choosing the publishing side. It is a business in which success builds success – a good edition goes on selling. After seventeen years, we still sell several sets of Malthus every year, and have about 100 sets left in stock, from an initial print order of about 600. The creation of new critical editions of major authors is a more useful service to scholarship than the purchases of rare books from one collection to sell then to another. No one had published a comparable collected Darwin in a century or Defoe in two and a half centuries. These are jobs that need to be done, and will not need to be done again.

There is something very exciting about creating a small, independent business. I do not believe that any large publisher, with their overheads, could have made a success of building Pickering & Chatto, and I know none would have tried. It is a satisfying thought that any serious scholar of English literature, even in a hundred years' time, will still be using the books we have published, just as today there are the books William Pickering published in the 1820s and 1830s.

SEVENTEEN

R. v Secretary of State for Foreign and Commonwealth Affairs, ex parte Rees-Mogg

In the 1980s my political sympathies lay with Margaret Thatcher and Ronald Reagan. Between them they overcame inflation and liberated Eastern Europe.

Thatcher and Reagan were genuine kindred spirits on all the major fundamental issues of political life. Most political friendships are obviously self-interested. Nonetheless, Reagan had a real admiration for Margaret Thatcher, and she had a very considerable admiration and affection for him. The strength of their relationship played a very important part, particularly over the Falklands. Plenty of people in Washington wanted to support their South American friends. This included Anglophobe Mrs Kirkpatrick, the US Ambassador to the UN, but Reagan, apart from anything else, simply thought that he could not let Margaret Thatcher down by failing to provide technical and intelligence support.

Thatcher and Reagan had the same views of the Soviet Union, they had the same view of economics and they had the same belief in the importance of a good relationship between Britain and the United States. Reagan's early speeches show that he was already talking a very Thatcherite language about liberty under the law as the foundation principle of the United States.

I met Reagan in London when he came over before his presidential campaign. Philip de Zulueta, formerly Eden's private secretary, invited us to a dinner which Reagan and Harold Macmillan also attended. The purpose of the dinner was for Reagan and Macmillan to meet in the atmosphere of a small private dinner party. I do not know that I thought 'this is a great man'. However, I took Reagan to be very intelligent, a competent American. Later, in 1980, I went out to the West Coast to give, I recall, a talk in Berkeley. I travelled back going through Utah and Chicago, where I heard Reagan talk to a lunchtime meeting. I found that, as one went across from west to east, people in the west perfectly well understood what Reagan was about, perfectly well understood that he was by no means an abnormal politician. He was somebody they respected; somebody who had, they said, been a good Governor of California. This was also the view in the Midwest, but, by the time you got to New York, every New Yorker was telling you that Reagan was just a cowboy. I never met him after he became President. My view of him is necessarily a superficial one but, nevertheless, he turned out to be right: a very reasonable, particular kind of American politician, and by no means a raging right-winger. He proved to be much more moderate than I had thought. Reagan was never a neo-con.

The Falklands campaign marked the symbolic end of the post-war British decline, in a way that nothing else would have done. I never believed that Margaret was primarily thinking of the next election in her deliberations about the Falklands. Indeed, had she been, she would have reckoned that there was a considerable possibility of being unable to recapture the Falklands. She did it because she thought it was right, in a very simple and straightforward way. That belief was something that the British public perceived. As a result she increased her majority in the 1983 election.

* * *

Many of my political friends were moderates of the centre left. When he was Leader of the Liberal Party I had seen a great deal of Jeremy Thorpe and had discussed the possibility of a Liberal/ Conservative coalition both with him and Ted Heath in 1974. In *The Times* I had supported the idea of a Liberal/Labour alliance in the 1970s. I became progressively more concerned about the risk of a takeover of the Labour Party by militants which I thought would be ruinous for Britain. I hoped that the alliance between the Social Democrats and the Liberal Party in 1983 would prove strong enough to replace the Labour Party as the party of the left. Labour was then still hampered by its debilitating trade union connection and commitment to state ownership. New Labour was to be essentially such a replacement party: unsatisfactory in some ways, with some certainly surprising attributes, such as its relative willingness to engage in overseas wars, but no longer hamstrung by the unions.

Both because of my personal friendships and my political sympathy for the Labour moderates, I welcomed the formation of the Social Democratic Party, and indeed in the 1990s saw New Labour as a positive movement. However, both the SDP and New Labour seem now to have lost their influence; if anything, it is David Cameron who has become the most effective leader of centrist politics.

Like many people, my attitude to Britain's relations with Europe changed quite sharply over time. In the mid 1950s I was at most a very moderate pro-European still attaching importance to the remaining Commonwealth. In 1956 the defeat of Eden's policy over Suez led me to think that Europe and Britain's economic ties to Europe would be more important than anything the Commonwealth could offer. I was therefore a fairly convinced European in the 1960s and a supporter of Ted Heath's European policy.

It was only later, in the early 1980s, that I began to have doubts about the European project. I was never in favour of Britain joining a single European currency and became a firm opponent of the Maastricht Treaty on which I entered into litigation against the Foreign Secretary, Douglas Hurd, arguing that the British Government had no lawful right to make the transfers of sovereignty proposed by the Treaty.

These changes of attitude required U-turns for me, and indeed, for *The Times*. I was not worried by these U-turns; newspapers are committed to making day-to-day comments based on the ever-shifting pattern of the news. I have not greatly changed my views in the last twenty years. I was as hostile to the Lisbon Treaty as to Maastricht, and have consistently believed that the euro is an illogical currency which can be expected to break up under the pressures of economic change.

While I was moving to a Eurosceptic position, many of my friends were moving in the opposite direction. The European issue split the Labour Party and was the main reason for the creation of the Social Democratic Party by a small group of Labour politicians, most of whom I regarded as my friends. Shirley Williams had remained a friend since Oxford days and Roy Jenkins since the 1950s. We had also met David Owen, whom I have always admired and liked.

Roy had always been one of my most valued contacts. By the time *The Times* resumed publication, after its year-long strike, on Tuesday 13 November 1979 he had been appointed as the President of the European Commission. I thought that an early visit to Brussels would bring me up to date with European policy and allow me to resume my connection with Roy. He invited me to dinner in Brussels and we were able to have a good conversation and exchange ideas.

At that point Roy Jenkins was negotiating with the President of France, Giscard d'Estaing. What I had not realized before this conversation was that Roy had become committed to the idea of a European currency. I was concerned that it would make it impossible for governments to use devaluation to correct whatever imbalances might arise in the future. At the end of the 1970s, that great decade of inflation, currencies were particularly unstable and the risks of a fixed European currency were particularly high.

Roy explained his favoured policy to me, rather assuming that I would support it. However, I put the difficulties, as I saw them, to him. His responses showed that he was no longer interested in the problems of a single currency; he was determined to carry the project forward and had already secured substantial European support.

In the course of the conversation I realized that he was slightly irritated, in a courteous way, by the objections which I raised, issues which did lead to the breakdown of the European Exchange Rate Mechanism and are a threat to the survival of the euro.

My relationship with Roy never recovered completely from our conversation in Brussels. Before that he had regarded me as a fully committed European integrationist, but after that conversation he knew that there were boundaries to my Europeanism. I had gone to Brussels thinking to revive a long-standing friendly relationship. The friendship remained but the relationship had been redefined.

I followed the economic logic of my discussion with Roy when, in autumn 1990, John Major decided, as Chancellor, to take Britain into the Exchange Rate Mechanism. I wrote an article for the *Independent* which compared that decision to Churchill's to go back on the Gold Standard at the wrong rate in 1925. I was convinced that it was the wrong rate, because I had been to Hong Kong and talked to Hong Kong foreign exchange dealers, all of whom said that the rate was too high relative to the D-Mark and that it would prove very difficult to sustain. So I criticized the decision from a purely pragmatic point of view. Major's decision started a revision of my whole view of Europe which led in the early 1990s to an increasingly Eurosceptic position. In this I was very much influenced by my family. My children were by this stage growing up, and none of them were Eurofanatics. Our younger children, particularly, felt that Britain was handing away an essential element of independence. This impressed me, not only because obviously one is impressed by the views of members of one's own family, but because it was in such contradiction to the propaganda that the young are in favour of a United States of Europe, or of a very integrated European policy. In my own household it was manifestly not true that all young people love the European Union and have no desire to maintain the independence of the sovereign state.

I was a believer in markets. I was a monetarist but I did not believe in economic and monetary union. I found that, like my family, I was a believer in British independence. I was, as I have remained, a Lockean individualist, rather than a believer in some kind of Hegelian state. When the movement of my mind came, it came fast, and almost inevitably.

There was significant opposition to the Maastricht Treaty both in the House of Lords and in the House of Commons. Perhaps more in the House of Lords. In the House of Commons the problem was that the John Major Government had a very small majority after the 1992 election, a majority which eventually eroded to almost nothing. The Tory Eurosceptics in the House of Commons were consequently able, by voting against or by abstaining, to embarrass the Government on a whole series of votes. The Labour Party, although they were supporters of the Maastricht Treaty and, while John Smith was alive, very keen supporters, were nevertheless pleased to take the opportunity to embarrass the Government. Labour would sometimes vote with the Eurosceptics in order to make the Government's life difficult. In the House of Lords the majority of the hereditary peers were unsympathetic to the Maastricht Treaty and it would therefore have been very difficult to give them a free vote because if they had had a free vote they would have voted at any rate for the referendum.

Throughout this period the public had been more Eurosceptic than Parliament, with members of Parliament taking a professional political view, being persuaded that the Maastricht Treaty was the natural progression. Given, therefore, the support of the leadership of all three parties, the Maastricht policy was the accepted policy of the professional political class. It was never the accepted policy of the ordinary citizen.

For the politician and the civil servant the European project is a world of opportunity in which very interesting continental decisions can be taken. For the ordinary citizen, by contrast, it imposes regulations, and removes power. There exists, therefore, a direct conflict of interest between the political class and the rest of the community.

However, the Maastricht Treaty precipitated the destruction of the Establishment consensus in favour of, not just Europe, but of accelerating European integration. The critical vote was the vote on whether there should be a referendum on the Maastricht Treaty. The case for a referendum was very strong because the Maastricht Treaty certainly represented a major change in the constitutional relationship between Britain and Europe. Interestingly this point was repeatedly made in 2003 by

Government spokesmen, concerning the new draft Constitution, which preceded the Lisbon Treaty.

In 1992, the Government could not have won the vote against a referendum without imposing the Whip. All three parties imposed the Whip on the vote. Even then, many members of the House of Lords voted against Maastricht. I was among those who voted against. I found myself in complete agreement with the very remarkable speech that Margaret Thatcher made in favour of a referendum. There was, of course, no referendum on Maastricht, despite the very best efforts of a substantial number of members of the House of Lords.

I believed that, after the refusal of a referendum, a major change was being made in the British Constitution which transferred essential powers from the Westminster Parliament to the basically non-democratic European structures. This included the transfer, under the second and third pillars, of powers over foreign affairs and defence as well as those powers required for economic and monetary union. When the opportunity to oppose it in the courts came I was keen to take it.

I was approached by solicitors who had originally briefed Leolin Price, the leading constitutional lawyer, to make a case for judicial review. They had done a lot of work themselves, and had reached the point where they needed two things. Firstly, someone to fund the case; secondly, somebody to be named as plaintiff. Jimmy Goldsmith agreed to fund the case; I agreed to be named as plaintiff. The action became known as R. v Secretary of State for Foreign and Commonwealth Affairs, ex parte Rees-Mogg.

The case went to the Court of Appeal where it was held that the Government had acted perfectly properly, that they should be allowed to go ahead and sign the Treaty. Nonetheless, the Court reaffirmed two important points. One was the previously expressed view of Lord Denning that, as Parliament had enacted British membership of the European Community by statute, Parliament could repeal the statute. This was important because it might have then been thought that the UK's membership was irrevocable. The reaffirmation was of value.

The Court's second point had a considerable effect on the second and third pillars of the Maastricht Treaty. The Court of Appeal held that the Government were not entitled to abandon any part of the prerogative, by use of the prerogative. The only way to give up a part of the prerogative is, they stated, by statute. This meant that the second and third pillars of Maastricht remained mere aspirations.

We considered a further appeal in the House of Lords. Jimmy Goldsmith and I were discussing whether it was worth the very substantial extra cost of going to the House of Lords. My daughter Annunziata, then aged thirteen, heard the discussion and said to me 'if you go a stage further will you get a better judgement?' Not necessarily was our conclusion. Worse still, we would quite likely lose some of the favourable points in the judgement of the Court of Appeal if we went to the House of Lords.

The action was as much of a success as one could have expected it to be. It did not stop Maastricht. It did not radically change public opinion. Still, it reaffirmed that there was a legal position to be considered. It increased the feeling that Euroscepticism had become, or was becoming, a serious cause rather than something that could just be brushed aside. It lent, I now believe, a certain intellectual weight to the Eurosceptic cause.

The last conversation I had with Jimmy Goldsmith came a few months before his death. We met at his campaign office in Wilton Place. Although I did not know it, he fought his campaign for the Referendum Party already suffering from the cancer which proved fatal. I remember him talking to me about two subjects, Europe and his reasons for devoting his life to amassing his huge fortune. That amounted at his death to a couple of billion dollars, or thereabouts. One can never be precise about other people's wealth.

On Europe, he used a vivid metaphor. He felt that he was like someone seeing off his family and friends on a train that was doomed to crash. He did not, I think, fear that the Europe which was being created at Maastricht could last for a thousand years. He would have hated that, but he did not think it possible. He thought the Europe that was being contracted was absolutely certain to fail, and that the failure was going to do great damage.

As a boy, he had become aware that he came from a family, the Goldsmiths, which had at one time been very rich, and he had Rothschild cousins, but had become comparatively poor. His father was a hotelier, rich enough by ordinary standards, but not by those of serious wealth. He wanted his family once again to become seriously wealthy, and was prepared to take calculated risks to achieve that. He was successful. His personality was an extraordinary one. He exuded an energy which would have done credit to a nuclear power station. This, in effect, enlarged his personal space, so that I always sat as far away from him as possible. I did not at all wish to be subject to his dominance. Yet I liked him and found him a warm-hearted man, a reliable colleague and a friendly acquaintance.

EIGHTEEN

'An Humbler Heaven'

Until 1977, Jamie Hamilton, a charming and gifted publisher, had never, in all his distinguished career, published a book on religion. I had written a short book on my own religious views and experiences. His firm, Hamish Hamilton, had been bought by the Thomson Organization, which then owned *The Times*. I took my book to Jamie. He read it over a weekend and decided to publish it. It was a very minor publishing success, gaining friendly reviews, being reprinted, and later appearing in paperback. I gave it a title taken from Pope's *Essays on Man*. I called my book *An Humbler Heaven*.

There was one passage which attracted particular attention, and has subsequently been quoted by other authors. I wrote about an unusual experience which had occurred after my father's death, at some time in the spring of 1964. I can still remember it, but it is now more than forty years since it happened, so I shall quote the passage as I wrote it in 1976:

> I married Gillian in March 1962, to my great happiness. [That is even more true after almost fifty years of marriage.] My father-in-law, Tom Morris, was the Mayor of St Pancras; we were married at the Church of the Holy Redeemer, and had our reception at the Town Hall.

Already at the time of our wedding my father, to whom I was and since his death remain devoted, was seriously ill. He was barely able to last out the ceremony and reception, and after further deterioration in the summer he died on 12 December 1962, five days before the birth of our eldest daughter, Emma, on 17 December. I went to the funeral from the maternity hospital and back to the maternity hospital from the funeral …

Not immediately after his death, but about fifteen months later, we lived briefly in the house in which he had spent his last years, and our bedroom was the room in which he had died. I experienced then, not invariably in that room, brief periods of tranquillity and ecstasy, such as many people have experienced, which convinced me of the harmony of the universe and the love of God. I have had such experiences elsewhere and at other times, but never so frequently and intensely as in that house then.

At the same period, one day when I was just about to have an afternoon nap in that bedroom, I had a very brief experience of a kind that I have never otherwise experienced. Momentarily I was walking on the left hand side behind a coffin in Cameley church, the church where my father was buried. The man in front of me was wearing a green great-coat in a coarse heavy material I have never seen before; under my feet there was the crunch of straw or rushes as though I had been walking in a barn. I did not then know, but have since established, that in the eighteenth century it was still customary to spread rushes on the church floor …

In the literature, glimpses of precognition, such as a glimpse of the sinking of the *Titanic* before the ship had sailed, seem to be common relative to glimpses of retrocognition, but other examples of retrocognition are recorded. I suppose that the sightings of ghosts may be sightings of past events rather than an intrusion by the apparitions themselves into the present day. I do not think that my experience has any evidential value for anyone but myself, but it has been very important for me. As I commented in *An Humbler Heaven*, 'If for a half second – as I have reason to believe but no-one else does – I followed an eighteenth century coffin, then I lived for that half second a century and a half before my own birth, and perhaps forty years before my great grandfather was born. If those days still exist, why should I suppose that I shall disappear from reality at the time when my own death comes?'

One of the books which has influenced me most is William James's *Varieties of Religious Experience*. On my seventieth birthday, Pickering & Chatto (Publishers) gave me a copy of the First Edition, which had at one time belonged to Anita Loos, the unexpectedly intellectual lady who was the author of *Gentlemen Prefer Blondes*. It has her attractive Jazz Age bookplate. My particular experience belongs more to the paranormal than to the religious, but it certainly had a religious impact. It convinced me of what James calls 'the reality of the unseen'. From that came a conclusion which can also be put in James's words: 'Were one asked to characterise the life of religion in the broadest and most general terms possible, one might say that it consists of the belief that there is an unseen order, and that our supreme good lies in harmoniously adjusting ourselves thereto.' It is obviously easier to believe in the unseen if one has at some point experienced it, however briefly. Unless people throughout history had had religious experiences of one sort or another, there would be no religion. Religious beliefs are derived from experience and validated by it.

Several years later I had the good fortune to meet an Anglican clergyman, Martin Israel, who was a mystic. When I first met him, he was handicapped by a nervous voice which made him seem very shy and hard to hear, but he had a great atmosphere of living in the spirit. I had a minor financial crisis, when I was selling my bookshop and did not know whether the American buyer would complete the transaction. My capacity as an entrepreneur has always been limited by the anxiety I feel over debt, an anxiety I share with my mother and both my grandfathers. I rang Martin, and he suggested that we say a prayer, which we did. That was some time in the early 1990s.

A year or two later, I heard that Martin had been ill and got back into touch with him. He had been through an unusual experience. He had gone into hospital with a Parkinsonian attack. He was in a coma which lasted for three or four weeks. In the course of this attack he had a near-death experience which could be regarded as a negative one. He was in a large space which was full of people who were lost in the next world. He found himself able to help them find the way, which he did. After a time he came back to life. Much of his former nervousness had disappeared. He felt that he had been able to use his experience to help people. I used to visit him three or four times a year and we would pray together. Martin Israel had a remarkable power of creating a space of absolute peace when he prayed. We discussed religious issues. Martin had been brought up in South Africa as a Jew, had, as a result of earlier experiences, become a Christian, had practised as a pathologist and then become an Anglican clergyman, widely known for his retreats, in which work he had never been troubled by his nervousness.

I found that my conversations with Martin Israel helped me to have a deeper spiritual approach, though I am still far from being the Christian I would wish to be. Nevertheless, I have found myself with a feeling of gratitude to all the people who have helped me to develop in my life.

My own early religious education I owe to my mother. My father was a member of the Church of England, but never went to church, except at Christmas and Easter, when he came to Mass with us. He had been bored by the long sermons of his childhood, and had disliked the clerical schoolmasters he came across at Charterhouse. He was himself the grandson and great-grandson of Anglican clergymen. He had not lost his faith in God, and he enjoyed the cadences of the King James Version of the Bible. His own beliefs, however, tended to the modernist rationalism of the French doctors he had worked with in the First World War. He was, however, entirely happy to allow my mother to bring us up as Roman Catholics. His war experiences had also influenced him in favour of the Catholic Church. He had seen Irish priests go into no-man's-land to administer the last rites to the dying, at great risk to themselves. The only thing he had against the Church was that we said Mass in what he regarded as a dog Latin; he had been educated in the Latin of the golden age.

As an Irish-American Roman Catholic my mother had her religious descent from distant historic Irish roots – the Irish Church of her childhood seemed to descend directly from St Patrick coloured by a good deal of Celtic superstition, which was evident in the family stories passed down to her.

In 1798, her great-grandfather Thomas Fox, who was, I think, a schoolteacher, supported the Irish rebellion, became a colonel in the United Irishmen, and eventually had his lands confiscated; at least three of his in-laws were executed by the British. That much is true. The family story then goes on. Thomas ran away from the British troops that had been sent to capture him. He got to the family cottage, and hid in the rafters. The Redcoats ran in and demanded to know where he was. The family was struck dumb. It was the cat which found her voice. 'He went thataway.' The Redcoats rushed out in the direction the cat suggested, and were all drowned in the bog.

Thomas Fox's wife, Ellen Nolan, seems to have become the family banshee, visiting members of the family and foretelling the deaths of their close relations. She appears in the costume of an Irish woman of the early nineteenth century with a long apron. I have a drawing by the English artist Cornelius Varley of just such an Irish woman of that period. One of my mother's aunts saw her. She told the story of waking up at night, probably in the late 1860s, and seeing her grandmother, who was dead, sitting in a rocking chair beside the bed and groaning, 'poor Johnny, poor Johnny'. Johnny was then five years old; the next day he was killed by being kicked by a horse, a common enough nineteenth-century accident.

I had not heard that story when Ellen Nolan first visited me in a dream. It was to warn me of a death in our family, which duly occurred. She came again before my father died; I knew he was going to die for about ten months before it happened; I was able to do much of my grieving while he was still alive. I last saw her in 1973, when we were going abroad for a family holiday in Israel, leaving my mother at home. Ellen Nolan, if indeed it is her, came to me again in a dream, and I knew that she was warning me of my mother's impending death, which I could not accept. In the dream I seized her broom and pushed the old lady rudely out of the room. While we were away on holiday, my mother, who was then eighty-one, had a bad, life-threatening, fall, but survived it. The old lady's warning may have been frustrated by my intemperate reaction. At any rate, she seems to have taken offence, for I have never seen her again. I am not alone in having seen the family banshee; she has appeared to at least one of my American cousins.

The Foxes were related to the Cullens, a family which produced the famous Cardinal Cullen, who ran the Church in

Ireland with a rod of iron, and drafted the definition of papal infallibility for the First Vatican Council in 1870.

Despite this background, my mother's father was not devout; his family teased him because he suffered from a Sunday liver, which prevented him going to Mass as often as might have been wished, but was miraculously cured by the time he had to take the train for Grand Central Station on a Monday morning. He was also descended from Protestant roots, probably from one of Cromwell's colonels who had been given land in Ireland. The family had converted to Catholicism a couple of generations before his time, when a younger son married a Catholic girl.

My mother's own religion, though orthodox, was very well balanced. She was influenced by the work of Pierre Teilhard de Chardin. I did not have a rigorous Catholic childhood, though I heard occasional sermons about hellfire. We went to Mass in Somerset at Midsomer Norton, in a converted medieval tithe barn, which was served from Downside, a Benedictine Abbey. I owe a large part of my formal religious experience and my attitude to spirituality to the moderation and wisdom of the Benedictine order, and, through our Parish priests, to the Rule of St Benedict.

In particular, I learned from Father Benet Innes, of the Order of St Benedict, who was the Parish priest at Midsomer Norton in the 1960s – that is during my thirties when our first four children were born. He was one of those relatively rare monks who, but for their vocation, would have enjoyed an active life in business or practical affairs. He was not a person who retreated into a monastery, but someone for whom the monastic limitation on his energies must often have been irksome. I found my mother's matter-of-fact attitude to the Church and Father Benet's practical attitude helped me to avoid an overanxious feeling about sin and guilt. I did not suffer the agonies of some of my Catholic friends.

I have admired, and known, several of the leading Roman Catholics of the post-war period, particularly Basil Hume. *The Times* had something to do with the appointment of Basil Hume as Archbishop of Westminster. After the death of Cardinal Heenan, a skilful Irish prelate who managed to maintain the unity of the Roman Catholic Church in England during the aftermath of the Second Vatican Council, I was invited by the Apostolic Delegate, Archbishop Heim, to lunch at his house in Wimbledon. When I arrived, I found the Duke of Norfolk and a couple of other lay Catholics already there. We were asked our views on the succession. Both the Duke of Norfolk and I stressed the need for spirituality and at least implied that Basil Hume, then Abbot of Ampleforth, possessed this quality. Archbishop Heim could have put both of us down as favouring Hume's appointment. Hume was his favourite candidate and he thought he would be ours. I do not doubt that he had chosen to ask our advice because he knew what it would be.

At that time, I had never met Basil Hume. I had, however, taken the precaution of discussing him with Hugo Young, later the excellent *Guardian* columnist, who was then still working for the *Sunday Times*. Hugo had been at Ampleforth. He gave a favourable, but guarded judgement. I suspect that the two men were too similar to each other to have been altogether easy in the relationship of schoolmaster to student; both were men of a strongly developed masculine character whose friendship was guarded by an ultimate reserve.

I also consulted Peter Nichols, who was for many years the extraordinarily well-connected *Times* correspondent in Rome. He valued his Rome contacts so highly that when I offered him the Washington post, he declined to go. Cardinal Benelli, the

Cardinal Secretary of State, was Peter's chief contact in the Vatican. In effect, at that time, Benelli, a man I came to admire, was Prime Minister to Pope Paul VI.

In the Vatican there were doubts about Hume's appointment to Westminster. Benelli, who was himself a great administrator, somewhat favoured an administrator. He was not opposed to Hume, but he doubted whether a Benedictine monk, even an Abbot, would be able to carry the administrative load. Peter Nichols reinforced the message that was coming from Archbishop Heim, telling Benelli that English Catholic opinion was strongly in favour of a change, and wanted an overtly spiritual leadership, which might be provided by a candidate with a monastic vocation. England had lost interest in ecclesiastical civil servants, however industrious. Benelli did not press whatever objections he had, and Basil Hume, in some ways reluctantly, was made Archbishop.

I greatly admired Cardinal Hume, when I came to know him. He came to lunch at Smith Square with the children; we also invited Shirley Williams, who is the godmother of our elder son, Thomas. Hume later asked me to sit on a committee on nuclear weapons for which he took the Chair. We used to attend Masses at Westminster Cathedral. He was superb in the performance of the liturgy. I have not known a priest for whom the Mass seemed more vividly real, or who made it more real for the congregation. He was a holy and spiritual man, and an inspiration to Christians of all denominations.

There is a theory that the papacy alternates between fat men and thin men. This theory worked reasonably well in the mid twentieth century. Pope Pius XII, the wartime pope, who is now widely criticized for his diplomatic approach to the Nazis, was a thin man, of ascetic and spiritual appearance. In 1953, as a *Financial Times* journalist, I was invited by the oil company

Shell Italiana to visit a tiny Italian oilfield. The real purpose was to lobby against ENI, the Italian State oil company. We were taken on a tour of beautiful Italian cities, including Orvieto, where we sampled the white wine. We were even shown a remote oil rig; I caught my foot in the platform and was much praised for my English sangfroid in waiting calmly to be extricated. We were also given an audience with Pope Pius XII, who had a sprinkling of English. I received his blessing with gratitude, but was too embarrassed to kiss his ring, so he may have taken me for a Protestant. I am not sure that he was a strong pope – certainly not a heroic one – but he left a memorable impression of personal sanctity.

In Rome, Shell could arrange a private audience, though it would take place among twenty or thirty miscellaneous businessmen. When I got to *The Times*, I found that Peter Nichols had even better access than Shell, and could provide an entrée to his amazingly diverse contacts in every area of Italian life, religious, artistic, journalistic and political. Gillian and I had audiences with Pope Paul VI, another thin man, and undoubtedly another holy man. One of the greatest popes of the twentieth century, in my view, was John XXIII, the pope of the Second Vatican Council, who came in between Pius and Paul. I never had the good fortune to meet him. The other great pope was Pope John Paul II, whom I saw regularly when I was on the Pontifical Council for Culture. It is ironic that two such great popes should have been elected in the second half of the twentieth century, which can be regarded as a period of global bewilderment.

John XXIII described his successor, Paul VI, as '*Omlettico*' – Hamlet-like – and there may have been truth in that epithet. At any rate, he seemed both highly spiritual and highly intelligent, but uncertain about the direction in which he should lead the

Church. Gillian, who is an excellent judge of character, liked him. He gave her a beautiful rosary, though she is not a Catholic, which my mother used in her last days. I felt a greater affinity with him than I had felt for Pius XII.

I was still Editor of *The Times* when John Paul II was elected, and remember the rush of dictating the leading article on the occasion straight onto the typewriter. I was on the Pontifical Council for Culture from 1982 to 1987, after I had left *The Times*. Members of the Council used to meet John Paul II every year. On one occasion, we even had lunch with him. I had given up wine at the time, because of some new but now old-fashioned blood test, but I broke my fast with a glass of the papal wine. In 1986 Emma joined Gillian and myself in Rome. With the rest of the Pontifical Council we had an audience with Pope John Paul II. The cardinal who greeted us and gave us a glass of wine was Cardinal Ratzinger, later to become Benedict XVI. He seemed a rather formidable figure; as pope his image has been milder.

John Paul II was quite another thing. He had a quite different physical presence, not the thin intellectual, like Pius or Paul, and certainly not the jolly fatness of Pope John, but the body of a man who had done manual work, which was the case during the war. That background is rather unusual in popes, or in the clergy generally.

At the meeting of the Pontifical Council for Culture, he talked to us mainly, of course, about culture, and of the importance of relating the Christian message to the culture of different countries. He was heroic, conservative and Polish. He had suffered under the Nazis and under the communists. When I first met him, he had already been shot, and seriously wounded, by the Turkish would-be assassin, presumably on the orders of the KGB. His faith, his courage and his willpower were absolute. Yet, at the same time, he left a strong impression of Christian humility.

I have no doubt that he was the greatest statesman-pope of the twentieth century. He was one of the most impressive human beings I have ever met, a heroic figure in the same sense as Winston Churchill. Both John XXIII and John Paul II were revolutionary popes, but John XXIII's revolution was the greater one in spiritual terms, in that the Second Vatican Council was a revolution in the whole of the Church and in religion.

Despite the leaven of melancholy in my temperament, my life has been exceptionally fortunate and happy. I have not, I think, isolated myself in my family life, but I have benefited enormously. I am conscious that Gillian has looked after me in a way no one could deserve; she has been a blessing in my life and so have my children and my grandchildren. As I write this, I am looking forward to seeing Maud, who is now at university, and I lunched yesterday with Jacob, Helena and their children. My children played a large part in teaching me, and my grandchildren make me feel in very good spirits. Mary, who is two, probably understands reality better than I do.

We have had a very fortunate and happy marriage, and are now on the verge of our Golden Wedding, which, God willing, will be due on 5 March 2012. We have had five children, Emma, Charlotte, Thomas, Jacob and Annunziata. Emma married David Brooks, and they decided to take his mother's name, Craigie, as their married name. They have four children, Maud, Wilfrid, Myfanwy and Samuel; they lost Stanley, a twin to Wilfrid, but not before I had bonded by holding his hand in the premature unit of the Bath Royal United Hospital.

Charlotte has not married; Thomas married Modwenna Northcote, a descendant of Sir Stafford Northcote, whose Northcote-Trevelyan Report was the foundation of the modern civil service. His statue is in the Central Lobby of the Palace of Westminster. Modwenna's grandmother was a daughter of Mrs Belloc Lowndes and, therefore, a niece of Hilaire Belloc. Their children are William, Beatrice, David and Constance.

Jacob married Helena de Chair, the daughter of Somerset de Chair, writer and Member of Parliament, and through her mother, Lady Juliet Tadgell, she is descended from Thomas Wentworth, who was the first minister to Charles I; they have had three children, Peter, Mary and Thomas. Our youngest daughter, Annunziata, married Matthew Glanville in Lucca last year, and their daughter Isadora has just been born. The Glanvilles have strong Somerset connections; Joseph Glanville was the Vicar of Shepton Mallet in the 1660s and later of Bath Abbey.

At the 2010 General Election both Jacob and Annunziata fought Somerset constituencies. Jacob was elected as Member for North East Somerset, where the Moggs or Rees-Moggs have lived since 1620; Annunziata was defeated in the adjoining constituency of Somerton and Frome, in which the Moggs were living from about 1300 to 1620. During the campaign, Annunziata was living in Mells with us; Mells is a village which has belonged to the Horner and Asquith families since the Dissolution of the Monasteries, but before that belonged to Glastonbury Abbey.

My religion and my family are interwoven in my mind, and have been the basis of the happiness of my life. There is a charming letter written in 1721 by Alexander Pope to his friend Edward Blount, in which Pope writes 'Let Mrs Blount know that she is in the list of my "Memento, Domine, famulorum, famularumque".' The Latin phrase is taken from the memento of the living in the Canon of the Catholic Mass. I was brought into my religious faith by my family, and my belief – itself imperfect – is strengthened by the sense of responsibility for the eighteen people who belong to our family, children and grandchildren. One can always pray for one's family as Pope did for Mrs Blount, who was herself born in the Catholic family of Guise. The Moggs themselves were not one of the Catholic families whose faith remained unchanged, but they did retain a strong sense of their religion, whether that religion was Catholic (and Irish) or Protestant (and English).

In my eighties, I know that my happiness is supported by the care and affection of all my family. All of our grandchildren have homes in Somerset, within a few miles of where we live. Somerset is a county of many qualities, great physical beauty, a fascinating history, the romance of Glastonbury and the Arthurian myths. But perhaps its finest quality is that it is an excellent county for the extremes of life, for childhood and old age. It has the quality of Alexander Pope's youthful poem:

> Happy the man, whose wish and care,
> A few paternal acres bound,
> Content to breathe his native air,
> In his own ground.

In the closing passage of Plato's *Republic*, he tells the story of the process of reincarnation, in which the souls returning to earth choose their own destinies. Any wandering soul which chooses family life in Somerset chooses well.

ACKNOWLEDGEMENTS

I am very grateful to all the people who have helped me write these memoirs, particularly to my daughter Emma Craigie, who has researched and edited the text, and to Matthew Slater who played a vital role in helping to establish the basic narrative. I am also grateful to Mary Howell, my assistant; Rose Wild of The Times Archive; Sir Ronald Grierson, James Powell and Elizabeth Bruegger whom I consulted on particular sections; Maud Craigie and Magnus Dennis for photographs; Arabella Pike and Sophie Goulden of HarperCollins and Gillian, who looked after me.

INDEX